D0891698

Harvard Economic Studies / Volume CXXX

An Econometric Model of Canada under the Fluctuating Exchange Rate

Lawrence H. Officer

HARVARD UNIVERSITY PRESS

CAMBRIDGE, MASSACHUSETTS 1968

Distributed in Great Britain by Oxford University Press, London

Library of Congress Catalog Card Number 68-14270

Printed in the United States of America

To My Parents

Preface

This study is a revised and extended version of my dissertation. It has profited from the advice of Richard E. Caves, H. S. Houthakker, and Thomas A. Wilson. These persons are not responsible for any errors, nor do they necessarily approve of the methods or accept the conclusions of the study.

The arithmetical work was performed at the computation centers of Harvard University and the Massachusetts Institute of Technology. Research funds were provided by a Ford Foundation doctoral dissertation fellowship and small grant, and an H. B. Earhart Fellowship. However, the conclusions, opinions, and other statements in the study are those of the author and not necessarily those of the Ford or Earhart Foundations.

Lawrence H. Officer

Cambridge, Mass.
February 1966

Contents

CHAPTERS

APPENDICES

TABLES

DIAGRAMS

An Econometric Model of Canada under the Fluctuating Exchange Rate

I / Introduction

The following statement was issued by the Canadian Minister of Finance on September 30, 1950: "Today, the Government, by Order in Council under the authority of the Foreign Exchange Control Act, cancelled the official rates of exchange which, since September 19 of last year, had been calculated on the basis of a 10 per cent premium for the United States dollar in Canada. It has been decided not to establish any new fixed parity for the Canadian dollar at this time, nor to prescribe any new official fixed rates of exchange. Instead, rates of exchange will be determined by conditions of supply and demand for foreign currencies in Canada."[1] Thus began the most recent Canadian experience with a fluctuating exchange rate. The decision did not constitute an innovation for policy-makers. The rate had been unpegged over most of the period between the two world wars, but this experience was divided by adherence to the gold standard in 1926–1929. In 1939, with the outbreak of war in Europe, the Canadian government pegged the Canadian dollar by offering to sell spot U.S. dollars at 111 Canadian cents per dollar and to buy at 110. Except for a narrowing of the spread between buying and selling prices in 1945, the next change in the rate occurred in 1946 when the Canadian dollar was appreciated to par with the U.S. dollar.[2] Then in September 1949 Canada took part in the series of currency depreciations by increasing the selling and buying rates to 110½ and 110, respectively. Belief that the Canadian currency was

1. *The Unpegging of the Canadian Dollar: A statement issued by Mr. Douglas Abbott, Minister of Finance, at Ottawa on September 30, 1950, regarding the Canadian exchange rate*, Department of External Affairs (Ottawa), p. 1.

2. The official rates (in Canadian cents per U.S. dollar) were 100½ selling and 100 buying.

undervalued and would soon be appreciated led to a capital inflow which became intolerably massive in the third quarter of 1950. The government responded with the declaration of September 30, and the foreign exchange market reopened.[3] It was not until twelve years later—on May 2, 1962—that the floating exchange rate was abandoned and a par value of 108 Canadian cents per U.S. dollar set up under the International Monetary Fund.

The experience of 1950–1962 combined with the abundance of Canadian quantitative data provides a unique opportunity for testing theories concerning an economy—and the Canadian economy in particular—under the influence of a fluctuating exchange rate. One method is to set up a model of the Canadian economy over the relevant time period and to estimate its parameters. Comparison of the a priori and the estimated values of parameters, together with examination of other relevant statistics, constitutes this approach. Then the impact of the predetermined upon the explained set of variables may be assessed by obtaining the matrix of impact multipliers from the estimated model. In particular, the policy implications of the system are discovered in this manner. These three tasks—formulation of the model, estimation of its parameters, deduction of implicit impacts—form the substance of the study.

Econometric macro-models in the Clark-Klein tradition are extended Keynesian income determination systems.[4] The model-builder traverses both the income and expenditure sides of the national accounts and sets up equations which explain those items he decides to treat as endogenous. In the process attention may be paid as well to the financial, labor, and—to some extent—foreign sectors of the economy. The present study diverges from this tradition in two respects. First, rather than constructing the model

3. Discussion of technical aspects of the Canadian foreign exchange market is found in Sidney A. Shepherd, *Foreign Exchange in Canada: An Outline* (Toronto, 1961), esp. pp. 21–26.

4. For example: L. R. Klein and A. S. Goldberger, *An Econometric Model of the United States 1929–1952* (Amsterdam, 1955), L. R. Klein, R. J. Ball, A. Hazlewood, and P. Vandome (denoted as KBHV), *An Econometric Model of the United Kingdom* (Oxford, 1961), James S. Duesenberry, Otto Eckstein, and Gary Fromm, "A Simulation of the United States Economy in Recession," *Econometrica*, 28: 749–809 (October 1960).

by examining the national accounts and taking that array of items as the focal point, this work places the exchange rate—specifically, the spot exchange rate[5]—on a pedestal. The spot exchange rate is designated as the first-order variable. Certain variables—call them second-order variables—are *directly* involved in the explanation of the spot exchange rate. Other variables—say, third-order variables—help explain those second-order variables that are not predetermined. Variables of the same or higher order—in this case, of first or second order, respectively—may also be included as explanatory variables. In general, variables of order n are predetermined or are explained. If predetermined, since there is no current inward causality, they do not give rise to variables of higher order. If not predetermined, they may be explained by any combination of variables of the same, lower, or higher order. Only variables of higher order—in this case, order $n + 1$—can conceivably give rise to variables of still higher order. Eventually, if the model is to be completed, all variables of some order N are either predetermined or explained by variables of the same or lower order. Construction of the model is then methodologically at an end.

The second respect in which the model differs from tradition is closely related to the first. An outstanding feature of the Canadian economy is its openness to external influences. The foreign sector is not to be added to a basic model as a mere adjoint. If the traditional method of model construction were adopted in this work, the balance of payments would be treated in the same manner as the national accounts. (This is not to deny that the two accounts are related as a matter of definition.) Under the methodology adopted, given the identity of the first-order variable, the balance of payments receives attention not only because of its interrelationships with the national accounts but also because it plays a primary role in determination of the first-order variable.[6]

5. Throughout this work the term exchange rate refers to the spot exchange rate, unless otherwise implied or stated.

6. An example of the traditional methodology according unsatisfactory attention to the balance of payments is found in KBHV. Because the United Kingdom had a pegged rate (albeit there was a change in the par value) in the period covered by the KBHV model and because the British economy in extent of openness is far closer to Canada than to, say, the United States,

One aspect of Canada's openness is of crucial importance to the model-builder. External influence is skewed in the direction of the United States. The effect of the United States on the Canadian economy is so pervasive that the model-builder is compelled to give special attention to this fact. However, as compensation this very asymmetry simplifies construction of the model. The United States is correspondingly the primary source of variables representing external forces. With respect to Canada's transactions with other countries, the United Kingdom is predominant. This, too, is a situation useful for model-building as well as a fact that requires consideration for its own sake.

In addition to special procedures imposed by the methodology adopted and the peculiarities of the country of study, there are general problems to be solved. At some stage in his research the model-builder must determine the period to be covered, the time-interval of observations, and the forms of the relationships of the system. It is not necessary that these decisions be made prior to hypothesis specification, nor need they be irrevocable after estimation of parameters. But in this study the three decisions were made before these two events.

Because the purpose of the study is construction of a model of the Canadian economy under the fluctuating exchange rate of 1950–1962, the first constraint operating on the overall time period might appear to be the limits of the interval during which a fluctuating exchange rate was in effect. Therefore it seems that the only observations of interest are contained between the dates September 30, 1950 and May 2, 1962. But the decision to impose such a restriction is not independent of a theoretical position. In fact the principal justification of this constraint is the conviction that an economy whose currency is freely fluctuating is struc-

a first-order variable corresponding to the exchange rate in the case of an economy with an unpegged currency should be the change in official reserves. However, as KBHV write, "Since we do not treat the balance of payments in its entirety but confine ourselves to the goods traffic alone, we cannot determine gold and dollar reserves in our model" (p. 90). The fact that KBHV do not "adhere rigidly to a design built around the national accounting framework" (p. 3) is irrelevant since the methodology of the model is clearly traditional. Only lack of data induced KBHV to formally abandon the national accounts as an entity.

turally different from the economy with a pegged exchange rate. Of course, structure is a matter of degree, and it is not inconceivable that one might go beyond the time limits (in either direction) and take account of difference in structure by corresponding alterations in the relationships. The question is one of information relative to the problem at hand.

Even within the time period so delimited, the government's exchange policy is not uniform. In 1939 the Canadian government imposed a system of exchange control. Although this system and its administration had been altered over the years, it remained in force after the Canadian dollar had been set free. As the Minister remarked in his statement unpegging the currency: "From what has been said, it will be seen that the change from a fixed rate of exchange to a market rate does not involve the abandonment of the foreign exchange control system."[7] Exchange control was terminated a year later, on December 14, 1951. Should, then, all observations prior to that date be excluded? This is the procedure adopted by Rudolf R. Rhomberg for his models.[8] Again, on the other end of the scale, the Minister of Finance announced a change in exchange rate policy one year before the fluctuating rate was formally brought to an end. In his budget speech of June 20, 1961 the Minister declared:

> No one can say today what the appropriate level of our exchange rate would be when our balance of payments is in a position better suited to our present economic circumstances. But the rate will certainly be lower than it has been of late and it may well be appropriate for it to move to a significant discount. It will be government policy to facilitate such a movement. Accordingly the exchange fund will be prepared, as and when necessary, to add substantial amounts to its holdings of United States dollars through purchases in the exchange mar-

7. *The Unpegging of the Canadian Dollar*, p. 2.

8. Rudolf R. Rhomberg, "Fluctuating Exchange Rates in Canada; Short-Term Capital Movements and Domestic Stability," unpub. diss., Yale University, 1959; "Canada's Foreign Exchange Market: A Quarterly Model," International Monetary Fund *Staff Papers*, 7: 439–456 (April 1960); "A Model of the Canadian Economy under Fixed and Fluctuating Exchange Rates," *Journal of Political Economy*, 72: 1–31 (February 1964).

> ket. This would have the effect of increasing the foreign exchange reserves available to Canada to be used in case of need. As many competent observers have pointed out, these reserves have not grown over the past decade in line with Canada's international transactions. Once an exchange rate more closely in line with Canada's economic position is achieved, the government will use the resources of the exchange fund to ensure that the rate is kept within a range appropriate to Canada's changing economic situation.[9]

Until this announcement it was not the policy of the government to use its reserves of gold and U.S. dollars in order to undertake a persistent one-way position in the exchange market.[10] Therefore there is reason to consider terminating the time period at June 20, 1961.

The *outer* limits discussed above are adopted as constraints to the time period because the purpose of the study is to estimate the parameters of a model of the economy under a *fluctuating* exchange rate. Observations under another exchange rate system would be useful only insofar as they improved estimation of the parameters *under the fluctuating rate*. To the extent that the structure under which the additional observations occurred differs from the structure under the fluctuating rate, these observations are harmful. Only if the difference in structures can be "netted out" by appropriate alteration of the relationships could these observations be included in the estimation process. The changes in structure beyond the two outer limits are too complicated to be represented by alterations in the relationships. But it is assumed that one can legitimately proceed beyond each of the *inner* limits, thus increasing the number of observations, taking account of

9. *Budget Speech, June 20, 1961* (Ottawa), pp. 12–13.

10. "The resources of the exchange fund are not used to reverse persistent trends but only to contribute to orderly conditions by limiting excessive short-run movements in either direction which might otherwise occur." *Budget Speech, April 5, 1955* (Ottawa), p. 6.

"The exchange rate is determined by the interplay of forces operating in the exchange market through their effect on the supply of and demand for United States and Canadian dollars. While our exchange fund is used to limit the effect of short-run fluctuations in these forces, we do not attempt to reverse persistent market trends." *Budget Speech, June 17, 1958* (Ottawa), p. 7.

differences in structure by tractable alterations in the relationships of the model.

Formal beginning of the model is January 1, 1951. This excludes the first three months of the fluctuating rate, thus allowing scope for transitional effects on the economy (because of the shift from a pegged to a floating rate) to have taken place before the first observation of the relevant time period. The vestiges of exchange control that carried over into 1951 were too unimportant to significantly affect the structure of the model. The exchange control system was considerably loosened following the change to the fluctuating rate. To some extent this was inherent in the shift to an unpegged rate. But restrictions were also removed as a matter of policy. In fact one observer remarked: "As the Canadian control in 1951 lay lightly on the Canadian economy some have argued that the machinery should have been retained as a precautionary measure; but to retain it would have involved substantial paper work for the public and if every application were automatically to be approved, the controllers would have had no decisions to make."[11]

The date of termination of the time period covered is March 31, 1962. This locates the end point only one month from the date of reversion to a pegged currency. The fact that a discontinuous change in the government's policy with respect to use of its official reserves of gold and foreign exchange occurred some time before the second quarter of 1962 cannot be dismissed as insignificant. This and related governmental action (see equation 15 in chapter II) directly affects the structure of the model. Relationships must be constructed in such a way as to give suitable attention to such effects.

The unit of observation is the quarter-year. There are then forty-five observations running from the first quarter of 1951 to the first quarter of 1962, inclusive. An annual model would allow eleven observations, a number clearly inferior with respect to size of sample. Moreover, annual observations would swallow substantial intra-annual movement of variables which it is desired

11. Alan O. Gibbons, "Foreign Exchange Control in Canada, 1939–51," *Canadian Journal of Economics and Political Science*, 19: 54 (February 1953).

to explain. Of course, a quarterly observation unit implies that intra-quarterly movements are not explained, and a monthly model would constitute an improvement. It is lack of monthly measurements of data crucial to the model, namely, the national accounts and balance of payments, which prevents adoption of the month as the observation interval. An intra-annual observation unit entails the problem of seasonal variation. Thus, the relative size of sample as a measure overstates the increase in information of the quarterly over the annual model (and similarly for the monthly over the quarterly). The problem of seasonality and its treatment in this study are discussed below.

There are three types of relationships included in the model. The first category is the identity. It is a non-stochastic equation. No a priori specification of the form of these equations is made. For example, they are not constrained to be linear. In themselves the identities involve no problem of parameter estimation. The second type of relationship is the stochastic equation. The parameters of such relationships are unknown and need to be estimated. These equations are formulated such that they are linear in the parameters. This restriction is serious and requires justification. One advantage is the resulting tractability of the equation with respect to both estimation and interpretation of parameters. Advances in computer technology should imply that mathematical tractability is no longer of overwhelming importance. Another advantage is that the theorems of estimation require this assumption. Theorems concerning estimation of parameters that enter equations in certain non-linear fashions may perhaps be developed if the need arises. There is a third kind of relationship: the semi-identity; it is a mixture of qualities of the two primary categories and is discussed in chapter III (see equations 106–108).

Seasonal variation in quarterly econometric models has been discussed by Klein[12] and Nerlove.[13] The problem is one of spurious information. A given number of observations entails less information than is apparent because of repetitive seasonal patterns. The Canadian economy is especially susceptible to seasonal

12. KBHV, pp. 40–44.

13. Marc Nerlove, "A Quarterly Econometric Model for the United Kingdom," *American Economic Review*, 52: 165–166 (March 1962).

influences. One reason is the importance of agriculture, by nature a seasonal activity.[14] Another factor is climate. Winter in Canada forces a slow-down in construction and closes a natural transportation route for international trade, the St. Lawrence River. Furthermore, Canada's openness implies that seasonal variation in the economies of other countries influences the Canadian economy as well.

There are four basic methods of coping with seasonality. One "solution" is simply to ignore the problem; but then the degrees of freedom in stochastic equations are overstated and estimates of parameters will be adversely affected because the residuals of relationships will themselves tend to follow seasonal patterns. Moreover, the problem in the Canadian case is too acute to be ignored. A second method is to revert to an annual model, and involves throwing away information (though not as much as three quarters of the information is lost). The third method deals with the problem before estimation begins. An attempt is made to purge the observations of any given variable of their seasonal "component." The traditional ways of this seasonal adjustment have been effectively attacked by Klein and Nerlove. The fact that no knowledge of structure of the economy is used in the seasonal elimination means that the seasonal component may be understated, and some spurious information will be left in the sample, or overstated, and some information will be lost. The fourth method is to make the stochastic equations themselves functions of the season of the year and to leave the observation matrix in its raw (seasonal) form. Therefore a typical equation may be written

$$f_i(X_1, \ldots, X_n | a, b, c, \ldots) + E = 0 \qquad i = 1, 2, 3, 4$$

where $X_1, \ldots, X_n$ are variables, $a, b, c, \ldots$ are parameters, E is an error term, and i corresponds to the ith quarter of the year.

The advantage of this method is that the effect of seasonality may be estimated simultaneously with the parameters. This is done by including seasonal components themselves as (dummy)

14. However, the intensity of seasonality in agricultural activity is overstated in the national accounts. See Appendix A.

variables. Given the linear form of the relationships, one possibility is to make the intercept a function of the quarter, and an arbitrary stochastic relation is then:

$$X_1 = a + b(X_2) + \dots + e(X_n) + f(Q1) \\ + g(Q2) + h(Q3) + E$$

where Q1, Q2, and Q3 are predetermined variables defined as follows:

$$\mathrm{Q}i = \begin{cases} 1 \text{ if quarter } i \\ 0 \text{ otherwise} \end{cases} \qquad i = 1, 2, 3$$

This is the form of the stochastic equations adopted for the model. All variables remain in seasonally unadjusted form. X_1 is the explained (dependent) variable. The Qi may be interpreted as proxies for variables not included in $X_2, \dots, X_n$ but exerting influence on X_1. Given the nature of the Canadian economy, it is a good assumption that such variables follow a seasonal pattern. The intercepts corresponding to the first, second, third, and fourth quarters are $a + f$, $a + g$, $a + h$, and a, respectively.[15]

In addition there could be interaction effects by including variables such as QiX_j. In fact any parameter in the equation may be made a function of the quarter. Also, if the form adopted for the equations were double-logarithmic, a possibility would be proportional seasonal effects as follows.

$$X_1 = (B)^a(X_2)^b \dots (X_n)^e(P1)^f(P2)^g(P3)^h(B)^E$$

15. A comparison of the various techniques of seasonal adjustment is performed by Michael C. Lovell, "Seasonal Adjustment of Economic Time Series and Multiple Regression Analysis," *Journal of the American Statistical Association*, 58: 993–1010 (December 1963). Lovell shows that the inclusion of seasonal dummy variables in a stochastic equation while all variables are left in seasonally unadjusted form (method four) is equivalent to a particular seasonal adjustment of the *variables* in the equation (method three). This approach is what he calls "least-squares adjustment" and involves regressing each variable on the same set of seasonal dummies as is applied in method four. In the present model this would be the variables Qi.

where B = the base of the logarithms

$$\text{and } Pi = \begin{cases} B \text{ if quarter } i \\ 1 \text{ otherwise} \end{cases} \qquad i = 1, 2, 3$$

Taking logarithms,

$$\log X_1 = a + b(\log X_2) + \cdots + e(\log X_n) + f(\log P1) + g(\log P2) + h(\log P3) + E$$

$$\text{and } \log Pi = \begin{cases} 1 \text{ if quarter } i \\ 0 \text{ otherwise} \end{cases} \qquad i = 1, 2, 3$$

Interaction seasonal effects are excluded because of the consequences for degrees of freedom if used in general. This exclusion does not prevent their use in individual instances, but such occasion does not arise. However, a different kind of interaction variable is included in the structure.

Proportional seasonality is a priori a better assumption than seasonality which alters merely the intercept. Both slopes and intercept are affected and in a predictable manner; yet only three degrees of freedom are used. However, this method requires that variables be transformed into their logarithms. Therefore every observation of a variable thus transformed must be strictly greater than zero. This condition does not hold for all variables of the model. The method could be employed only for those equations all the variables of which meet the condition. It is not used in order to have a uniform treatment of seasonality throughout the system.

II / Stochastic Equations

This chapter has a dual purpose. On the one hand, it outlines theoretical aspects of the model by discussing the stochastic equations used to explain the jointly determined variables. On the other, it presents estimates of the parameters of these equations.

Yet both tasks are only incompletely fulfilled. The model comprises not only stochastic but also non-stochastic relationships: identities and semi-identities are exposited in chapter III. Furthermore, until the end of that chapter no attempt is made to relate the structure to the methodology adopted in chapter I. Indeed the equations are discussed in a logical sequence; but that order is independent of methodological decisions. The outline of each relation is headed by a title referring to the corresponding determined variable. By convention the variable explained by the equation is written on the left-hand side.

After a discussion of the theoretical background of an equation —involving a symbolic portrayal of its parameters—the equation is rewritten in estimated form. This sequential form of presentation is appropriate because the procedure of the study involves testing the underlying hypotheses. Below each parameter estimate (and parenthesized) is its standard error. The Durbin-Watson statistic (DW) and the usual measure of squared correlation between actual and estimated values of the dependent variable (RSQ) are then listed. Associated with certain of the equations are additional statistics, denoted by p, RSQC, and RSQT. Briefly, p is the first-order autoregressive coefficient of the residuals of a first-stage regression on the determined variable; RSQC is similar to RSQ except that variables are corrected for any transformation, that is, they are expressed in their original form; and RSQT is RSQ (and necessarily RSQC) for the first-stage regression on a current endogenous explanatory variable. Each RSQT measure is a function of the corresponding variable. The bracketed symbol following on the same line as the estimated equation denotes the method of estimation. The statistics and methods of estimation are discussed in Appendix B.

Comments on actual values of parameter estimates are deferred to Appendix C because intelligent analysis of results may require knowledge of not only the overall theoretical model (chapters II and III) but also methods of estimation (Appendix B).

The following notation is used in this chapter and throughout the rest of the study:

* multiplication
/ division
+ addition
− subtraction

This is notation of the Fortran programming language and the corresponding hierarchy of operations is followed; that is, multiplication and division are performed before addition and subtraction. This hierarchy can be overridden by means of parentheses. Fortran notation is used because variable names consist of different numbers of characters and because some non-stochastic relations involve complicated arrangements of operations. Pure Fortran symbols are used in the equations themselves; but conventional notation—sometimes in combination with Fortran—appears in the text.

The order of presentation of the stochastic equations (represented by their dependent variables) is systematically outlined as follows.

Exchange Rates

1. Spot exchange rate
2. Forward exchange rate

Balance of Payments

Merchandise Exports

3. Exports of merchandise to the United States
4. Exports of merchandise to the United Kingdom

5. Exports of merchandise to OECD and Japan
6. Exports of merchandise to "other countries"

Merchandise Imports

7. Imports of merchandise from the United States
8. Imports of consumer goods
9. Imports of investment goods
10. Imports of industrial materials
11. Imports of fuels and lubricants

Services

12. Net payments for travel
13. Net payments for freight and shipping
14. Net payments for business services and miscellaneous transactions

Interest and Dividends

15. Payments of dividends
16. Receipts of Dividends
17. Net payments of interest

Capital Account

18. Direct investment in Canada
19. Net new issues of securities
20. Trade in outstanding securities
21. Balance of transactions in treasury bills

Financial Sector

22. Short-term interest rate
23. Long-term interest rate
24. Net new issues of non-federal marketable long-term securities

Personal Income

25. Earned wage income
26. Earned non-wage personal income

Consumption

27. Personal expenditure on consumer non-durable goods
28. Personal expenditure on consumer durable goods
29. Personal expenditure on consumer services

Investment

30. Residential construction
31. Non-residential construction
32. Machinery and equipment
33. Change in non-farm business inventories
34. Change in farm inventories

Labor

35. Labor force
36. Employment of paid workers
37. Employment of unpaid workers
38. Number of hours worked per paid worker
39. Numbers of hours worked per unpaid worker

Prices

40. Price index of final sales
41. Price index of consumer non-durable goods
42. Price index of consumer durable goods
43. Price index of investment goods
44. Base-weighted price index of merchandise exports
45. Price index of industrial materials
46. Price index of consumer services
47. Wage rate in consumer service industries
48. Price index of foreign tourist expenditure in Canada
49. Current-weighted price index of merchandise exports
50. Price index of new machinery, equipment, and non-residential construction

Equations 2, 27, 28, 29, and 42 involve special techniques of estimation. Standard errors of estimates of certain parameters of these equations are not listed in chapter II. Full details are presented in Appendix B.

1. Spot Exchange Rate

There are essentially three different theories designed to explain the movement of a fluctuating exchange rate. First, it can be argued that the exchange rate is determined by the purchasing power parity, in absolute or relative terms. As a long-run theory the PPP has some value. For the short run it is not satisfactory unless, perhaps, there is hyperinflation. This is not to deny that prices of goods and services in Canada and abroad affect the exchange rate. But they are not *direct* determinants; rather they enter appropriately elsewhere in the model. The second theory makes speculation the fundamental determinant of the exchange rate. Rhomberg is an exponent of application of this theory in the Canadian case.[1] This study accepts a third theory. It makes a return to the orthodox theory of determination of the exchange rate. It is the basic items, the autonomous elements, in the balance of payments that directly determine the rate. This theory is adopted not for all situations but rather for the case of Canada in the period considered. To the extent that speculative factors influence components of the balance of payments they are included in the appropriate relationships. Autonomous elements of the balance of payments are not uniquely placed into categories. Decision-making is required. The first decision is to take such explanatory variables as net rather than gross flows. The second is to consider different exchange market slopes associated with five categories of autonomous items, namely, merchandise trade, non-merchandise current transactions, long-term capital, short-term capital, and official reserves. The resulting equation is:

$$\begin{aligned} \mathrm{RS} = a_1 &+ b_1 * \mathrm{BM} + c_1 * \mathrm{BS} + d_1 * \mathrm{BLK} + e_1 * \mathrm{TBN} \\ &+ f_1 * \mathrm{OR} + g_1 * \mathrm{Q1} + h_1 * \mathrm{Q2} + i_1 * \mathrm{Q3} + E_1 \end{aligned}$$

where RS = spot exchange rate, number of United States dollars per Canadian dollar

BM = balance of merchandise trade, in millions of dollars[2]

1. For example, "Canada's Foreign Exchange Market: A Quarterly Model." However, Rhomberg presents an unusual definition of speculation, viz., "By 'speculative position' is meant a holding or a claim which gives rise to an uncovered foreign exchange risk. The term thus includes both active and passive speculation. Active speculation is the assumption of positions in foreign exchange for the purpose of making an exchange profit. The failure to cover in the forward market a foreign exchange position ancillary to some other transactions constitutes passive speculation" (p. 441).

2. Throughout the study the term dollar refers to the Canadian dollar unless otherwise stated.

BS = balance of non-merchandise current transactions, in millions of dollars
BLK = balance of long-term capital, in millions of dollars
TBN = balance of transactions in Canadian treasury bills and United States treasury bills and certificates, in millions of dollars
OR = change in official reserves due to exchange market operations, in millions of dollars
Q1 = 1 if first quarter, 0 otherwise
Q2 = 1 if second quarter, 0 otherwise
Q3 = 1 if third quarter, 0 otherwise
E_1 = error term

The balance of payments variables are so defined that the net flows are credits. BM and BS are exports (or inward transfers) minus imports (or outward transfers), BLK and TBN are capital imports minus capital exports, and an increase (decrease) in official reserves due to exchange market operations implies that OR is negative (positive). These definitions have implications for the signs of b_1, c_1, d_1, e_1, and f_1. They should all theoretically be positive.

The left-hand side variable of all equations, both stochastic and non-stochastic, is current endogenous.

The following explanatory variables are endogenous: BM, BS, BLK, TBN.

OR is taken as predetermined. Under a pegged exchange rate OR would be endogenous. It would be an accommodating item. Under the fluctuating rate the government may use its official reserves (and its Canadian dollar holdings) to enter the exchange market on either side and *at its discretion*. OR is then a policy variable.

Q1, Q2, and Q3 are seasonal dummy variables and therefore predetermined.

In general E_i is the error term of the ith stochastic equation.

Equation 1 in estimated form is:

$$\begin{aligned} \text{RS} = {} & \underset{(0.018)}{0.91} + \underset{(0.000070)}{0.00038} * \text{BM} + \underset{(0.000045)}{0.00011} * \text{BS} \end{aligned}$$

$$
\begin{aligned}
&+ \underset{(0.000080)}{0.00042} * BLK + \underset{(0.00084)}{0.0064} * TBN \\
&+ \underset{(0.000047)}{0.00016} * OR + \underset{(0.0080)}{0.033} * Q1 + \underset{(0.014)}{0.074} * Q2 \\
&+ \underset{(0.016)}{0.10} * Q3 \qquad\qquad\qquad\qquad\qquad\qquad (AJT)
\end{aligned}
$$

$$
\begin{gathered}
p = 0.44 \quad DW = 1.46 \quad RSQ = 0.72 \quad RSQC = 0.01 \\
RSQT(BM) = 0.71 \quad RSQT(BS) = 0.94 \\
RSQT(BLK) = 0.48 \quad RSQT(TBN) = 0.07
\end{gathered}
$$

It is noticed that parameter estimates and their standard errors are presented to two significant digits. The other statistics are rounded to the second decimal place.

The five balance of payments variables do not represent the whole of the balance of payments, that is, they do not sum identically to zero. The excluded elements may be outlined as follows:

(1)′ Canada as a gold-producing country includes a category "gold production available for export" in its balance of payments. This item is composed of gold taken into Canada's official reserves and (non-monetary) gold exported. The balance of merchandise trade includes the latter component of this item but does not include the component representing increase in reserves, which is clearly not part of (international) merchandise trade.

(2) The balance of long-term capital does not include certain items—although they would be taken as autonomous movements—because the data are lacking. Even as a group observations are not available prior to the first quarter of 1960. These elements are:

(i) "Borrowings from non-residents by finance companies." (Little is known about these flows. It is uncertain whether they are long-term in nature.)

(ii) "Loans by Government of United Kingdom to a Canadian corporation."

constraints, market imperfections, and other considerations, par ticipants may expect a larger return if foreign exchange cur money market arbitrage is postponed or hastened, as the case may be. If the absolute value of the forward exchange differential i expected to increase (decrease), arbitrageurs will slow dowr (speed up) their actions, unless the sign of the forward exchang differential is expected to change. Expectation of a change in th sign in itself may speed up (or slow down) arbitrage. The im portance of this effect depends on the relative accessibility o funds and comparable money market instruments at home anc abroad. This factor may have been of some importance in th early years of the fluctuating rate when the Canadian mone market was in a primitive state of development. Assume that al such expectations are a function of the rate of change of the for ward exchange differential. Because the time period of the mode is discrete, this reduces to the change in the forward exchang differential over the previous quarter, which is defined by the identity

$$CRFD = RFD - RFD1$$

where CRFD = change in forward exchange differential, number of United States dollars per Canadian dollar

RFD1 = forward exchange differential, number of United States dollars per Canadian dollar, lagged one quarter

CRFD is adopted as an explanatory variable in addition to SA.

)ne more influence on the forward exchange rate must be idered. This is a factor peculiar to the Canadian case. It is lled that the Canadian dollar was unpegged just because of onsequences of the expectation that the dollar would be ap ted. After the dollar was freed, the expectation of apprecia evailed, though alteration in the exchange rate would now result of market forces rather than a discontinuous change gged value. Therefore the general public (excluding the tended to sell forward United States dollars in large s. The government was determined to avoid a large and

(In 1951–1953 the United Kingdom financed facilities with respect to production of aluminum in Canada in return for assurance of supply. Quarterly allocation of this flow is not available.)

(3) TBN does not include United States treasury bills and certificates held by Canadian banks, because the corresponding movements cannot be isolated from flows representing official reserves in these forms. Nor does it include movements of United Kingdom treasury bills because of lack of information concerning such transactions by Canadian residents. Satisfactory data exist only for 1955.

(4) The items "change in Canadian dollar (deposit) holdings of foreigners" and "bank balances and other short-term funds abroad (excluding official reserves)" are excluded because they are taken to be non-autonomous components of the balance of payments. All such flows are not necessarily passive results of movements of autonomous items in the balance of payments. If increases and decreases of Canadian and U.S. private deposit balances were a vehicle for *speculation* on the exchange rate, these movements would be classified as autonomous rather than accommodating. But it is extremely unlikely that such forms of speculation actually took place in measurable quantities in the period of interest. Other methods of speculation existed and were more profitable.

(5) The residual item "all other transactions including changes in loans and accounts receivable and payable" is omitted because it consists of a large number of elements—some autonomous and some accommodating—including a balancing item representing errors and omissions. In any event this item, even without a breakdown, is not available prior to 1960.

(6) OR excludes (i) decreases in reserves due to subscriptions in gold and U.S. dollars to international financial agencies and (ii) increases in reserves due to Canadian gold production. (However (i) is included in BLK.) These exclusions are made because the relation requires a definition of change in official reserves net of movements which do not directly affect the exchange rate.

2. Forward Exchange Rate

The theory adopted for explaining the forward exchange rate is based on the assertion that the spot and forward exchange rates and the corresponding (in terms of maturity) appropriate short-term interest rates at home and abroad *under perfect arbitrage* must satisfy a definite relation. This relation may be derived as follows.[3] Let

rs = spot exchange rate, number of units of foreign currency per unit of domestic currency
rf = forward exchange rate of maturity *m*, number of units of foreign currency per unit of domestic currency
cis = domestic interest rate of duration *m*, in percent
usis = foreign interest rate of duration *m*, in percent
cs = number of units of spot domestic currency
cf = number of units of forward (duration *m*) domestic currency
uss = number of units of spot foreign currency
usf = number of units of forward (duration *m*) foreign currency

Given competition the following relations hold simultaneously.

$$cf = (1 + cis/100) * cs \qquad \text{(i)}$$
$$usf = (1 + usis/100) * uss \qquad \text{(ii)}$$
$$uss = rs * cs \qquad \text{(iii)}$$
$$usf = rf * cf \qquad \text{(iv)}$$

Furthermore, the relations are invertible in the sense that (i), (ii), (iii), and (iv) yield expressions for *cs*, *uss*, *cs*, and *cf*, respectively.

Substituting (iii) in (ii), and (i) and (ii) in (iv),

$$(1 + usis/100) * rs * cs = rf * (1 + cis/100) * cs$$

Assume $cs \neq 0$. Then

$$(1 + usis/100) * rs = rf * (1 + cis/100)$$

Solving for *rf*,

$$rf = [(1 + usis/100)/(1 + cis/100)] * rs \qquad \text{(v)}$$

3. The presentation derives from Jaroslav Vanek, *International Trade: Theory and Economic Policy* (Homewood, 1962), pp. 58–60.

Let *rsa* denote the right-hand side of (v). Then *rsa* is the basic variable explaining the forward exchange rate, but it must be specialized to fit the Canadian case. There is not a unique maturity of forward exchange. However, the only published data refer to a maturity of ninety days. Interest rates must have a corresponding maturity, and they are measured by the rates on three-month treasury bills. It is not expected that relation (v holds exactly. The interest rates chosen are not the appropria ones under all circumstances, there are costs of transactions, arbitrageurs and their agents may not act in a purely compet manner. Therefore (v) cannot be included in the mode non-stochastic behavioral relation. For the same reasons efficient of *rsa* is not constrained to be unity. Moreover, a term adjusted by seasonal dummy variables is includ equation along with an error term. These consideratio following variables to the model.

RF = ninety-day forward exchange rate, numb States dollars per Canadian dollar
RSA = spot exchange rate adjusted for Uni Canadian short-term interest rates, number dollars per Canadian dollar
CIS = interest rate on government of C treasury bills, percent per quarter
USIS = interest rate on United States thre percent per quarter

The following identity holds.

RSA = [(1 + USIS/100)/(1

A measure of the profit to be ear the forward exchange differential,

RFD = RF

where RFD = forward exchan States dollars per Canadian

This suggests an addition forward from the adjusted sp

(In 1951–1953 the United Kingdom financed facilities with respect to production of aluminum in Canada in return for assurance of supply. Quarterly allocation of this flow is not available.)

(3) TBN does not include United States treasury bills and certificates held by Canadian banks, because the corresponding movements cannot be isolated from flows representing official reserves in these forms. Nor does it include movements of United Kingdom treasury bills because of lack of information concerning such transactions by Canadian residents. Satisfactory data exist only for 1955.

(4) The items "change in Canadian dollar (deposit) holdings of foreigners" and "bank balances and other short-term funds abroad (excluding official reserves)" are excluded because they are taken to be non-autonomous components of the balance of payments. All such flows are not necessarily passive results of movements of autonomous items in the balance of payments. If increases and decreases of Canadian and U.S. private deposit balances were a vehicle for *speculation* on the exchange rate, these movements would be classified as autonomous rather than accommodating. But it is extremely unlikely that such forms of speculation actually took place in measurable quantities in the period of interest. Other methods of speculation existed and were more profitable.

(5) The residual item "all other transactions including changes in loans and accounts receivable and payable" is omitted because it consists of a large number of elements—some autonomous and some accommodating—including a balancing item representing errors and omissions. In any event this item, even without a breakdown, is not available prior to 1960.

(6) OR excludes (i) decreases in reserves due to subscriptions in gold and U.S. dollars to international financial agencies and (ii) increases in reserves due to Canadian gold production. (However (i) is included in BLK.) These exclusions are made because the relation requires a definition of change in official reserves net of movements which do not directly affect the exchange rate.

2. Forward Exchange Rate

The theory adopted for explaining the forward exchange rate is based on the assertion that the spot and forward exchange rates and the corresponding (in terms of maturity) appropriate short-term interest rates at home and abroad *under perfect arbitrage* must satisfy a definite relation. This relation may be derived as follows.[3] Let

rs = spot exchange rate, number of units of foreign currency per unit of domestic currency
rf = forward exchange rate of maturity m, number of units of foreign currency per unit of domestic currency
cis = domestic interest rate of duration m, in percent
$usis$ = foreign interest rate of duration m, in percent
cs = number of units of spot domestic currency
cf = number of units of forward (duration m) domestic currency
uss = number of units of spot foreign currency
usf = number of units of forward (duration m) foreign currency

Given competition the following relations hold simultaneously.

$$cf = (1 + cis/100) * cs \qquad \text{(i)}$$
$$usf = (1 + usis/100) * uss \qquad \text{(ii)}$$
$$uss = rs * cs \qquad \text{(iii)}$$
$$usf = rf * cf \qquad \text{(iv)}$$

Furthermore, the relations are invertible in the sense that (i), (ii), (iii), and (iv) yield expressions for cs, uss, cs, and cf, respectively.

Substituting (iii) in (ii), and (i) and (ii) in (iv),

$$(1 + usis/100) * rs * cs = rf * (1 + cis/100) * cs$$

Assume $cs \neq 0$. Then

$$(1 + usis/100) * rs = rf * (1 + cis/100)$$

Solving for rf,

$$rf = [(1 + usis/100)/(1 + cis/100)] * rs \qquad \text{(v)}$$

3. The presentation derives from Jaroslav Vanek, *International Trade: Theory and Economic Policy* (Homewood, 1962), pp. 58–60.

Let *rsa* denote the right-hand side of (v). Then *rsa* is the basic variable explaining the forward exchange rate, but it must be specialized to fit the Canadian case. There is not a unique maturity of forward exchange. However, the only published data refer to a maturity of ninety days. Interest rates must have a corresponding maturity, and they are measured by the rates on three-month treasury bills. It is not expected that relation (v) holds exactly. The interest rates chosen are not the appropriate ones under all circumstances, there are costs of transactions, and arbitrageurs and their agents may not act in a purely competitive manner. Therefore (v) cannot be included in the model as a non-stochastic behavioral relation. For the same reasons the coefficient of *rsa* is not constrained to be unity. Moreover, a constant term adjusted by seasonal dummy variables is included in the equation along with an error term. These considerations add the following variables to the model.

RF = ninety-day forward exchange rate, number of United States dollars per Canadian dollar
RSA = spot exchange rate adjusted for United States and Canadian short-term interest rates, number of United States dollars per Canadian dollar
CIS = interest rate on government of Canada three-month treasury bills, percent per quarter
USIS = interest rate on United States three-month treasury bills, percent per quarter

The following identity holds.

$$\text{RSA} = [(1 + \text{USIS}/100)/(1 + \text{CIS}/100)] * \text{RS}$$

A measure of the profit to be earned by means of arbitrage is the forward exchange differential, defined as

$$\text{RFD} = \text{RF} - \text{RSA}$$

where RFD = forward exchange differential, number of United States dollars per Canadian dollar

This suggests an additional reason for the divergence of the forward from the adjusted spot exchange rate. Because of liquidity constraints, market imperfections, and other considerations, participants may expect a larger return if foreign exchange cum money market arbitrage is postponed or hastened, as the case may be. If the absolute value of the forward exchange differential is expected to increase (decrease), arbitrageurs will slow down (speed up) their actions, unless the sign of the forward exchange differential is expected to change. Expectation of a change in the sign in itself may speed up (or slow down) arbitrage. The importance of this effect depends on the relative accessibility of funds and comparable money market instruments at home and abroad. This factor may have been of some importance in the early years of the fluctuating rate when the Canadian money market was in a primitive state of development. Assume that all such expectations are a function of the rate of change of the forward exchange differential. Because the time period of the model is discrete, this reduces to the change in the forward exchange differential over the previous quarter, which is defined by the identity

$$\text{CRFD} = \text{RFD} - \text{RFD1}$$

where CRFD = change in forward exchange differential, number of United States dollars per Canadian dollar
RFD1 = forward exchange differential, number of United States dollars per Canadian dollar, lagged one quarter

CRFD is adopted as an explanatory variable in addition to RSA.

One more influence on the forward exchange rate must be considered. This is a factor peculiar to the Canadian case. It is recalled that the Canadian dollar was unpegged just because of the consequences of the expectation that the dollar would be appreciated. After the dollar was freed, the expectation of appreciation prevailed, though alteration in the exchange rate would now be the result of market forces rather than a discontinuous change in a pegged value. Therefore the general public (excluding the banks) tended to sell forward United States dollars in large quantities. The government was determined to avoid a large and sudden rise in the forward exchange rate, and hence "the Exchange Fund Account undertook forward transactions with the banks to assist them in making forward rate protection available to their customers on reasonable terms."[4] Thus the Exchange Fund ended up a net buyer of forward United States dollars. In fact, for some time it offered to purchase forward United States dollars at a fixed discount from the spot rate.

The government ceased its active role some time in the last quarter of 1951. A government publication mentions "the forward exchange facilities made available by EFA to commercial banks in 1950 and up to December 1951."[5] In fact the net forward position of the Exchange Fund Account became negative at the end of November 1951.[6] Clearly the governmental action here described tended to depress the forward exchange rate from what it would have been in the absence of such action.[7] The relation explaining the forward rate includes a jump factor altering the intercepts in the year 1951, thus giving some attention to the role of the government.

It is interesting that the public was able to be a large and persistent net seller of forward United States dollars even though exchange control was in effect. The regulation governing forward transactions from the freeing of the exchange rate until the abolition of exchange control on December 14, 1951, was as follows:

> Banks may, without permit from the Board, enter into forward contracts with resident customers for either the purchase or sale of exchange, regardless of the term or purpose of the contracts. A bank may, however, deliver foreign exchange under a forward contract only where at the time of delivery the exchange is to be used for an authorized purpose.[8]

4. Foreign Exchange Control Board, *Annual Report for 1951*, p. 20.
5. Bank of Canada, *Statistical Summary, Financial Supplement, 1955*, p. 52, footnote 3.
6. *Ibid.*, p. 52.
7. It has been argued that the spot exchange rate as well was lowered by this policy. See Harry C. Eastman and Stefan Stykolt, "Exchange Stabilization in Canada, 1950–4," *Canadian Journal of Economics and Political Science*, 22: 230–231 (May 1956).
8. Foreign Exchange Control Board, *Annual Report for 1950*, p. 19.

Inference from this experience can only be that exchange control did not have a significant effect on transactions in the forward exchange market after the exchange rate was unpegged. This supports the position that the existence of exchange control in 1951 did not alter the general structure of the model.[9] The equation adopted is:

$$\begin{aligned} RF = {} & a_2 + b_2 * RSA + c_2 * CRFD + d_2 * FA + e_2 * Q1 \\ & + f_2 * Q2 + g_2 * Q3 + E_2 \end{aligned}$$

where FA = 1 if 1951, 0 otherwise

It is expected that the sign of b_2 is positive and that of d_2 negative. The coefficient c_2 is a function of the type of expectations arbitrageurs possess. Its sign cannot be designated a priori.

RSA and CRFD are current endogenous variables. FA is predetermined.

The estimated equation:

$$\begin{aligned} RF = {} & 0.063 + 0.94 * RSA - 2.4 * CRFD - 0.013 * FA \\ & - 0.0021 * Q1 + 0.000021 * Q2 - 0.00088 * Q3 \end{aligned} \qquad \text{(AOT)}$$

$$p = 0.18 \quad DW = 1.86 \quad RSQ = 0.88 \quad RSQC = 0.99$$

3. Exports of Merchandise to the United States

Explanation of Canadian merchandise exports proceeds by dividing them into areas of destination. In the period 1951 to 1961, inclusive,[10] the United States was by far Canada's best customer, taking 58 percent of the total value of Canadian ex-

9. See chapter I. Discussion of the experience is found in Eastman and Stykolt, pp. 228–231 and in Harry C. Eastman, "Aspects of Speculation in the Canadian Market for Foreign Exchange," *Canadian Journal of Economics and Political Science*, 24: 362 (August 1958).

10. Although for the purpose of estimating parameters of the model observations run from the first quarter of 1951 to the first quarter of 1962, inclusive, the practice of omitting the final observation is followed in assigning weights for index number construction and also in general for comparisons over the sample period. This is done to avoid giving undue importance to the first quarter of the year.

ports. It is clear that a relation to explain Canadian exports to the United States itself is warranted.

This and the accompanying equations explain real rather than current-dollar flows. The dependent variable is obtained by deflating current-dollar exports by a current-weighted index of (Canadian) export prices. The deflator is a current- rather than base-weighted index because the objective is to yield a series which is a real flow—one from which changes in price have been eliminated. The time base of the price index is 1957, that is, its average value for that year is unity. Therefore the resulting variable is a measure of real exports *expressed in 1957 dollars.* The general result is readily seen by the use of symbols. Let q refer to quantity (volume), p price, n the current period, and o the base period. The current-dollar flow is $\sum q_n p_n$. This is deflated by the current-weighted price index $\sum p_n q_n / \sum p_o q_n$. Carrying out the division,

$$\begin{aligned}\sum q_n p_n / (\sum p_n q_n / \sum p_o q_n) &= \sum q_n p_n * (\sum p_o q_n / \sum p_n q_n) = \sum p_o q_n \\ &= \sum q_n p_o\end{aligned}$$

Indexes that are variables in the model have time base 1957, and all but those in one category are adjusted so the average value for the year 1957 is unity. The exception is constant-dollar flows of the national accounts, for which 1957 remains the time base but for which the sum of observations over the year 1957 equals the sum of the corresponding current-dollar values rather than four.

The relation here discussed sets a pattern for all equations explaining merchandise exports, by including both an income and a price effect. To measure the activity effect, the United States industrial production index is introduced as an explanatory variable. The alternative of taking a national accounts measure of activity is not readily applicable because a real variable is required, and deflated United States national accounts are not published in seasonally unadjusted form. In any event the index of industrial production would be chosen, because the bulk of Canadian exports to the United States are forest products and metals and minerals rather than food and fully manufactured goods. To help measure the price effect, an index of prices of exports competitive to Canada is constructed. This indicates the prices of goods substitutable for Canadian exports. A *base-weighted* index measures Canadian export prices, since in this case the concern is the use of prices for analysis rather than for deflation of corresponding current-dollar flows. The ratio of the two indexes serves to measure the price effect, but the Canadian price index refers to Canadian dollar values while the other index is based on foreign currencies. Therefore the price index of Canadian exports is multiplied by the spot exchange rate, thus converting it to prices in foreign currency.

The time structure of this equation is unusual. Industrial production is not lagged at all, whereas the price variable is lagged one quarter. The geographical location of the United States in relation to Canada, the close corporate links between the two countries—these links fostered by direct investment—the habitual trading relationships, and the commodity distribution of Canadian exports to the United States create a situation in which the activity variable enters the equation without lag. However, the price variable is lagged because the substitutability refers to competing exports on a worldwide scale rather than to import-competing industries in the United States.

Among other factors possibly influencing the flow of merchandise from Canada to the United States are the state of the United States gold stock and liquid liabilities, and tariffs and other restrictions on trade. Although it is conceivable that restrictions on merchandise trade could be a function of the international reserves and balance of payments positions of the United States, in fact this did not occur in the period of interest. Regarding changes in tariffs and other restrictions per se, it is assumed they were unimportant or did not operate systematically on Canadian exports. In general such changes were not discriminatory against Canada. Then the following equation explains merchandise exports to the United States:

$$\begin{aligned} \text{XUS} = {} & a_3 + b_3 * \text{USIP} + c_3 * \text{PXRPO1} + d_3 * \text{Q1} \\ & + e_3 * \text{Q2} + f_3 * \text{Q3} + E_3 \end{aligned}$$

where XUS = exports of merchandise to the United States, in millions of constant (1957) dollars
USIP = index of industrial production of the United States, 1957 = 1
PXRPO1 = ratio of product of base-weighted price index of Canadian exports and spot exchange rate to price index of exports competitive to Canada, lagged one quarter

A positive income and negative price effect implies that b_3 is greater and c_3 less than zero. USIP is exogenous to the model. PXRPO1 is endogenous but predetermined, because it is a lagged variable.

The estimated equation is:

$$\begin{aligned} XUS = & -\underset{(140.0)}{190.0} + \underset{(110.0)}{700.0} * USIP + \underset{(150.0)}{240.0} * PXRPO1 \\ & - \underset{(10.0)}{84.0} * Q1 - \underset{(12.0)}{28.0} * Q2 - \underset{(11.0)}{6.8} * Q3 \qquad \text{(ALS)} \end{aligned}$$

$$p = 0.55 \quad DW = 1.99 \quad RSQ = 0.79 \quad RSQC = 0.86$$

4. Exports of Merchandise to the United Kingdom

Canada's external economic relationships are skewed not only in the direction of the United States but also in the direction of the United Kingdom. Britain took 16 percent of the value of Canadian merchandise exports in the period 1951–1961, inclusive. Therefore the United States and United Kingdom together account for virtually three quarters of Canadian exports. As in the equation explaining exports to the United States, the index of industrial production is adopted as an explanatory variable. It is true that food constitutes a far greater proportion of British imports from Canada than it does of United States imports. This suggests a role for disposable income, but it is assumed that this influence is sufficiently represented by industrial production. Official quarterly national accounts for the United Kingdom do not exist prior to 1954. The price variable is the same as that included in the equation explaining exports to the United States, but the lag is different. A longer lag underpins this relation, partly because of the factor of distance, partly because corporate links between Canada and the United Kingdom are not as pervasive as those between Canada and the United States.

Klein and his associates suggest that a variable indicating the reserves position of the United Kingdom be included in equations explaining British imports "—to show the influence of wealth on purchases and as a proxy for the stringency of controls."[11] The measure they choose is the ratio of gold and dollar reserves to total (merchandise) imports over the two preceding years. It is true that official reserves should not be considered *independent* of the need for reserves; but Klein's denominator does not give proper attention to the fact that the United Kingdom is a reserve currency country. This suggests that sterling liabilities outstanding serve as the denominator. Moreover—even apart from the fact that sterling is a reserve currency—reserves are held to meet balance of payments deficits of all types, not just those induced by merchandise imports. It is not feasible to divide reserves by the balance of payments deficit (or surplus) itself (appropriately lagged). Although official reserves have historically always been positive, the balance of payments may be in surplus or in deficit and may even have a zero balance. Use of sterling liabilities as the denominator is related to considering balance of payments deficits. The advantage is the provision of a base so that no negative (or zero) value can be obtained.

Official reserves of the United Kingdom consist of gold, U.S. dollars, and insignificant amounts of other convertible currencies. The totality of reserves constitutes the numerator of the variable. The denominator is not so easily selected. Overseas sterling holdings are broken down by areas. Sterling is also held by nonterritorial organizations such as the International Monetary Fund. If the denominator consists only of sterling holdings of the dollar area, the implicit (multilateral) theory *rejected* is that restrictions on imports—insofar as Canadian exports are affected—are a function of the *overall* reserves and balance of payments

11. KBHV, p. 62.

position of the United Kingdom. However, the opposing bilateral theory is rejected, and the multilateral one is accepted. The sterling balances of non-territorial organizations are also included, although exclusion could be defended. Ultimately any overseas sterling holding is a liability of the United Kingdom.

Thus the following relation is added to the model:

$$\begin{aligned} \text{XB} = {} & a_4 + b_4 * \text{BIP2} + c_4 * \text{PXRPO2} + d_4 * \text{RESB2} \\ & + e_4 * \text{Q1} + f_4 * \text{Q2} + g_4 * \text{Q3} + E_4 \end{aligned}$$

where XB = exports of merchandise to the United Kingdom, in millions of constant (1957) dollars

BIP2 = index of industrial production of the United Kingdom, 1957 = 1, lagged two quarters

PXRPO2 = ratio of product of base-weighted price index of Canadian exports and spot exchange rate to price index of exports competitive to Canada, lagged two quarters

RESB2 = beginning-of-quarter ratio of British official reserves to overseas sterling holdings, lagged two quarters

BIP2 and RESB2 are lagged exogenous variables. PXRPO2 is endogenous but lagged. Therefore all three variables are predetermined. A priori it is expected that b_4 is positive and c_4 negative. It is assumed that an increase (decrease) in the value of RESB2 induces the British government to adopt less restrictive (more restrictive) controls on imports. Therefore d_4 is theoretically greater than zero.

Equation 4 in estimated form is as follows.

$$\begin{aligned} \text{XB} = {} & \underset{(47.0)}{71.0} + \underset{(34.0)}{230.0} * \text{BIP2} - \underset{(52.0)}{110.0} * \text{PXRPO2} \\ & + \underset{(74.0)}{76.0} * \text{RESB2} - \underset{(8.3)}{19.0} * \text{Q1} - \underset{(8.0)}{6.5} * \text{Q2} \\ & - \underset{(8.1)}{2.2} * \text{Q3} \qquad \text{(LS)} \end{aligned}$$

$$\text{DW} = 1.91 \quad \text{RSQ} = 0.69$$

5. Exports of Merchandise to OECD and Japan

The third area considered as recipient of Canadian exports consists of the members of the Organization for Economic Cooperation and Development (excluding Canada, the United States and the United Kingdom) together with Japan. Although an observer to the OECD, Yugoslavia is excluded from this group. However, Spain is included in this area. Its relation to the OECD and OEEC was much closer than that of Yugoslavia. This group of countries accounts for 13 percent of Canadian exports in the time period 1951–1961, that is, somewhat more than half of non-U.S.–, non-U.K.–destination exports. Western Europe and Japan are lumped together because their economies grew at high rates for much of the time period of interest; and the element of distance, associated with which is the lag structure of the relationship, should not differ significantly. It is true that Japan is now a member of OECD, but it joined in 1963—beyond the time period of the study. Both Japan and Western Europe are developed areas, although some countries of the OECD are not highly developed. In general, however, growth and change in Western Europe were contagious. A complete list of the countries in the area under consideration is as follows: Belgium, Netherlands, Luxembourg, France, West Germany, Italy, Norway, Sweden, Switzerland, Austria, Denmark, Iceland, Greece, Spain, Portugal, Turkey, Ireland, and Japan.

Price and activity variables similar to those in the equations explaining exports to the United States and Britain are included in the relation dealing with exports to the OECD countries and Japan. The price variable is unchanged. It could be argued that this variable should be altered in one respect depending on the relation which it enters. The price index of competing exports could be constructed with weights depending on the commodity distribution of Canadian exports to the area under consideration. However, joint area-commodity breakdowns of Canadian exports exist in readily available and useful form only for the United States and United Kingdom and only since 1953. Moreover, the current-weighted price index which is used to deflate current-dollar exports exists only for Canada's overall exports.

The variable used to measure the income effect consists of a weighted average of measures of activity in the countries which constitute the area. Insofar as availability of data permits, these measures are taken to be indexes of industrial production. Other measures used are indexes of employment and of volume (as distinct from monetary value) of exports. A grand index of activity is constructed by weighting the country indexes by the respective totals of current-dollar imports of Canadian merchandise over the years 1951 to 1961, inclusive.

A variable to measure the effect of gold and dollar reserves is not included. Such a variable is included for the United Kingdom and not for the OECD and Japan because: (1) The United Kingdom is a single governmental entity, whereas the OECD and Japan consist of eighteen countries. The reserves positions of eighteen countries may differ widely. (2) Reserves are a priori more crucial for the United Kingdom because it is a reserve currency country. (3) A satisfactory indicator of the need for reserves, namely, sterling liabilities, exists for Britain. (4) The reserves position was more serious and balance of payments difficulties more prevalent for the United Kingdom over the time period of interest.

The above considerations lead to the following relationship:

$$\begin{aligned} \text{XWEJ} = {} & a_5 + b_5 * \text{WEJIP2} + c_5 * \text{PXRPO2} + d_5 * \text{Q1} \\ & + e_5 * \text{Q2} + f_5 * \text{Q3} + E_5 \end{aligned}$$

where XWEJ = exports of merchandise to OECD countries and Japan, in millions of constant (1957) dollars

WEJIP2 = index of production in OECD countries and Japan, 1957 = 1, lagged two quarters

All explanatory variables in the relation are predetermined. The theoretical sign of b_5 is positive and that of c_5 negative.

The estimated relationship is:

$$\begin{aligned} \text{XWEJ} = {} & \underset{(61.0)}{160.0} + \underset{(20.0)}{140.0} * \text{WEJIP2} - \underset{(67.0)}{120.0} * \text{PXRPO2} \\ & - \underset{(7.1)}{43.0} * \text{Q1} - \underset{(7.8)}{29.0} * \text{Q2} - \underset{(7.1)}{13.0} * \text{Q3} \qquad \text{(ALS)} \end{aligned}$$

$p = 0.26 \quad \text{DW} = 1.92 \quad \text{RSQ} = 0.73 \quad \text{RSQC} = 0.80$

6. Exports of Merchandise to "Other Countries"

Canada's exports to communist countries constituted one percent of total exports in the period 1951–1961, but were heavily concentrated in 1961—primarily because of wheat sales to Communist China. Communist countries are defined as Albania, Bulgaria, Czechoslovakia, East Germany, Hungary, Poland, Rumania, the Soviet Union, Communist China and Yugoslavia. These countries are state-trading, that is, foreign trade is a monopoly of the state. The one exception is Yugoslavia, which since 1959 adopted a decentralized approach both for the domestic economy and foreign trade. Canadian exports to these countries are discontinuous and volatile in the period of interest. Canada had most-favored-nation arrangements with Czechoslovakia, Poland, Yugoslavia, and Communist China throughout the period covered by the model and with the Soviet Union since 1956. But the foreign trade monopoly, coupled with the economic policies of these centrally planned economies, subjects trade with Canada (as with other non-state-trading economies) to vicissitudes depending on the state of the economic plan. In addition these countries tend to adopt a policy of bilateralism in trade with free economies. This policy restricts and warps trade. For all these reasons constant-dollar exports to communist countries are a predetermined variable in the model.

The rest of the world accounts for the remaining 12 percent of Canadian exports. These exports are endogenous to the model. It is true that some of the remarks in the preceding paragraph apply to certain "other countries" of the world as well as to communist countries. However, Canada's exports to the former countries are more regular because politically Canada is on better terms with them and trade relations are better developed. Also foreign (especially direct) investment is generally allowed (though possibly restricted) in these countries. This is an important factor fostering predictable trading relationships.

The rest of the world ("other countries")[12] includes both developed and underdeveloped economies, but most are underdeveloped. Moreover, their growth has not been as rapid as that of Western Europe and Japan. Exports to "other countries" are basically explained by means of a price and an income variable, as is the case with other export equations. The price variable is identical to that included in the other relations explaining merchandise exports. The income variable is a weighted average of indexes of activity in these various countries. The weight for a given country is the sum of Canadian current-dollar exports to that country over the years 1951 to 1961. Measures of activity are indexes of production, employment, or *real* exports, as the case may be. Every "other country" for which a suitable measure of activity can be found is included in the overall index. There are two situations in which it is decided that the measure is unsuitable. The first is the case of Tunisia. Exports to Tunisia are nil prior to 1960. An index of mining production exists, but shows greater values in earlier years. This index is not included in the overall activity variable. In any case its weight would be very small. The second situation concerns those countries for which the only available measure is *current-dollar* exports. This is not considered to be a suitable measure of activity, and therefore is excluded from the overall index.[13]

During the period under discussion, some of these countries at times had acute balance of payments problems. Some had exchange control. It would be very difficult to set up a variable measuring—even by proxy—restrictions on trade for all these countries together. And the relevant data would be scattered.

12. To avoid ambiguity the term "other countries" is enclosed by quotation marks if, and only if, it refers to all countries other than Canada, United States, United Kingdom, OECD area, Japan, and communist states. Unless otherwise implied, the *unenclosed* term means all countries other than Canada and the United States.

13. In explaining British exports to the dependent sterling area, KBHV make use of current-dollar exports to construct a measure of activity, deflating the values by the price index of *British* exports (KBHV, p. 70). This procedure is legitimate for colonies of the United Kingdom with respect to British exports because the principal supplier is Britain itself; but such a justification has no applicability to the case of Canada.

Moreover for some countries, such as South Africa and oil-producing states of the Middle East, the balance of payments position could hardly be sufficiently unfavorable to induce restrictions on imports.

However, another variable is included in the relation, namely, Canada's foreign aid to "other countries." Foreign aid consists of official contributions (grants) and drawings on government of Canada loans. The only official loans during the period of interest were advances to India and Ceylon in 1958 and 1959 to finance imports of Canadian wheat and flour. Only a small proportion of official donations represents technical assistance; the bulk constitutes a debit entry in the balance of payments corresponding to merchandise exports forwarded abroad as a donation. Because of its virtual one-to-one relationship with Canadian merchandise exports, it is clear that this variable should not be lagged. It is divided by the base-weighted index of export prices. Deflation by a current-weighted price index is inappropriate because foreign aid is not a national accounts expenditure flow. Deflation by a current-weighted price index takes place only when it is desired to obtain a base-weighted quantity index. This does not apply in the present case.

The equation explaining exports to "other countries" is:

$$\mathrm{XO} = a_6 + b_6 * \mathrm{OIP2} + c_6 * \mathrm{PXRPO2} + d_6 * \mathrm{OCDPXB} + e_6 * \mathrm{Q1} + f_6 * \mathrm{Q2} + g_6 * \mathrm{Q3} + \mathbf{E}_6$$

where XO = exports of merchandise to "other countries," in millions of constant (1957) dollars

OIP2 = index of production in "other countries," 1957 = 1, lagged two quarters

OCDPXB = drawings on government of Canada loans plus official contributions to "other countries," divided by base-weighted index of export prices, in millions of deflated dollars[14]

OIP2 and PXRPO2 are predetermined. OCDPXB is current endogenous because its denominator is a current endogenous

14. The term "deflated" rather than "constant" is used because the latter implies that deflation of a current-dollar series is performed by means of a *current-weighted* price index (or approximation to that measure).

variable. The a priori signs of b_6 and c_6 are positive and negative, respectively. It is expected that e_6 is positive. It should be in the order of unity but not identically one because foreign aid may have effects—either stimulatory or depressive—on other exports in addition to those it directly finances. However, Canada's foreign aid is perhaps too small to give scope to additional effects.

The estimated equation:

$$\begin{aligned} XO = {} & \underset{(70.0)}{240.0} + \underset{(51.0)}{69.0} * OIP2 - \underset{(72.0)}{160.0} * PXRPO2 \\ & + \underset{(0.85)}{0.029} * OCDPXB - \underset{(5.7)}{13.0} * Q1 + \underset{(6.5)}{3.2} * Q2 \\ & - \underset{(6.1)}{11.0} * Q3 \qquad \text{(AOT)} \end{aligned}$$

$$p = 0.50 \quad DW = 1.96 \quad RSQ = 0.40 \quad RSQC = 0.38$$
$$RSQT(OCDPXB) = 0.72$$

7. Imports of Merchandise from the United States

In the period 1951 to 1961 the United States was the source of 70 percent of the total value of Canada's imports. The relation to explain this flow deals with real imports rather than imports measured in current dollars. To obtain the dependent variable, current-dollar imports from the United States must be deflated by an index of prices. Strictly speaking, a current-weighted price index should be used. But the weights of the only existing current-weighted price index of Canadian merchandise imports refer to *all* imports regardless of origin. Because of the nature of the equation it is better to use a price index referring to United States exports alone. A current-weighted price index of United States exports exists, but (1) it includes service components of the balance of payments, and (2) it is seasonally adjusted. These two disadvantages make the index clearly unsatisfactory for the purpose of deflating seasonally unadjusted merchandise exports.

Therefore deflation takes place by means of the official index of unit value of United States exports. Because expression of the dependent variable in Canadian dollars is desired, the deflator is itself divided by an index of the spot exchange rate. The resulting variable is said to be expressed in constant (1957) dollars, although this is not a precise statement since deflation by the appropriate current-weighted price index is required.

Because the United States is the origin of such a high proportion of Canadian imports, the totality of merchandise imports (in constant dollars) is itself an explanatory variable. In fact the theory adopted is that imports from the United States are some fraction of total imports, but this proportion tends to be altered because of price effects and seasonal factors. In order to obtain a variable to measure the price effect it is necessary to construct an index of the export prices of other exporters to Canada, that is, exporters other than the United States. This is done by weighting measures of export prices (one for each country included in the index) by the country's total exports (in current dollars) to Canada in the period 1951 to 1961, inclusive. The index includes measures of export prices of all countries from which Canada's imports are not negligible and for which the requisite price information is available. The price variable is then the ratio of the unit value index of United States exports to the export price index of other exporters to Canada.

Actually only those countries from which Canada imports merchandise competitive with United States exports should be included in the denominator of the ratio. One way to attempt to accomplish this would be to include export price measures only of countries similar to the United States, say, developed countries. This procedure is not followed, but it nevertheless turns out that the bulk of the weight in the index refers to developed countries. Even so, some countries included in the index may export commodities that are complements to Canadian imports from the United States. But in the overall index it is assumed that the substitution effect predominates. This is highly likely, because countries such as the United Kingdom, Japan, and West Germany dominate the index and their exports tend to be competitive with U.S. exports to Canada, since they concentrate on exports of manufactured goods. This is not to deny that complementarity exists even among manufactured goods, but it is assumed that the substitution effect dominates.

Both numerator and denominator of the price variable should be base-weighted indexes. But the only available official measure for United States exports is the index of unit value. With respect to the denominator of the ratio the overall index is base-weighted as explained above. (The base is the entire period 1951–1961.) The component indexes, however, are not all base-weighted indexes of export prices. Other measures such as indexes of wholesale prices of export goods or indexes of unit value are used, if no base-weighted index exists. The price variable is lagged one quarter. The lag is the same as that of the price variable in stochastic equation (3) because the considerations are the same. If the price effect under examination were the result of substitution between United States imports and Canadian domestically produced goods, the variable would enter without lag. Then the following equation is adopted:

$$\text{GMUS} = a_7 + b_7 * \text{GM} + c_7 * \text{PMUSP1} + d_7 * \text{Q1} + e_7 * \text{Q2} + f_7 * \text{Q3} + E_7$$

where GMUS = imports of merchandise from the United States, in millions of constant (1957) dollars

GM = total imports of merchandise, in millions of constant (1957) dollars

PMUSP1 = ratio of price index of United States exports to price index of exports of other countries exporting to Canada, lagged one quarter

GM is a current endogenous variable while PMUSP1 is predetermined. b_7 is theoretically greater than zero. It is assumed that the substitution effect with respect to price predominates. Therefore c_7 should be negative.

The estimated form of the equation is:

$$\begin{aligned} GMUS = {} & \underset{(270.0)}{420.0} + \underset{(0.11)}{0.67} * GM - \underset{(380.0)}{410.0} * PMUSP1 \\ & + \underset{(20.0)}{50.0} * Q1 + \underset{(20.0)}{19.0} * Q2 - \underset{(17.0)}{8.2} * Q3 \qquad \text{(AOT)} \end{aligned}$$

$$p = 0.34 \quad DW = 1.91 \quad RSQ = 0.79 \quad RSQC = 0.91$$
$$RSQT(GM) = 0.94$$

8. Imports of Consumer Goods

The following four equations explain stochastically various commodity groups of imports. Each classification relates to imports irrespective of country of origin. As regards the explanation according to area, imports from countries other than the United States are discussed under equation 62. The criterion used to divide imports into commodity classes is an end-use classification. The categories are (1) consumer goods, (2) investment goods, (3) industrial materials, and (4) fuels and lubricants.

This equation and the three subsequent ones explain *real* imports. The current-dollar flow of imports is deflated by a current-weighted price index itself divided by the index of the spot exchange rate in order to convert to Canadian currency. (All base-weighted and current-weighted indexes of prices of imports are defined exogenously, that is, net of movements in the exchange rate.) Therefore the resultant variable is expressed in constant dollars. Moreover, all four equations contain both price and income effects. The consumer goods equation includes disposable income as an explanatory variable. Because the dependent variable is deflated, so is this explanatory variable. Disposable income is divided by a base-weighted price index of imports of consumer goods itself divided by the index of the spot exchange rate. The divisor is not the *current*-weighted price index because it is not desired to obtain a base-weighted quantity index. A base-weighted quantity index of an income—as distinct from expenditure—variable in the national accounts is not a meaningful concept. It is assumed that the distribution of disposable income is not of significance in this relation. The equation explains not *sales* to consumers but rather *imports*. What is relevant is the total demand of the personal sector. If sales are one element by which Canadian importers determine orders, then disposable income is a proxy for sales; it is a more "basic" factor.

To measure the price effect the following variable is introduced: the ratio of the base-weighted price index of imports of consumer goods divided by the index of the spot exchange rate to the price index of domestically produced consumer goods. The problem here is that there are no raw data by means of which a price index of *domestically produced* consumer goods can be constructed from first principles, that is, by taking a weighted average of price indexes of individual commodities. The base-weighted price index of imports of consumer goods is easily computed from first principles. In addition an index of consumer goods—both imported and domestically produced—can be obtained by weighting the durable and non-durable goods components of the official consumer price index. This information allows four possible ways of obtaining the required price index.

Solution (a): Use the price index of (all) consumer goods as a proxy for the price index of domestically produced consumer goods. The disadvantage of this method is that both the numerator and denominator of the price ratio include prices of imports. This solution is acceptable only when the volume of imports is insignificant in relation to that of goods produced domestically.

Solution (b): Let P_o = price index of (all) consumer goods

P_m = price index of imports of consumer goods divided by index of spot exchange rate

P^c_o = measure of price index of domestically produced consumer goods

P_o and P_m are known. Consider P_o to be a weighted average of P_m and P^c_o, thus

$$P_o = (A * P_m + B * P^c_o)/(A + B)$$

Rearranging terms,

$$P_o^c = [(A + B) * P_o - A * P_m]/B$$

The difficulty is assigning of the weights. The problem refers to not only substance but also time period. Ideal weights might be A = imports of consumer goods, B = domestic output of consumer goods. However, the data concerning domestic output of consumer goods do not exist. Moreover, should the weights be lagged variables? Should they constitute moving averages?

Solution (c): Estimate the coefficients a and b in the following equation:

$$P_o = a + b * P_m + e$$

where e is an error term.

Let $$P_o^c = P_o - \hat{b} * P_m = \hat{a} + \hat{e}$$

be the measure of the price of domestically produced consumer goods.

The problem is that this solution tends to overestimate the importance of imports because of collinearity between P_o and P_m. Moreover, it does not give attention to the structure of determination of the price index of (all) consumer goods.

Solution (d): This is the method adopted. It extends (c) to consideration of *structure*. Take the weighted average of the durable and non-durable components of the consumer price index, but first purify each component of its import content of consumer goods by means of the equation in the model which explains the appropriate component of the consumer price index. Among the variables which explain the price index of durable (or non-durable) consumer goods is the base-weighted price index of imports of durable (non-durable) consumer goods. Subtract the adjusted price index (including exchange rate variation) of imports of durable (non-durable) consumer goods from the price index of (all) durable (non-durable) consumer goods, and multiply all observations of the result by an appropriate factor in order to obtain 1957 as the time base. The index of prices of domestically produced consumer goods is a weighted average of the two resulting indexes. The weights here are the sums of the weights of the durable and non-durable components, respectively, of the base-weighted price index of imports of consumer goods.

Both price and income variables enter the equation without lag. It is true that this is only an approximation to a true relationship; it really represents a mean "lag." In the period 1953 to 1961, inclusive,[15] 65 percent of the value of imports of consumer goods came from the United States. The lag is short because of factors discussed under equation 3 above, namely, the location of the United States in relation to Canada, the close corporate links between the two countries, and habitual trading relations. An additional reason is the size of the Canadian economy in relation to that of the United States. Imports can be ordered and sent with little delay because there is no need of production prior to dispatching, since the Canadian economy is small relative to the United States economy. Another justification of a short lag is independent of Canada's special relationship with the United States: the imports under consideration represent final goods. With the exception of imports of parts of passenger automobiles, they are not required as inputs for purposes of producing final goods. These imports in general are to be directly distributed for purposes of sales to consumers (or inventories to cover such sales). In summary the equation adopted is:

$$\text{GMC} = a_8 + b_8 * \text{YDMC} + c_8 * \text{PMCRPD} + d_8 * \text{Q1} + e_8 * \text{Q2} + f_8 * \text{Q3} + E_8$$

where GMC = imports of consumer goods, in millions of constant (1957) dollars

YDMC = disposable income divided by base-weighted price index of imports of consumer goods itself divided by the index of the spot exchange rate, in millions of deflated dollars

PMCRPD = ratio of base-weighted price index of imports of consumer goods divided by index of spot exchange rate to price index of domestically produced consumer goods

15. Information for 1951 and 1952 does not exist.

Both YDMC and PMCRPD are current endogenous variables. The income effect b_8 is theoretically positive. The price effect c_8 is a priori negative because both the imports and domestic output to which the price ratio refers are final consumer goods.

The estimated equation is:

$$\begin{aligned} \text{GMC} = {} & \underset{(270.0)}{260.0} + \underset{(0.0065)}{0.079} * \text{YDMC} - \underset{(250.0)}{280.0} * \text{PMCRPD} \\ & - \underset{(8.5)}{21.0} * \text{Q1} + \underset{(9.4)}{23.0} * \text{Q2} - \underset{(9.3)}{83.0} * \text{Q3} \qquad \text{(AJT)} \end{aligned}$$

$$p = 0.30 \quad \text{DW} = 1.98 \quad \text{RSQ} = 0.87 \quad \text{RSQC} = 0.90$$

$$\text{RSQT(YDMC)} = 0.97 \quad \text{RSQT(PMCRPD)} = 0.34$$

9. Imports of Investment Goods

Imports of investment goods have the United States as their preponderant origin. Of the total value of such imports in the years 1953 to 1961, inclusive, 84 percent came from the United States. These imports are explained by means of an activity variable and a price variable. The activity variable is business gross fixed capital formation. This is expresed in constant dollars and is not lagged. A portion of imports of investment goods constitutes part of gross fixed capital formation by definition. But in addition domestic fixed investment has a causal effect on imports of investment goods—even those imports that, say, enter inventories. The definition of investment goods includes some commodities (such as construction materials) that are intermediate in nature. The criterion is end-use, namely, fixed investment. The price variable is of the same nature as the corresponding variable in the relation explaining imports of consumer goods. It is the ratio of the base-weighted price index of imports of investment goods divided by the index of the spot exchange rate to the price index of domestically produced investment goods. The price index of domestically produced investment goods is obtained in a manner similar to that by which the price index of domestic output of consumer goods is constructed. The model includes an equation which explains the (overall) price index of investment goods. One of the variables included in that relation is the base-weighted price index of imports of investment goods. The effect of this factor is removed from the overall price index and what remains (appropriately based) is taken to be the price index of domestically produced investment goods. No lag is given to the price variable because of the nature of the commodities imported and the distribution of their origin. These considerations add the following equation to the model.

$$\begin{aligned} \text{GMI} = {} & a_9 + b_9 * \text{GDI} + c_9 * \text{PMIRPD} + d_9 * \text{Q1} \\ & + e_9 * \text{Q2} + f_9 * \text{Q3} + E_9 \end{aligned}$$

where GMI = imports of investment goods, in millions of constant (1957) dollars

GDI = business gross fixed capital formation, in millions of constant (1957) dollars

PMIRPD = ratio of base-weighted price index of imports of investment goods divided by index of spot exchange rate to price index of domestically produced investment goods

GDI and PMIRPD are current endogenous variables. The theoretical sign of b_9 is greater than zero; that of c_9 is less than zero if it is assumed that the substitution effect predominates. Because complementarity of capital goods is of substantial importance in production, it is conceivable that c_9 is of opposite sign. Suppose prices of some domestically produced investment goods fall. Then imports of capital goods complementary to these in production will increase.

The estimated equation:

$$\begin{aligned} \text{GMI} = {} & \underset{(690.0)}{500.0} + \underset{(0.18)}{0.25} * \text{GDI} + \underset{(460.0)}{480.0} * \text{PMIRPD} \\ & + \underset{(47.0)}{77.0} * \text{Q1} + \underset{(25.0)}{51.0} * \text{Q2} - \underset{(25.0)}{19.0} * \text{Q3} \qquad \text{(AJT)} \end{aligned}$$

$p = 0.81$ DW = 1.82 RSQ = 0.76 RSQC = 0.53

RSQT(GDI) = 0.76 RSQT(PMIRPD) = 0.66

10. Imports of Industrial Materials

The previous two equations dealt with imports of final goods; now imports of goods that are intermediate in nature will be considered. Although a price and an income variable are adopted as explanatory variables in the relation to explain imports of industrial materials, both a peculiar lag structure and an additional variable are required to take account of the fact that intermediate goods are at issue. The activity variable is the Canadian economy's output of goods which constitute final sales. This variable is measured in constant dollars, because real—rather than current-dollar—imports are under consideration. The variable is composed of expenditure on goods by consumers and governments, business gross fixed capital formation, and exports of goods; merchandise imports are subtracted. The resultant variable is not the total output of goods, because change in inventories is not included. But it is not total output of goods that is required as a variable. What is needed is that indicator of activity level which is most relevant to this equation. Because industrial materials are used to produce goods, service components of gross national expenditure are excluded. It is true that increased expenditure on services implies a greater demand for goods (a) directly (for example, a barber shop requires more chairs) and (b) indirectly (through multiplier effects). But the result of these demands is included in the activity variable. For precision, only those merchandise imports which are included in the components of the activity variable itself should be subtracted from the gross variable. Those imports included in change in inventories are already implicitly subtracted because of the exclusion of that change. However, such a division of imports is statistically impossible. Moreover, it can be argued that *all* merchandise imports should be subtracted from gross output of goods. To the extent that merchandise imports are industrial materials, they are included in the dependent variable. Therefore they should not be included in the explanatory variable. To the extent that imports are finished goods, an increase in imports does not require an increase in industrial materials (imported or otherwise). But this last remark is not always true because of complementarities in production. Imports of investment goods may be used in production processes which require industrial materials. Taking account of all these factors, it seems better to subtract merchandise imports from gross output of goods rather than to include them.

In the period 1953–1961, 70 percent of imported industrial materials originated from the United States. The activity variable is unlagged, partly because some explanatory variable should be so constructed in order to take account of the preponderance of the United States as the source of imports and partly because it may be considered as the current complement of the lagged explanatory variable to be discussed next.

Because the imports under consideration are raw materials, stocks should be included in their explanation. A stock-flow variable is warranted. The variable selected is the ratio over all manufacturing industries of beginning-of-quarter inventories to sum of shipments over the previous four quarters. The numerator is an all-inclusive measure. It includes inventories of domestic as well as imported goods. (Data confined to imports do not exist.) For each industry inventories divide into raw materials, goods in process, and finished products. Should the inventories of the inventory-shipment ratio be confined to raw materials, or should all three categories of inventories be included? Superficially it can be argued that because imports of only industrial materials are to be explained, the former procedure is appropriate. However, this reasoning ignores the fact that "raw materials" is not an absolute concept. What are raw materials for one industry may represent finished goods for another. To the extent that imports of industrial materials are raw materials (according to statistics of inventories), the first procedure is applicable. To the extent that they are finished goods as well, the second procedure is better; and it is this method which is adopted.

Because imports of industrial materials are expressed in constant dollars, it is desirable to deflate both numerator and denominator of the stock-flow variable. However, because of the problems discussed below both are left in current dollars. The ideal attainable price index for deflation of inventories would be the official measure relating current- to constant-dollar value of the stock of inventories over all manufacturing industries. Unfortunately this index cannot be obtained. An alternative is deflation by an index of wholesale prices. Such a meausre is readily available or can be constructed. "This method should, however, be used with caution. While each industry has its own average turnover rate which can be estimated roughly, it is difficult to estimate a rate which can accurately be applied to raw materials, goods in process and finished goods. Moreover, all firms within a given industry do not value inventories on the same basis, the most common methods being lower of cost or market and standard cost. These considerations make it difficult to determine the length of time necessary before a change in wholesale prices will be reflected in inventory values. Added to this is the fact that the wholesale price index and the index of inventory values are compiled differently. The wholesale price index is computed from selling prices, and weighted according to quantities sold; while, as noted above, most firms report inventories at some variation of cost and the index is automatically weighted according to quantities held."[16] These factors are all the more applicable, because in the case at hand inventories are not confined to an individual industry but refer to *all* manufacturing industries.

The problem of deflating shipments is not as acute, because the time periods are known and use of the wholesale price index does not involve inherently extraneous weights. However, it is absurd to deflate only the denominator of a stock-flow variable. Because the variable is a ratio of two current-dollar series, it is hoped that its divergence from the "true" variable (involving constant-dollar values) is not great, especially since the appropriate deflators would be lagged not only for inventories but also for shipments.

The price variable—corresponding to such variables in the import equations earlier discussed—is the ratio of the base-weighted

16. Dominion Bureau of Statistics, *Inventories, Shipments and Orders in Manufacturing Industries* (December 1953), p. 120.

price index of imports of industrial materials divided by the index of the spot exchange rate to the price index of industrial materials of domestic production. As in the previous cases, the price index of domestically produced industrial materials is obtained by correcting an overall price index (itself determined stochastically) for the price index of imports of industrial materials (one of the explanatory variables). This variable enters with a lag of one quarter because of the tremendous importance of stocks in regard to intermediate as distinct from finished goods. Intensive use of stocks tends to lag adjustments because increases in output can be satisfied by means of inventories on hand. The lag can be safely extended the greater are stock holdings not only in relation to the appropriate flow (the denominator of the inventory-shipment variable) but also absolutely. Therefore imports of industrial materials are explained by the relation:

$$\text{GMIM} = a_{10} + b_{10} * \text{YG} + c_{10} * \text{SMANI} + d_{10} * \text{PIMPD1} + e_{10} * \text{Q1} + f_{10} * \text{Q2} + g_{10} * \text{Q3} + E_{10}$$

where GMIM = imports of industrial materials, in millions of constant (1957) dollars

SMANI = ratio of beginning-of-quarter inventories in all manufacturing industries to sum of shipments over preceding four quarters

PIMPD1 = ratio of base-weighted price index of imports of industrial materials divided by index of spot exchange rate to price index of domestically produced industrial materials, lagged one quarter

YG = output of goods which constitute final sales, in millions of constant (1957) dollars

All explanatory variables except YG are predetermined. The sign of b_{10} is expected to be positive. Theoretical considerations dictate a negative sign for c_{10}. Shipments in the preceding four quarters serve manufacturers as a proxy regarding future demand. (Parenthetically it may be remarked that YG is an index of present demand. It is because YG is included in the equation that unfilled orders—measured at the beginning of the current quarter—are not added to the denominator of the stock-flow variable.) Ability to meet demand depends in part on the stock of industrial materials on hand.

The coefficient of the price variable is theoretically negative, assuming substitutive rather than complementary effects dominate. It is likely that substitution is predominant, because the overall price index is constructed in such a way as to resemble the import price index in weighting structure.

The estimated form of the equation is:

$$\begin{aligned} \text{GMIM} = {} & \underset{(180.0)}{400.0} + \underset{(0.012)}{0.039} * \text{YG} - \underset{(580.0)}{1300.0} * \text{SMANI} \\ & - \underset{(50.0)}{25.0} * \text{PIMPD1} + \underset{(15.0)}{13.0} * \text{Q1} + \underset{(9.9)}{31.0} * \text{Q2} \\ & - \underset{(7.2)}{19.0} * \text{Q3} \qquad \text{(AOT)} \end{aligned}$$

$$p = 0.34 \quad \text{DW} = 2.10 \quad \text{RSQ} = 0.78 \quad \text{RSQC} = 0.84$$
$$\text{RSQT(YG)} = 0.97$$

11. Imports of Fuels and Lubricants

Determinants of imports of fuels and lubricants are of the same nature as determinants of imports of industrial materials. However, attention must be given to the commodity structure of the classification "fuels and lubricants." The classification divides into four principal groups: (1) anthracite coal, (2) bituminous coal, (3) crude petroleum, and (4) gasoline, fuel oils, and lubricating oils. The important fact is that the commodities in group (4) are essentially refined petroleum. Crude petroleum enters as an input in the production function of gasoline and refined oils. Another peculiarity of this commodity class of imports is the reliance on overseas sources of supply. Fifty-eight percent of the total value of imports in the years 1953 to 1961 did *not* come from the United States.

An appropriate activity variable should take account of the fact that fuels and lubricants are used in residences, factories, vehicles, retail outlets, etc. YG (defined above) is used as the basis of such a variable; to it is added (constant-dollar) expenditure on consumer services. This addition is required to take account of the relationship between demand for fuel and expenditure on shelter. Household operation is an important factor. A technical matter is that the variable includes foreign tourist expenditure in Canada but not Canadian expenditure abroad. This is clearly a proper treatment. The variable is lagged, mainly because only 42 percent of imports originate from the United States, also because of the nature of the commodity group under explanation: stocks are of considerable importance.

The nature of fuels and lubricants makes it imperative that a stock-flow relationship be included in the relation. The variable adopted is a weighted average of two sub-ratios. One is the ratio of beginning-of-quarter stocks of coal and coke to sales of these commodities over the preceding four quarters. These quantities are in physical units and are as reported by retail fuel dealers. The other component is the ratio of beginning-of-quarter inventories of refined petroleum products (group 4 in the above classification) to sales of these commodities over the previous four quarters. The inventories here refer to both refinery and market. Refinery inventories are those at the manufacturing plant (the plant that manufactures petroleum products). Marketing inventories are stocks at district or regional outlets under the control of the refinery or of a large-scale distributor marketing its own brands. Retail inventories are excluded. Physical units are used in this ratio as well as in the preceding one. However, the units are different from those in the first sub-ratio. Coal and coke are measured in tons, and refined petroleum products are measured in gallons. The joint ratio involves weighting *after* the two sub-ratios have been computed; this removes the problem of noncomparable units.

The price variable is of a nature different from the corresponding variable in the other import equations. It is defined symmetrically with the others, namely, as the ratio of the base-weighted price index of imports of fuels and lubricants divided by the index of the exchange rate to the price index of domestically produced fuels and lubricants. The difference is that the price index of domestic output is constructed directly. There is no need to consider an "overall" index of prices of fuels and lubricants. Because of data limitations (on the domestic side) only (2) bituminous coal and (4) refined petroleum products are included in the price indexes which compose the variable. The price (as well as the activity) variable is lagged one quarter.

The equation:

$$\text{GMFL} = a_{11} + b_{11} * \text{YGFL1} + c_{11} * \text{SFL} + d_{11} * \text{PFLPD1} + e_{11} * \text{Q1} + f_{11} * \text{Q2} + g_{11} * \text{Q3} + E_{11}$$

where GMFL = imports of fuels and lubricants, in millions of constant (1957) dollars

YGFL1 = output of goods constituting final sales plus personal expenditure on services, in millions of constant (1957) dollars, lagged one quarter

SFL = ratio of beginning-of-quarter inventories of fuels and lubricants to sum of sales over preceding four quarters

PFLPD1 = ratio of base-weighted price index of imports of fuels and lubricants divided by index of spot exchange rate to price index of domestically produced fuels and lubricants, lagged one quarter

All explanatory variables are predetermined. The theoretical sign of b_{11} is positive and that of c_{11} negative. The sign of d_{11} is a priori ambiguous. The commodity class—namely, (3) crude petroleum—which has the greatest weight in imports is not represented in the price variable. A rise in PFLPD1 induces more crude petroleum imports because *domestic* gasoline and oils are now cheaper relative to imports; therefore domestic output will tend to expand. But crude petroleum is required as an input to produce refined products! Therefore imports of crude petroleum will increase. On the other hand, imports of refined petroleum products will decrease. It is true that gasoline and oils do not have the larger weight in the inventory-sales variable; however, crude petroleum constitutes the greatest part of imports themselves. These offsetting factors prevent a priori designation of the sign of the price effect.

The estimated equation:

$$
\begin{aligned}
\text{GMFL} = {} & \underset{(34.0)}{59.0} + \underset{(0.0032)}{0.0080} * \text{YGFL1} - \underset{(120.0)}{98.0} * \text{SFL} \\
& + \underset{(28.0)}{45.0} * \text{PFLPD1} - \underset{(2.5)}{39.0} * \text{Q1} - \underset{(5.2)}{15.0} * \text{Q2} \\
& + \underset{(3.9)}{3.5} * \text{Q3} \qquad \text{(ALS)}
\end{aligned}
$$

$p = 0.53$ DW $= 1.85$ RSQ $= 0.90$ RSQC $= 0.82$

12. Net Payments for Travel

Some of the remaining components of the current account are explained in real terms, others in current dollars. Travel (tourist) expenditure enters the former category. It is possible to include two relations—one to explain travel receipts, the other payments. Instead the net flow is explained, and only one relation is necessary. In this case the net flow is of greater interest than the gross flows, because interest settles on the effect of travel expenditure on the exchange rate rather than its role in providing additions to (or deletions from) gross national expenditure. Because a *real* equation is desired, the problem is to construct a *deflated* net flow of tourist payments. The method of construction is used to obtain deflated net flows of other service components of the balance of payments, and is therefore outlined in detail.

Let P_c = travel payments, in millions of (current) dollars

R_c = travel receipts, in millions of (current) dollars

P_p = price index of travel payments, 1957 = 1

P_r = price index of travel receipts, 1957 = 1

Then gross deflated payments are defined as:

$$P_k = P_c/(P_p/r),$$

and gross deflated receipts:

$$R_k = R_c/P_r$$

Net deflated payments are:

$$\text{TRN} = P_k - R_k \qquad \text{(i)}$$

It should be emphasized that (i) is not an identity which serves to *explain* net deflated payments. Rather it is a symbolic illustration of the *method of construction* of the variable. (TRN is explained *stochastically* and the equation is set forth below.) It is clear that (i) is not an equation of the model, because P_k and R_k are undefined symbols with respect to the model. P_c and R_c are the respective balance of payments flows. The price index of tourist expenditure in Canada (P_r) and that of Canadian tourist expenditure abroad (P_p) should preferably be current-weighted, but the only available indexes are base-weighted. The weights are a function of the distribution of tourist expenditure. Division of the price index of Canadian expenditure abroad by the exchange rate index is required in order to express the resultant variable in Canadian dollars.

In accordance with the tradition thus far established, TRN is explained by both an income and a price variable. The income variable is essentially a ratio of disposable incomes in Canada and abroad. In the period 1951 to 1961, inclusive, the United States accounted for 91 percent of Canada's travel receipts and the United Kingdom for 4 percent. These proportions are used to weight indexes of disposable incomes in the United States and Britain. The result is called the index of disposable income abroad. The income variable is the ratio of the index of Canadian disposable income deflated by the price index of Canadian tourist expenditure abroad itself divided by the index of the spot exchange rate to the index of disposable income abroad converted to Canadian currency (by division by the spot exchange rate) and deflated by the price index of tourist expenditure in Canada. This variable enters the equation lagged one quarter. The lag occurs chiefly because of the planning involved in travel.

The price variable is the ratio of the price index of Canadian tourist expenditure abroad divided by the index of the exchange rate to the price index of tourist expenditure in Canada. These price indexes are identical to those discussed above. The price index of travel *payments* includes only United States prices. The United States was the recipient of 78 percent of Canadian tourist expenditure abroad in the years 1951–1961. The United Kingdom accounted for nearly 10 percent of the total flow, and this might suggest the inclusion of suitable British prices in the price index of Canadian tourist expenditure abroad. The problem is that the weighting scheme of the index refers to expenditure in the United States only. Weights for travel to the United Kingdom would certainly differ; air and sea transportation would have to enter the price index and such price information is not readily available.

The price variable is unlagged because prices at the time of travel or tourism are the relevant ones.

A possible variable, but one which is not included, is a measure of the intensity of Canadian restrictions on travel expenditures relative to those of the United States and the United Kingdom. Changes in such a variable over the relevant time period would probably be insignificant. In addition it may be argued that the exchange rate plays a psychological role in tourist expenditure, quite apart from its use in converting Canadian and foreign prices to one another. One way to take account of this factor might be to increase (decrease) the value of the exchange rate by some percentage when the rate is above (below) unity, and use the resulting series (suitably indexed) in place of the index of the spot exchange rate in the price variable and possibly in the income variable as well. This is not done. The distribution of disposable incomes at home and abroad into, say, wage and non-wage incomes may be a factor, but it is ignored. The use of more than one ratio of disposable income would entail an undue complication of the relation, which in its adopted form is:

$$\begin{aligned} \mathrm{TRN} = {} & a_{12} + b_{12} * \mathrm{RYD1} + c_{12} * \mathrm{PTR} + d_{12} * \mathrm{Q1} \\ & + e_{12} * \mathrm{Q2} + f_{12} * \mathrm{Q3} + E_{12} \end{aligned}$$

where TRN = net travel payments, in millions of constant (1957) dollars

RYD1 = ratio of index of Canadian disposable income deflated by the price index of Canadian tourist expenditure abroad itself divided by the index of the spot exchange rate to index of disposable income abroad deflated by the price index of tourist expenditure in Canada, lagged one quarter

PTR = ratio of price index of Canadian tourist expenditure abroad divided by index of spot exchange rate to price index of tourist expenditure in Canada

RYD1 is lagged and therefore predetermined, but PTR is current endogenous. It is expected that the sign of b_{12} is positive and that of c_{12} negative. The coefficients are not to be interpreted as ratios of income and price coefficients of Canadian travellers and foreigners traveling to Canada. The reason is that TRN is not a ratio—it is a difference—even though RYD1 and PTR are ratios. A proper interpretation of the theory underlying this relation is that Canadian tourist expenditure abroad and foreign tourist expenditure in Canada are induced by the same basic factors.

The estimated form of this relation is:

$$\begin{aligned} \text{TRN} = {} & \underset{(140.0)}{110.0} + \underset{(40.0)}{120.0} * \text{RYD1} - \underset{(100.0)}{180.0} * \text{PTR} \\ & + \underset{(6.9)}{40.0} * \text{Q1} + \underset{(7.9)}{35.0} * \text{Q2} - \underset{(6.2)}{55.0} * \text{Q3} \qquad \text{(AOT)} \end{aligned}$$

$$p = 0.31 \quad \text{DW} = 2.03 \quad \text{RSQ} = 0.96 \quad \text{RSQC} = 0.95$$
$$\text{RSQT(PTR)} = 0.97$$

13. Net Payments for Freight and Shipping

Freight and shipping, a second service component of the balance of payments, is explained stochastically in net deflated form. The method of construction of the variable is identical to that outlined in connection with travel expenditures. Current-dollar gross payments and receipts now refer to the freight and shipping account. Price indexes used as deflators are based on wage rates in transportation. They are base-weighted because current weights are not available on a quarterly basis. It is possible to obtain pseudo-current-weighted price indexes by using annual weights, which are available. But this approach is not followed. The components of the respective price indexes are wage rates in the main categories of commodity transportation, namely, rail and shipping. Merchandise trade also moves by means of truck and plane; and petroleum and natural gas are transported by pipeline. Price measures (wage rates) with respect to these three modes of transportation are not included in the index because of lack of information with respect to both prices and weights. Direct data on prices of transportation services are not available; wage rates are used as proxies. Alternatively, deflation could take place by means of price indexes for merchandise trade—that for imports deflating payments and that for exports receipts. Wage rates may be regarded as a principal constituent of the true prices. The wage rates composing the index which deflates payments refer only to the United States, which was the recipient of 68 percent of freight and shipping payments over the period 1951–1961, inclusive. It is true that the percentage would be less in the case of water as distinct from land transportation (in which by geographic constraint it is 100 percent).

The flow of commodity movements is a major determinant of the freight and shipping account. It is expected that exports will tend to use relatively more transportation inducing freight and shipping receipts, and imports relatively more transportation inducing payments. A major reason for this is the fact that the freight and shipping account excludes both purely domestic transactions, that is, freight and shipping payments from Canadian importers to Canadian suppliers of freight and shipping services, and purely foreign transactions, defined analogously for exports. But the area distribution of trade in goods is also important, because in the nature of things rail transportation is limited to trade with the United States, whereas ocean transport predominates in trade with other countries. These considerations lead to the two following explanatory variables:

BMTUS = imports from the United States minus exports to the United States, in millions of constant (1957) dollars

BMTO = imports from other countries minus exports to other countries, in millions of constant (1957) dollars

BMTUS and BMTO represent principally net flows of merchandise trade, but slight modifications are required to take account of movements of goods that are not included in merchandise trade.[17]

The period the model covers witnessed a precipitous decline in the size of the Canadian merchant marine. This no doubt had a significant effect on shipping receipts, as is suggested in Table 1.

TABLE 1. Canadian ocean-transported trade[a] carried in Canadian-flag ships.

Year	Percentage	Year	Percentage
1951	7.9	1956	1.4
1952	6.4	1957	1.0
1953	4.3	1958	0.2
1954	2.1	1959	0.0[b]
1955	2.4	1960	0.2

Source: Fifteenth Report of the Canadian Maritime Commission, June 29th, 1962, p. 25.

[a] Dry cargo only. Both exports and imports are included. Trade with or via the United States is excluded.

[b] Less than 0.05.

Clearly a variable such as the following should be included in the relation:

CMARIN = Canadian ocean-going merchant fleet, in thousands of gross tons

One practice that the decrease in the merchant marine may have stimulated is the chartering of foreign ships by Canadian operators. The effect on the freight and shipping account is twofold: outpayments for the charter itself, inpayments of freight earnings.

The equation does not include a price variable. The existence of shipping rings in ocean transportation operates to depreciate price effects. As regards railways, regulation of freight rates both

17. For details see equations 63 and 64 in chapter III.

by government and by agreement among railway systems tends to minimize the importance of a price variable. This conclusion is reinforced in the case of railways by the barriers to entry, imposed both by government and by the nature of the capital stock required to do business. There is no parallel to the phenomenon of tramp shipping, that is, a freight ship that has no regular schedule and therefore has a wide scope to alter its routes in order to maximize return. Of course, railways compete against truck and water transportation, the latter including both inland (say, via the Great Lakes) and coastal routes. The competition at issue, however, is between Canadian-owned forms of transport *of all types* and those which are not Canadian-owned.

The equation is:

$$\begin{aligned} \text{FRSN} = a_{13} &+ b_{13} * \text{BMTUS} + c_{13} * \text{BMTO} \\ &+ d_{13} * \text{CMARIN} + e_{13} * \text{Q1} \\ &+ f_{13} * \text{Q2} + g_{13} * \text{Q3} + E_{13} \end{aligned}$$

where FRSN = net freight and shipping payments, in millions of constant (1957) dollars

BMTUS and BMTO are current endogenous variables; CMARIN is predetermined. The sign of d_{13} is expected to be less than zero because a smaller merchant marine implies less shipping receipts, hence more net payments. On the other hand, the theoretical sign of b_{13} and c_{13} is greater than zero, on the grounds that the balance of freight and shipping and that of commodity trade should move together because of the stronger affinity of exporters to domestic as distinct from foreign-owned transportation (and because of the exclusion of purely domestic and purely foreign transactions from the freight and shipping account). This affinity, of course, is due to more than subjective circumstances. By nature it is usually easier to deal with domestic- rather than foreign-based transport. Communication is simple (though not necessarily simpler than communication with foreign transport) and so are legal factors. Government policy may also foster such a relationship—if only indirectly; railways are a prime example, though here the nature of the capital stock again is important.

The estimated equation:

$$\underset{(7.0)}{FRSN = 29.0} + \underset{(0.026)}{0.024} * BMTUS + \underset{(0.033)}{0.033} * BMTO$$
$$- \underset{(0.0088)}{0.023} * CMARIN - \underset{(3.2)}{10.0} * Q1 + \underset{(4.1)}{4.6} * Q2$$
$$+ \underset{(2.6)}{9.6} * Q3 \qquad \text{(AOT)}$$

$$p = 0.51 \quad DW = 1.82 \quad RSQ = 0.63 \quad RSQC = 0.67$$
$$RSQT(BMTUS) = 0.89 \quad RSQT(BMTO) = 0.79$$

14. Net Payments for Business Services and Miscellaneous Transactions

The component of the balance of payments discussed here is heterogeneous in nature. It breaks down into three categories: (1) personal and institutional remittances, (2) miscellaneous income transactions, (3) business services and other transactions. Unfortunately, items (1) and (2) cannot be separated from (3) on a quarterly basis; however, insight into explanation of this component can be gained by considering that "business services and other transactions" accounted for 66 percent of total receipts and 68 percent of total payments over the years 1951 to 1961, inclusive.

The variable entering the model is expressed in net deflated form. The problem of deflation is imposing because of the heterogeneity of the item under consideration. Each category and even sub-category of the component should have its own deflator.[18] For example, personal remittance payments by Canadians should perhaps be deflated by the price index for consumer goods in Canada, since remittances are a way of spending income. However, such precision cannot be achieved—not even at the tripartite level—because the component flows cannot be

18. However, the deflator of miscellaneous income should be identically one, that is, it is illegitimate to deflate such transactions. See equation 15.

isolated. One good feature of the item is that business services and related transactions constitute a preponderant portion of the flow; the use of wage rates to achieve real flows of these services is reasonable. Therefore receipts for business services and miscellaneous transactions are deflated by an index of Canadian wage rates in business and miscellaneous services. Payments are deflated by a similar price index referring to the United States. This geographical restriction is legitimate because in the years 1952–1960 the United States was the recipient of 76 percent of overall payments of this balance of payments item, and 87 percent of the payments relating to the sub-component business services and other transactions.

The important determinant of the flow under consideration is Canada's links with non-resident companies via direct investment. A large segment of the item refers to payments by a branch or subsidiary to the head office abroad for designing, engineering, accounting, advertising, and other services. The corporate links that have been developed because of direct investment foster exchange of business services. Direct investment in Canada, both as stock and flow, is in general far greater than Canadian direct investment abroad. This imbalance is of importance in determining *net* payments and suggests the following explanatory variable:

SDINP = beginning-of-quarter ratio of stock of foreign direct investment in Canada to Canadian direct investment abroad.

Because SDINP is a *ratio* the components of which are expressed in dollars, no problems of deflation arises.

The main influence of SDINP is on business services associated with direct investment; but because of financial links between companies in Canada and abroad—these links induced principally by direct investment—it also affects the miscellaneous income component. Miscellaneous income does not refer to dividends and interest on bonds. It includes transfers of profits with respect to branch operations of banks and insurance companies and interest on loans extended by a resident to a non-resident company (and vice-versa).

The activity level in Canada is a second explanatory variable. Although a *net* flow is under consideration, the large size of payments in relation to receipts and the preponderant influence of direct investment on the Canadian economy when compared to the scope of Canadian direct investment abroad require the inclusion of an effect relating to current expenditure in Canada. The variable chosen to measure this effect is business gross fixed capital formation but excluding residential construction: in other words, expenditure on machinery, equipment, and non-residential construction. The dependent variable is a real flow; therefore the activity variable is also expressed in constant dollars. It may be viewed as the current complement to the lagged variable SDINP.

Because the balance of payments item here discussed is so heterogeneous, many other factors can be considered. Personal remittances are functions of immigration to Canada and of Canadian emigration. Such items as rental of films may depend on Canadian disposable income. If "business services and miscellaneous transactions" could be divided into components, equations could be set up to explain items appropriately designated, and consideration would then be given to the factors mentioned in this paragraph as well as other influences. But in the absence of the requisite information the overall item must be explained; and because of its dominating role it is feasible to concentrate on business services. Therefore the relation is:

$$\text{OTHERN} = a_{14} + b_{14} * \text{SDINP} + c_{14} * \text{CME} + d_{14} * \text{Q1} + e_{14} * \text{Q2} + f_{14} * \text{Q3} + E_{14}$$

where OTHERN = net payments for business services and miscellaneous transactions, in millions of constant (1957) dollars
CME = new machinery, equipment, and non-residential construction, in millions of constant (1957) dollars

SDINP is a predetermined variable; CME is current endogenous. The expected sign of both b_{14} and c_{14} is positive.

In estimated form the relationship is:

$$\underset{}{\text{OTHERN}} = \underset{(13.0)}{-70.0} + \underset{(3.8)}{20.0} * \text{SDINP} + \underset{(0.012)}{0.020} * \text{CME} + \underset{(5.1)}{22.0} * \text{Q1} + \underset{(4.5)}{12.0} * \text{Q2} + \underset{(5.0)}{9.2} * \text{Q3} \qquad \text{(AOT)}$$

$$p = -0.15 \quad \text{DW} = 2.03 \quad \text{RSQ} = 0.72 \quad \text{RSQC} = 0.65$$
$$\text{RSQT(CME)} = 0.91$$

15. Payments of Dividends

Both merchandise and service components of the balance of payments have been explained stochastically; and the relations dealt with constant-dollar as distinct from current-dollar flows. Equations that determine interest and dividends components of the balance of payments will now be set forth. These flows are expressed in current dollars. It is absurd to deflate investment income. There is no underlying commodity or service for which the real flow must be established. It is true that the convention that investment income is a payment for service of capital is generally adopted, but this "service" does not use any factors of production. In this respect it is unlike bona fide services of the balance of payments.

Gross rather than net payments of dividends are explained. (This is not to imply that dividends include reinvested earnings; they do not.) Receipts of dividends are included in the relation to be subsequently discussed.

Investment income is surely expected to bear some relation to total capital. Therefore one explanatory variable is a stock measurement. This consists of direct investment in Canada and also those portfolio investments on which dividends are received. It can be argued that only the portion of direct investment partaking some form other than bonds should be included. However, this ignores the fact that because interest payments on bonds are fixed, a desire to adjust earnings in relation to capital invested might take the form of adjustment in dividends. Therefore the totality of direct investment enters the variable, which in turn enters the relation with a lag. The lag itself is variable and dependent on the nature of the investment as well as the outcome. Sometimes it is nil, as might be the case when a well-established Canadian company passes to foreign control. Other times the lag can be very long indeed—for example, direct investment taking the form of setting up a mining company where there is no pre-existing organization and where exploration for minerals is the first task. The variable is expressed as at the beginning of the quarter and is lagged two quarters, which is an arbitrary lag (in the absence of information) but certainly better than no lag at all.

Dividend payments are a function not only of invested capital but also of earnings. Earnings refer to total surplus available for distribution. This measure is composed not only of profits (net of taxes) but also—as measured by the national accounts—capital consumption allowances and miscellaneous valuation adjustments.[19] These flows refer to corporations only; a quantitatively insignificant portion of direct investment consists of unincorporated branches of foreign corporations. The variable can be regarded as a measure of liquidity. It refers to the totality of corporate liquidity in Canada; an alternative might be to confine the measure to direct investment companies alone. Information is available but not on a quarterly basis. Moreover, this alternative neglects earnings of portfolio investment.

The earnings variable is lagged one quarter. The theory is that earnings in the previous quarter help to determine this quarter's dividend payments, but that the determined flow of payments can be increased or decreased—that is, dividend transfers over a longer time horizon can be more concentrated or less concen-

19. Discussion of "capital consumption allowances and miscellaneous valuation adjustments" is in Dominion Bureau of Statistics, *National Accounts, Income and Expenditure, 1926–1956*, pp. 111–113 and 152–156 and *National Accounts, Income and Expenditure by Quarters, 1947–61*, p. 89. Miscellaneous valuation adjustments may be regarded as combining with capital consumption allowances to produce an extended measure of depreciation allowances and related charges. The concept is exclusive of the "inventory valuation adjustment."

trated in the current quarter—depending on a speculative factor. This speculative factor is the expected change in the exchange rate. It helps to determine not the amount of dividend payments (over a horizon longer than one quarter) but rather its time distribution. If the exchange rate is expected to increase (decrease), payments will tend to be postponed (expedited) because a given amount of transfer in Canadian dollars will, it is hoped, give rise to a greater amount in foreign currency. The change in the spot exchange rate over the preceding quarter constitutes a measure of the expectations.

A change in exchange control regulations affected the seasonal distribution of dividend payments; but this change went into effect in November 1950, that is, prior to the beginning of the period on which the model is based. Remittance of earnings by subsidiaries and branches of foreign companies had previously been permitted only on an annual basis; it was announced that distribution would heretofore be allowed with respect to quarterly earnings. Furthermore, the required minimum lag between remittance of funds and completion of the period during which the earnings under consideration had taken place was reduced from three months to forty-five days. This action induced a high concentration of dividend payments in the fourth quarter of 1950, but by the beginning of 1951 transition to these altered regulations had been completed.

The effects of government policy introduced toward the close of the period of the fluctuating rate cannot be dismissed. As early as March 1960 the Minister of Finance gave vague hints of a future policy to limit inflow of foreign capital when he remarked: "However, those who undertake commitments in terms of United States dollars or other external currencies expose themselves to the risk of having to repay at a time when the exchange rate for the Canadian dollar may be quite different from what it is today. This is a risk which the borrower, whether personal, corporate, provincial or municipal must bear himself and is a danger which I clearly wish to stress."[20] The effect of long-term capital inflow on the value of the exchange rate and the consequent effect on

20. *Budget Speech, March 31, 1960* (Ottawa, 1960), p. 8.

the balance of merchandise trade and on exports in particular continued to cause the government grave concern; and in his Budget Speech of December 20, 1960, the Minister declared: "At this stage of our national development it is appropriate to withdraw some of the special incentives which were designed in past years to attract foreign capital."[21] Canadian law provides for a general 15 percent withholding tax on income paid to non-residents, but this tax had little scope for operation because of a series of exemptions, special rates, and agreements with other countries. The government decided to discourage long-term capital inflow by increasing the restrictiveness of the system of withholding taxes. In terms of the balance of payments not only dividends but interest and miscellaneous income were the subjects of the new policy; and the new regulations, all of which were to take effect on December 21, 1960, may be conveniently listed as follows:

A. Dividends

(i) The tax on dividends paid to a non-resident parent corporation which owns all the voting shares of a Canadian (paying) corporation had been 5 percent. The rate was increased to 15 percent.

(ii) Canada has an agreement with the United States one provision of which is that each country will impose no more than a 5 percent tax on dividends paid by controlled subsidiaries[22] to the parent corporation across the border. The agreement allows unilateral cancellation of this particular provision. The Canadian tax rate was increased to 15 percent.

(iii) Canada has similar agreements with countries other than the United States, but which cannot legally be unilaterally altered. The Minister expressed the intention of negotiating with these countries as soon as possible with the aim of again increasing the tax rate to 15 percent.

21. *Budget Speech, December 20, 1960* (Ottawa, 1961), p. 13.

22. These are defined as subsidiaries for which the associated non-resident corporations hold more than 50 percent of the voting shares.

B. Interest

(i) Interest on government of Canada bonds had been exempted from the withholding tax. This exemption was withdrawn.

(ii) Interest from those bonds of Canadian provinces that are payable in Canadian currency had been subjected to a tax rate of 5 percent. This rate was tripled.

(iii) Interest on securities payable in foreign currency had been exempt from the withholding tax. The exemption was withdrawn.

These regulations apply to interest on new issues of securities, these issues taking place after December 20, 1960.

C. Miscellaneous Income

A tax of 15 percent (formally not a withholding tax) was imposed on certain transfers of miscellaneous income. However, banks, life insurance companies, and companies engaged in transportation or communication were exempt.

The importance of the above changes for both investment income and capital flows suggests that the following variable might enter appropriate relations of the model:

W = 1 if first quarter 1961 or beyond, 0 otherwise

W is used as a jump factor not to alter the intercept of the relation under consideration but rather to alter one of the slopes (coefficients). It affects expectations of the future value of the exchange rate. This procedure does not preclude the use of W in changing the level of *capital flow* equations but in itself—that is, apart from interacting with the change in the exchange rate—it does not affect *current* dividends.

Included in W are also the effects—insofar as these effects are not included in other variables in the relation—of direct intervention of the government into the foreign exchange market via official reserves.[23] It is true that this intervention was announced six months after the massive changes in the withholding tax. However, it can be considered to be a logical—even if not

23. See chapter I.

desirable—continuation of the changes with respect to the withholding tax; both policies had the objective of altering the valuc of thc exchange rate (and in the same direction). It would be unreasonable to introduce a second dummy variable which has unit value only for the final three quarters of the time period in the attempt to isolate its effects from those of W, where W under these circumstances refers only to the withholding tax.

The relation explaining payments of dividends can finally be exposited.

$$\begin{aligned} \text{DIVP} = a_{15} &+ b_{15} * \text{SOFIC2} + c_{15} * \text{CPC1} + d_{15} * \text{CRS} \\ &+ e_{15} * \text{WCRS} + f_{15} * \text{Q1} + g_{15} * \text{Q2} \\ &+ h_{15} * \text{Q3} + E_{15} \end{aligned}$$

where DIVP = payments of dividends, in millions of dollars

SOFIC2 = direct investment and portfolio investment on which dividends are received, invested in Canada at beginning of quarter, in millions of dollars, lagged two quarters

CPC1 = corporate profits, capital consumption allowances and miscellaneous valuation adjustments minus direct taxes, in millions of dollars, lagged one quarter

CRS = change in spot exchange rate, number of United States dollars per Canadian dollar

WCRS = change in spot exchange rate if first quarter 1961 or beyond, 0 otherwise

SOFIC2 and CPC1 are predetermined variables; CRS and WCRS are current endogenous. The theoretical sign of both b_{15} and c_{15} is positive. It is true that one effect of CPC1 may lower the magnitude of the coefficient. High earnings may alter its distribution in favor of capital expenditure. However, dividends need not be penalized since increased direct investment can help finance such expenditure. It is admitted that the total effect depends on the liquidity not only of the Canadian company but also—in the case of direct investment—of the parent corporation abroad. Furthermore, it is also to some extent a matter of intracompany accounting among groups of companies in which overall control is centralized.

The sign of d_{15} cannot be set forth a priori; it is a function of the type of expectations that relevant decision-makers possess. The coefficient of CRS after the withholding tax policy went into effect is $(d_{15} + e_{15})$.

The estimated equation is:

$$\begin{aligned} \text{DIVP} = {} & \underset{(13.0)}{61.0} + \underset{(0.0016)}{0.0029} * \text{SOFIC2} + \underset{(0.029)}{0.042} * \text{CPC1} \\ & + \underset{(270.0)}{500.0} * \text{CRS} - \underset{(560.0)}{940.0} * \text{WCRS} - \underset{(5.6)}{44.0} * \text{Q1} \\ & - \underset{(6.6)}{40.0} * \text{Q2} - \underset{(5.6)}{46.0} * \text{Q3} \qquad \text{(AOT)} \end{aligned}$$

$$p = -0.10 \quad \text{DW} = 2.14 \quad \text{RSQ} = 0.85 \quad \text{RSQC} = 0.81$$
$$\text{RSQT(CRS)} = 0.51$$

16. Receipts of Dividends

The relation explaining dividend receipts is similar to that explaining payments. The only lack of symmetry is that a variable equivalent to CPC1 is not included. Although Canada's investments abroad (from which dividend receipts are derived) are concentrated in the United States, which accounts for the fact that 65 percent of dividend receipts over the period 1951–1960, inclusive, originated from the United States, an earnings variable based on American corporations is not warranted because Canadian investment plays an extremely minor role in the United States economy, not only absolutely but also relative to the importance of the reciprocal relationship. The equation for dividend receipts is:

$$\begin{aligned} \text{DIVR} = {} & a_{16} + b_{16} * \text{SOCIA2} + c_{16} * \text{CRS} + d_{16} * \text{WCRS} \\ & + e_{16} * \text{Q1} + f_{16} * \text{Q2} + g_{16} * \text{Q3} + E_{16} \end{aligned}$$

where DIVR = receipts of dividends, in millions of dollars

SOCIA2 = direct investment and portfolio investment on which dividends are received, Canadian investment abroad at beginning of quarter, in millions of dollars, lagged two quarters

SOCIA2 is a predetermined variable. The sign of b_{16} is theoretically positive; those of c_{16} and d_{16} cannot be designated.

The estimated equation:

$$
\begin{aligned}
\text{DIVR} = & -\underset{(45.0)}{170.0} + \underset{(0.017)}{0.080} * \text{SOCIA2} + \underset{(2200.0)}{9800.0} * \text{CRS} \\
& - \underset{(440.0)}{1700.0} * \text{WCRS} - \underset{(2.2)}{9.0} * \text{Q1} + \underset{(7.3)}{20.0} * \text{Q2} \\
& - \underset{(4.4)}{30.0} * \text{Q3} \qquad \text{(JT)}
\end{aligned}
$$

$$\text{DW} = 1.69 \quad \text{RSQ} = 0.74 \quad \text{RSQC} = 0.00$$
$$\text{RSQT(CRS)} = 0.16$$

17. Net Payments of Interest

It can be argued that interest income in the balance of payments should be considered a predetermined variable, on the grounds that interest is entirely contractual, hence non-stochastically determined. This position is not accepted because (1) it ignores the role of the *current* exchange rate; (2) the fact that interest is contractual implies dependence on the contract itself; (3) the all-inclusive information needed to relate each part of interest income to corresponding holdings of securities does not exist. Therefore stochasticity has a role here, namely, in the estimation of an overall relationship.

Gross flows of interest are not determined by the model. Attention is centered rather on the net flow, that is, payments of interest minus receipts of interest. Moreover, it is not the net payments themselves which are explained; instead the *change* in net payments over the preceding quarter is taken as the dependent variable. To set forth the explanatory variables it is necessary to answer the following question: what causes the *change* (that is, an increase or decrease) in net interest payments in the current quarter with reference to the flow in the preceding quarter?

One element in the divergence is the interest paid on those new issues of bonds and debentures which bore no earnings in the previous quarter. Official publications of the Canadian balance of payments indicate there is approximately a two-quarter lag between new issues of bonds and the initial payment of interest. "Among the most immediate effects of borrowing through the sale of bonds abroad are interest payments on these securities held abroad, but even in this case the interest usually follows the change in investment by an interval of some six months."[24]

The variable entering the relation is the net balance (capital inflow) of new issues of bonds and debentures. In order to take account of divergent interest rates on domestic and foreign securities, the gross flows are respectively weighted by the Canadian and American long-term interest rate. Actually new issues sold to Canadians refer to a variety of issuers; United States bonds are probably not of overwhelming importance. Nevertheless the United States interest rate serves as a measure of all foreign rates. Fortunately, the imprecision of the measure used to weight foreign bonds cannot unduly affect the variable itself (and from it the relation) because new issues of *Canadian* bonds and debentures constituted 96 percent of total new issues (Canadian and foreign) of these securities in the time period running from the third quarter of 1950 to the third quarter of 1961, inclusive (the appropriate time period to consider in view of the lag mentioned above).

A second reason for the difference in net interest payments between the current and preceding quarter is the fact that outstanding securities change hands and securities are retired. Therefore the net balance (inflow of capital) with respect to retirements of bonds and debentures and trade in outstanding securities of that nature, constitutes a second explanatory variable. Interest rates do not enter as weighting factors because of lack of information on the dates when the securities under consideration were originally issued. Clearly the time distribution of appropriate measures of interest rates should be a function of these

24. Dominion Bureau of Statistics, *The Canadian Balance of International Payments, 1959*, p. 20.

dates. With respect to retirements the securities may have been issued well in the past. Outstanding securities that are traded may or may not have been of recent issue. There is no known basis for a choice of a weighting scheme.

Canada's official reserves of United States dollars earn interest; changes in such interest receipts are a third component of the divergence being examined. Information available concerning the form of official holdings of United States dollars is confined to year-end assets of the Exchange Fund Account. The Exchange Fund Account is the chief repository of reserves; it includes the totality of gold holdings and a preponderant portion of official reserves of United States dollars—96 percent of such reserves based on year-end figures from 1950 to 1961. The nucleus of a third explanatory variable is the change in official holdings of United States dollars; this *change* is lagged one quarter because of the natural lag between obtaining a security and the receipt of interest. Distribution of United States dollar holdings based on year-end figures from 1950 to 1961, inclusive, is presented in Table 2.

TABLE 2. Exchange Fund assets of United States dollars.[a]

Type	Percent
Treasury notes and certificates	52.4
Treasury bills	41.3
Deposits	6.3

[a] Based on Bank of Canada, *Statistical Summary Supplement*, 1961, p. 146.

It is appropriate to multiply dollar holdings by a suitable United States interest rate measure. Official reserves in the form of *deposits* earn no interest but are fortunately only a small part of the total. They cannot be removed from the total for lack of information. United States treasury bills have a maturity of three months, certificates have maturity no greater than one year, and notes have varying maturity but no greater than five years. The United States treasury bill rate is used for the purpose at hand. To take some account of the distribution by security type, holdings are multiplied not merely by the *current* bill rate but by a weighted average of current and past rates. The rather arbitrary weighting scheme is one half for the current quarter and one sixth for each of the three preceding quarters. This variable is expressed in Canadian dollars because the dependent and previously mentioned explanatory variables are so measured.

A second kind of official interest, namely, interest earned on government of Canada loans, is included in receipts of interest but is not given a special role in the relation. Repayments of such loans occurred throughout the period of interest, though drawings took place in only a few quarters.[25] However, the factors of overwhelming importance in receipts of interest on these loans are the varied terms of individual loans and the *changes* in these terms, both unilateral (non-payment by the borrower) and bilateral (for example, in 1956 and 1957 the United Kingdom made use of provisions of the 1946 loan agreement allowing suspension of interest payments).

The effect of the exchange rate on this equation requires careful examination. It should be recalled that both change in net payments of interest (the dependent variable) and the three explanatory variables discussed above are measured in Canadian dollars. Then if *all* payments and receipts of interest are denominated in Canadian dollars, the exchange rate plays no role in the relation (other than an implicit one in converting components of the explanatory variables from foreign to domestic currency). But if interest income is denominated in *foreign* currency, the exchange rate by that very fact has a direct effect on the dependent variable via conversion of such earnings to Canadian currency. The exchange rate affects the dependent variable not only through interest (denominated in foreign currency) associated with the three explanatory variables, but rather through *all* payments and receipts of interest so denominated. Foreign-pay securities are of particular importance on the payments side. For example, Canadian bonds and debentures payable optionally or solely in foreign currencies constituted 81 percent of total new issues of such securities in 1951 to 1961, inclusive. Therefore the exchange rate enters the relation directly as an explanatory variable. Because the *change* in net payments of interest is ex-

25. See equation 6.

plained, the appropriate variable is the change in the exchange rate, and the relation is:

$$\begin{aligned} \text{CINTN} = {} & a_{17} + b_{17} * \text{BNI2} + c_{17} * \text{BRTO1} + d_{17} * \text{OINT1} \\ & + e_{17} * \text{CRS} + f_{17} * \text{Q1} + g_{17} * \text{Q2} + e_{17} * \text{Q3} \\ & + E_{17} \end{aligned}$$

where CINTN = change in net payments of interest, in millions of dollars

BNI2 = net balance of new issues of bonds and debentures, the gross flows weighted by Canadian and American long-term interest rates, in millions of dollars, lagged two quarters

BRTO1 = net balance of retirements and trade in outstanding issues of bonds and debentures, in millions of dollars, lagged one quarter

OINT1 = change in official holdings of United States dollars, weighted by United States treasury bill rate, in millions of dollars, lagged one quarter

BNI2, BRTO1 and OINT1 are predetermined variables. BNI2 and BRTO1 are constructed in such a way that inflows of capital are taken as positive and outflows negative. Because increased interest payments (or decreased interest receipts) are associated with such inflows of capital and decreased payments (or increased receipts) with outflows, both b_{17} and c_{17} are theoretically greater than zero. But OINT1 is a capital outflow, and therefore the sign of its coefficient should be less than zero. With respect to the effect of CRS it is recalled that foreign-pay securities are its vehicle. If the exchange rate rises, this implies that less Canadian dollars are required to transfer a given amount of payment denominated in United States currency. Hence the expected sign of e_{17} is less than zero.

The estimated relationship is:

$$\begin{aligned} \text{CINTN} = {} & \underset{(3.0)}{-17.0} + \underset{(0.011)}{0.012} * \text{BNI2} + \underset{(0.024)}{0.0054} * \text{BRTO1} \\ & + \underset{(0.015)}{0.0028} * \text{OINT1} - \underset{(170.0)}{50.0} * \text{CRS} + \underset{(4.0)}{34.0} * \text{Q1} \\ & + \underset{(2.8)}{14.0} * \text{Q2} + \underset{(4.0)}{17.0} * \text{Q3} \end{aligned} \qquad \text{(AJT)}$$

$$p = -0.43 \quad DW = 2.47 \quad RSQ = 0.74 \quad RSQC = 0.71$$
$$RSQT(CRS) = 0.16$$

18. Direct Investment in Canada

Elements of the capital account of the balance of payments will now be discussed. Long-term flows are the first category treated, and direct—as distinct from portfolio—investment is the dependent variable of the equation under consideration. This variable is gross in the sense that it refers only to the flow of direct investment into Canada, thus excluding Canadian direct investment abroad. However, it is composed of the whole of the balance of payments item. It includes all kinds of direct investment in Canada: that which finances fixed capital formation; that which finances imports of investment goods; that used to acquire existing assets; and that used to provide funds to carry on day-to-day operations. Moreover, the variable is net in the sense that it takes account of the outflow of capital of non-resident controllers of Canadian enterprises. Therefore it is seen that direct investment is by no means a homogeneous flow, and selection of explanatory variables would have improved precision if the item could be divided into appropriate categories. In fact the distribution of direct investment by industrial group provides a two-way classification of direct investment. Because information for a disaggregated treatment is unavailable, explanatory variables for the gross flow are best selected so as to influence several (or all) categories.

One explanatory variable is chosen to represent the activity level in Canada. It is the current-dollar flow of new non-residential construction, machinery and equipment. Capital formation is of particular importance to that type of direct investment which serves to finance it. But as a measure of the state of the Canadian economy it also affects other kinds of direct investment. The explanatory variable is not deflated, because the dependent variable is itself in current-dollar form.

The first factor is related to the desire of foreign interests to invest in Canada; the second refers to their ability to do so. This second explanatory variable is a measure of the supply of foreign funds available for investment. In the period 1951–1961 three-quarters of the direct investment in Canada was performed by residents of the United States and 16 percent by those of the United Kingdom. Because of this skewness these two countries alone need be considered in the measure constructed, which is a weighted average of indexes of corporate liquidity in these countries. To give scope to the effect of the exchange rate the index is converted to Canadian dollars. Liquidity is defined as the sum of profits and capital consumption allowances less direct taxes. The component measures are required to be in index number form for a proper application of the weights. A variable derived from the underlying flows expressed in one or the other currency would involve an imprecise weighting pattern.

A dummy variable representing the Canadian government's new policy regarding taxation of investment income is discussed above (see equation 15). The measures adopted affected direct investment because the net return on investment via dividend receipts was lowered in proportion to the increase in the withholding tax. Moreover, W represents not only the effect of the tax policy but also the expectations and fears of further changes in government policy in this and other areas induced by the government's exchange fund policy[26] adopted in mid–1961. The intercepts of the equation are changed by the use of the dummy variable, and the relation itself is set forth below:

$$\text{DIC} = a_{18} + b_{18} * \text{MNRCC} + c_{18} * \text{SIF} + d_{18} * \text{W} + e_{18} * \text{Q1} + f_{18} * \text{Q2} + g_{18} * \text{Q3} + E_{18}$$

where DIC = direct investment in Canada, in millions of dollars
MNRCC = new machinery, equipment, and non-residential construction, in millions of dollars
SIF = index of liquidity of corporations in the United States and United Kingdom divided by index of spot exchange rate

Both MNRCC and SIF are current endogenous. Their coefficients are theoretically greater than zero. The fourth-quarter

26. The term "exchange fund policy" refers to the use of official reserves to influence an *unpegged* exchange rate.

intercept in the era of new government policy is $(a_{18} + d_{18})$. (Intercepts in other quarters are altered correspondingly.) It is expected that in this period the level of the relationship was lowered, that is, the theoretical sign of d_{18} is less than zero.

The estimated equation is:

$$\begin{aligned} \text{DIC} = \underset{(26.0)}{1.3} + \underset{(0.032)}{0.048} * \text{MNRCC} + \underset{(47.0)}{80.0} * \text{SIF} - \underset{(16.0)}{21.0} * \text{W} \\ - \underset{(12.0)}{11.0} * \text{Q1} - \underset{(12.0)}{9.7} * \text{Q2} - \underset{(12.0)}{28.0} * \text{Q3} \qquad \text{(OT)} \end{aligned}$$

$$\text{DW} = 2.03 \quad \text{RSQ} = 0.50 \quad \text{RSQC} = 0.48$$

$$\text{RSQT(MNRCC)} = 0.93 \quad \text{RSQT(SIF)} = 0.98$$

19. Net New Issues of Securities

There are many ways of arranging portfolio investment for purpose of analysis. A comprehensive breakdown would be by type of movement (new issues, retirements, trade in outstanding issues), by direction of movement (inflow or outflow), by country to or from which movement is directed (with respect to Canada), by country of issue, by nature of security (bond, debenture, common or preference stock), and by nature of issuer (level of government, industry). This study remains at a highly aggregative level in this respect, but does analyze separately new issues and retirements as distinct from trade in outstanding issues.

The dependent variable under consideration is the net inflow of portfolio capital in the form of new issues and retirements of Canadian and foreign securities. It is conceivable that new issues might be considered alone in such an equation, and retirements taken as predetermined or related to *past* new issues and trade in outstanding securities. However, net new issues are a more relevant variable than gross new issues. This is obvious if the data refer to only one issuer, but even in the aggregate this is a meaningful way to proceed. Moreover, retirements may be made to take place sooner than anticipated because of interest and exchange rate factors, which are given a role in the equation under consideration.

The first explanatory variable, representing the traditional theory, is an interest rate differential. It is the Canadian minus the American long-term interest rate. The American rate is taken because the United States is by far the most important transactor—accounting for 87 percent of new issues and retirements of securities (all flows taken as positive in this calculation) in the period 1951–1961. Regarding transactions with other countries, it can be argued that residents of such countries have a choice between American and Canadian securities. Hence the interest rate differential again is relevant.

With respect to the interest rate as well as other effects, it should be noted that there may be a difference in timing between contracting and delivering securities. For analytical purposes the sales contract is the relevant date, but in the balance of payments new issues are measured as at date of delivery. The difference between contract and delivery is composed of two parts: sales of earlier periods delivered in the current period and current sales the delivery of which is withheld. Given that the dependent variable is on the delivery basis, these components are of opposite sign, hence tend to cancel one another. The differences that remain in the two concepts inherently lessen as the period under consideration lengthens.

Of total new issues minus retirements (with all flows taken as positive) in the time period 1951–1961, Canadian securities accounted for 95 percent. This suggests the appropriateness of a factor pertaining only to Canadian issues. Such a variable is the supply of Canadian securities, representing demand for funds. To correspond with the nature of the dependent variable this factor is net new issues—gross new issues minus retirements—of long-term marketable securities.

Clearly the variable affects not only inflow of foreign capital but also (in an opposite direction) outflow of Canadian funds.

The influence of the foreign exchange market is taken into account by means of the variable CRS. The change in the spot exchange rate rather than the level of the rate is the relevant variable. Divergence from the "normal" value might be an even better measure; however, this would require definition of a normal value. To the extent that the normal value might be a (moving) weighted average of past values, CRS represents divergence from that normal value with all the weight concentrated in the preceding quarter.

The withholding tax on interest and dividends transferred abroad affects the relation in two ways. On the one hand, it depresses the intercept, because the prospect of a lower net return on portfolio investment restricts capital movements. On the other hand, because the variable CRS is included in the relationship, government policy affecting the foreign exchange market—first indirectly (restricting inflow of capital through the withholding tax) and then directly (intervention in the market as a large-scale trader)—alters expectations of exchange rate movements. Therefore the variable WCRS enters the relation in order to change the coefficient of CRS during the relevant time period.

The equation is:

$$\begin{aligned} \text{PNIR} = {} & a_{19} + b_{19} * \text{DIL} + c_{19} * \text{S} + d_{19} * \text{W} + e_{19} * \text{CRS} \\ & + f_{19} * \text{WCRS} + g_{19} * \text{Q1} + h_{19} * \text{Q2} + i_{19} * \text{Q3} \\ & + E_{19} \end{aligned}$$

where PNIR = net inflow of portfolio capital via new issues and retirements of Canadian and foreign securities, in millions of dollars

DIL = Canadian long-term interest rate minus American long-term interest rate, percent per quarter

S = net new issues of Canadian long-term marketable securities, in millions of dollars

DIL and S are current endogenous variables, and their coefficients are theoretically positive. The coefficient of W is expected to be negative, that is, the intercepts are lowered in the final five quarters of the period to which the model applies. The signs of e_{19} and f_{19} are functions of the type of expectations applicable to this relation.

The estimated form of the equation is:

$$\begin{aligned} \text{PNIR} = {} & \underset{(34.0)}{-77.0} + \underset{(180.0)}{490.0} * \text{DIL} + \underset{(0.057)}{0.20} * \text{S} - \underset{(190.0)}{250.0} * \text{W} \\ & + \underset{(1200.0)}{1600.0} * \text{CRS} - \underset{(14000.0)}{16000.0} * \text{WCRS} + \underset{(28.0)}{8.6} * \text{Q1} \\ & - \underset{(30.0)}{9.6} * \text{Q2} - \underset{(27.0)}{12.0} * \text{Q3} \qquad \text{(OT)} \end{aligned}$$

DW = 1.76 RSQ = 0.50 RSQC = 0.35

RSQT(DIL) = 0.76 RSQT(S) = 0.73 RSQT(CRS) = 0.50

20. Trade in Outstanding Securities

The model divides portfolio investment into two parts. New issues and retirements of securities are discussed above. Trade in outstanding securities is now the subject of examination. The dependent variable of the relation to be set forth is *net* portfolio capital inflow via trade in outstanding Canadian and foreign securities. This variable is the algebraic sum (where capital outflows are given a negative sign) of gross sales of securities—both Canadian and foreign-issued—to foreign residents and of Canadian gross purchases of such securities from foreigners. The total value of these transactions (with no netting of flows) may differ from the net flow by a factor of 20, 50 or even 100 or more over a given time period. Trade in outstanding securities is different in behavior from net new issues in three respects. First, although the variables DIL, W, CRS, and WCRS enter both relations, it is expected that their coefficients would differ.[27] Speculative factors might be expected to play a more important role (relative to other determinants) in the relation involving trade in outstanding issues. Second, the variable S does not enter

27. Justification for the use of DIL with respect to its inclusion of the United States interest rate is the fact that 83 percent of trade in outstanding issues—with all balance of payments flows (according to official statistics) taken as positive—are accounted for by the United States in the period 1951–1961.

this equation because the latter is limited to explaining trade in outstanding, as distinct from new, issues.

Third, from 1954 onward some ten American-owned but Canadian-registered investment companies played an important role in the market for outstanding Canadian securities, especially common and preference stocks. These companies are mutual funds. Both by law and stated purpose they seek diversification of their holdings rather than control, and for this reason their transactions are not included in direct investment. "As their essential characteristic is portfolio investment, notwithstanding their legal status as Canadian corporations, they are treated as representing United States portfolio investors, and their transactions in Canadian securities are included in statistics of international security trading."[28]

What distinguishes these companies from similar organizations which played a minor role in the market for outstanding Canadian securities before 1954 is the fact that the latter companies were not registered under the (United States) Investment Company Act of 1940. This Act forbids investment companies not created under the laws of the United States from using the mails or any form of interstate commerce to offer, sell, or deliver, any security it has issued. However, upon application by a foreign-registered investment company the Securities and Exchange Commission may rescind that restriction providing (1) it is feasible to enforce the provisions of the Act against that company and (2) the exemption is consistent with the "public interest" and the protection of investors.[29] In early 1951 the first such application was made by a Canadian-registered company. On April 27, 1954, the S.E.C. issued a rule setting forth conditions under which Canadian investment companies could be registered under the Act, and two such companies were registered. These companies expanded both in size and in number because of their taxation status coupled with the ability to sell their shares in the United States. On the one hand, Canada does not have a capital gains

28. *The Canadian Balance of International Payments, 1960*, p. 37.

29. *Investment Company Act of 1940 as amended March 31, 1961* (No. 768, 76th Congress, H.R. 10065), section 7(d), p. 12.

tax. On the other, United States investors in the companies are subject to no American taxes on their investments except in the case of earnings *transferred* or holdings *sold*, and in the latter case the received income is considered capital gains. In fact, "The U.S. tax position of the individual U.S. investors in registered foreign investment companies is generally comparable to that of a U.S. corporate investor making direct foreign investments abroad through operating subsidiaries."[30] These terms are clearly an inducement to management of the companies to reinvest earnings. Therefore the companies reinvest both interest and dividends received on their security holdings and profits arising from market transactions with respect to their portfolios. The purpose is to appreciate their issues, and when shareholders liquidate their holdings the income receives the favorable taxation treatment of capital gains.

All these factors indicate the significant role that the companies can play in the Canadian securities market; in fact, there have been times when they increased holdings of stocks of Canadian companies at the same time that other United States investors decreased such holdings. For purposes of the model, ideal treatment would be to consider transactions of these companies by means of an additional equation. But the required information is not available, and the procedure adopted is to change the level of the equation explaining the totality of trade in outstanding securities, this change applying to the period in which Canadian companies were registered under the United States Investment Act.

The three considerations discussed above lead to the following relation:

$$\begin{aligned}\text{PTOS} = {} & a_{20} + b_{20} * \text{DIL} + c_{20} * \text{W} + d_{20} * \text{CRS} \\ & + e_{20} * \text{WCRS} + f_{20} * \text{FIA} + g_{20} * \text{Q1} \\ & + h_{20} * \text{Q2} + i_{20} * \text{Q3} + E_{20}\end{aligned}$$

where PTOS = net inflow of portfolio capital via trade in out-

30. "A Proven Pattern for Boosting U.S. Private Investments Abroad: The Story of the Pioneering Role Played by Registered Canadian Investment Companies," *World's Business*, May 1958, p. 24.

standing Canadian and foreign securities, in millions of dollars
FIA = 1 if third quarter 1954 or beyond, 0 otherwise

FIA is a predetermined variable. With respect to the theoretical signs of b_{20}, c_{20}, d_{20}, and f_{20}, remarks made with respect to corresponding coefficients of equation 19 apply. It is expected that the operations of the special investment companies increase inflow of capital; therefore f_{20} is theoretically greater than zero. The relation involves three fourth-quarter intercepts, each applicable to a disjoint time period as follows: a_{20} from the first quarter of 1951 to the second quarter of 1954, $a_{20} + f_{20}$ from the third quarter of 1954 to the fourth quarter of 1960, and $a_{20} + f_{20} + c_{20}$ from the first quarter of 1961 to the first quarter of 1962. Because it is expected that $f_{20} > 0$ and $c_{20} < 0$, theoretical considerations dictate that $a_{20} + f_{20}$ exceeds the other two intercepts. Ranking of the latter intercepts is a function of the relative *magnitudes* of f_{20} and c_{20}.

The estimated equation:

$$\begin{aligned} \text{PTOS} = & \underset{(48.0)}{-57.0} + \underset{(180.0)}{260.0} * \text{DIL} - \underset{(110.0)}{230.0} * \text{W} \\ & + \underset{(3600.0)}{150.0} * \text{CRS} - \underset{(6800.0)}{17000.0} * \text{WCRS} + \underset{(23.0)}{35.0} * \text{FIA} \\ & + \underset{(11.0)}{7.7} * \text{Q1} + \underset{(15.0)}{8.1} * \text{Q2} + \underset{(13.0)}{5.8} * \text{Q3} \qquad \text{(AJT)} \end{aligned}$$

$p = 0.21$ DW = 1.79 RSQ = 0.35 RSQC = 0.00

RSQT(DIL) = 0.48 RSQT(CRS) = 0.21

21. Balance of Transactions in Treasury Bills

The only autonomous current endogenous *short-term* capital movement is the net inflow from transactions in Canadian treasury bills and United States treasury bills and certificates. This variable (in terms of its construction) is discussed above (see equation 1).

To some extent this capital flow is a medium for covered interest arbitrage. It is recalled that RFD, the forward exchange differential, is a measure of the profit to be earned by means of arbitrage. If foreign exchange and short-term money markets were perfect, arbitrage would take place if, and only if, RFD differs from zero. Transactions in treasury bills[31] constitute part of the process of arbitrage. Even under imperfect arbitrage the further RFD diverges from zero, in either direction, the larger the profit-guaranteed movement that should take place. Hence the greater the flow, in the appropriate direction, of short-term capital in the form of treasury bills. Therefore RFD is an explanatory variable.

The factor of speculation as distinct from arbitrage must be taken into account because not all interest-arbitrage transactions are *covered* in the forward exchange market. Speculation on the future value of the spot exchange rate is considered a function of the change in the rate. Therefore CRS is a second explanatory variable. As is the case throughout the model, CRS as affecting expectations of the future course of the exchange rate implies the relevance of a variable which measures the change in expectations induced by government policy. This variable is WCRS, and it simply changes the coefficient of CRS in the final five quarters of the time period. There is no reason to change the level of the function as a result of the changed government policy. W is not a relevant explanatory variable because the withholding tax changes with respect to interest on government of Canada securities referred to bonds only, and not to treasury bills. Then the relation is as follows:

$$\begin{aligned} \mathrm{TBN} = {} & a_{21} + b_{21} * \mathrm{RFD} + c_{21} * \mathrm{CRS} + d_{21} * \mathrm{WCRS} \\ & + e_{21} * \mathrm{Q1} + f_{21} * \mathrm{Q2} + g_{21} * \mathrm{Q3} + E_{21} \end{aligned}$$

The signs of c_{21} and d_{21} are functions of the type of expectations possessed by traders and hence cannot be designated a priori. However b_{21} is theoretically positive. This reflects the facts that

31. Movements of United States treasury bills cannot be isolated from those of treasury certificates. For analysis of interest arbitrage the joint flow is treated as consisting of bills only.

(1) if RFD is greater (less) than zero, arbitrage entailing purchases of Canadian (United States) treasury bills provides a positive return, and (2) TBN is positive (negative) under a net inflow (outflow) of capital.

The estimated relationship:

$$\begin{aligned} TBN = {} & \underset{(9.5)}{16.0} + \underset{(2200.0)}{2600.0} * RFD - \underset{(500.0)}{1000.0} * CRS \\ & + \underset{(1000.0)}{2900.0} * WCRS - \underset{(14.0)}{1.3} * Q1 - \underset{(12.0)}{13.0} * Q2 \\ & - \underset{(14.0)}{14.0} * Q3 \qquad \text{(AOT)} \end{aligned}$$

$$p = -0.28 \quad DW = 2.23 \quad RSQ = 0.25 \quad RSQC = 0.13$$

$$RSQT(RFD) = 0.85 \quad RSQT(CRS) = 0.50$$

22. Short-term Interest Rate

Three stochastic equations explain financial aspects of the Canadian economy. Two deal with interest rates. The short-term interest rate is measured by the tender (auction) rate on three-month government of Canada treasury bills. It might be thought that one explanatory variable would be the bank rate itself. However, throughout the period the model covers the causal relationship was reversed. The short-term interest rate determined the bank rate! This is obviously true from November 1, 1956 onward, for on that date the Bank of Canada announced that it would change the bank rate weekly and fix it at one quarter of one percent above the average rate on government of Canada treasury bills at the most recent tender. But even before November 1, 1956, changes in the bank rate followed rather than led changes in the short-term interest rate. "Prior to November 1st, 1956 the Bank had followed the practice of keeping its lending rate above the treasury bill rate by raising the Bank Rate at intervals of some months whenever the treasury bill rate approached or temporarily exceeded the previous level of the Bank

Rate."[32] In fact the only changes in the bank rate since October 17, 1950, occurred between February 14, 1955, and October 17, 1956, during which time there were seven alterations of the rate. It is of interest to observe that the fluctuating bank rate did not long survive the demise of the fluctuating exchange rate, for on June 24, 1962, the Bank of Canada reverted to a pegged rate system.[33]

Even though the short-term interest rate determines the bank rate rather than the reverse relationship, government policy plays an important part in determining the interest rate through three explanatory variables. The first such variable is the excess reserve position of the chartered banks. It is defined as the actual cash reserve ratio minus the legal or customary reserve ratio. Prior to July 1, 1954, the legal ratio was 5 percent, but the banks instead worked to achieve a ratio of 10 percent. It is clear that the consequences—other than legal ones—of violating a customary reserve ratio are of the same nature as those of violating a legal ratio. From July 1, 1954, onward the legal minimum reserve ratio was 8 percent, and it was effective in the sense that the chartered banks abandoned the customary ratio of 10 percent. The excess reserve ratio is a demand factor in the money market; it directly affects the treasury bill demand of the chartered banks, and indirectly that of investment dealers to the extent that they borrow from the banks.

In addition to the cash position of chartered banks their liquid assets position is also of relevance. In November, 1955, the banks agreed to maintain a minimum ratio of cash, treasury bills, and day-to-day loans[34] relative to Canadian deposit liabilities. The ratio was set at 15 percent. It can reasonably be assumed that the chartered banks accepted the liquid assets requirement only under pressure from the Bank of Canada. Though there is no legal

32. Bank of Canada, *Annual Report for 1956*, p. 45.

33. However, the fluctuating rate remained in effect for purchase and resale agreements with investment dealers as distinct from loans to chartered (commercial) banks.

34. Day-to-day loans are call loans made to money market jobbers on the security of treasury bills and government of Canada bonds maturing within three years.

basis for the restriction, the banks adhere to the agreed liquid assets ratio no less strictly than they adhere to the cash ratio. In this respect the agreed liquid assets ratio is similar to the customary cash ratio.

The excess liquid assets ratio is a second explanatory variable, adding a further dimension to determinants of demand for treasury bills. The problem is how to measure this variable prior to the agreement. The procedure adopted is as follows. The excess liquid assets ratio is defined as the actual liquid assets ratio minus (1) the required liquid assets ratio (15 percent) from the first quarter of 1956 onward or (2) the customary reserve ratio (10 percent) in earlier quarters. This measurement requires justification. First, it is clear that a liquid assets effect is applicable even prior to 1956. After all, banks hold secondary reserves even under no compulsion—legal or otherwise—just as they would hold cash reserves under such circumstances. Nevertheless, it is desired to show some tightening up in the minimum liquid assets ratio as a result of the agreement. Three periods are of interest. Prior to July 1954 the theory is that to the extent banks did not meet the customary reserve ratio, treasury bills filled the gap. These securities were the closest alternative to cash, since day-to-day loans were inaugurated only in June 1954. From July 1954 to December 1955 a different situation prevailed. There remained no agreed liquid assets requirement, but day-to-day loans had commenced in the previous month and the legal reserve ratio was raised to 8 percent at the beginning of this period. The minimum liquid assets ratio is left at 10 percent. This is arbitrary, but probably less arbitrary than selecting another figure since it can be argued that the banks clung to the 10 percent customary ratio by means of treasury bills and day-to-day loans even though they reduced the effective cash ratio to 8 percent very quickly. The third period—in which the desired minimum ratio is set at 15 percent—commences in the first quarter of 1956. It is true that the agreement was not to come into effect until May 31, 1956, but it was reached in November 1955. It seems reasonable to begin the 15 percent ratio as a goal in the first quarter of 1956. The banks knew that ratio had to be achieved by all within half a year. They obviously felt pressure immediately. If they waited, they might suffer the consequences of a rise in the price of treasury bills. This discontinuity—the jump from 10 to 15 percent—is thus conceivably better than an arbitrary smoothing of the jump, say, at a rate of 1 percent a month.

Two demand factors have been discussed. A supply factor is the amount of government of Canada three-month treasury bills issued at tender. None of these variables are lagged, on the grounds that the money market is a quickly adjusting one.

Attention must be given to the fact that the Canadian money market is not closed. The net inflow of capital through treasury bill movements enters as an explanatory variable. Both American and Canadian securities are included in this variable. An alternative is to consider only the gross capital inflow for the purpose of Canadian treasury bills. This is rejected because Canadian investment in United States treasury bills is not irrelevant if it is assumed that the funds might otherwise have been invested in Canadian treasury bills. Then the relation is as follows:

$$\text{CIS} = a_{22} + b_{22} * \text{R} + c_{22} * \text{RLA} + d_{22} * \text{TB} + e_{22} * \text{TBN} + f_{22} * \text{Q1} + g_{22} * \text{Q2} + h_{22} * \text{Q3} + E_{22}$$

where R = excess cash reserve ratio of chartered banks, percent
RLA = excess liquid assets ratio of chartered banks, percent
TB = government of Canada three-month treasury bills sold at tender, in millions of dollars

R, RLA, and TB are predetermined variables. Some comment is warranted. TB is a policy variable, since the government itself determines the amount of treasury bills it will supply. TB measures the amount of treasury bills sold, which is equal to the amount offered by the government. In general the amount offered is oversubscribed by private investors and the Bank of Canada acting as a normal trader. The amount offered is always sold because in practice (there is no legal compulsion) the Bank of Canada submits a "reserve" bid (at a lower rate than its "market" bid) for the entire issue. The purpose is to guard against an artificial high rate induced by collusion among bidders.

With respect to the variable R, the Bank of Canada in the first instance controls the amount of actual reserves rather than actual reserves minus required reserves (divided by deposit liabilities). R is considered a policy variable on the grounds that the Bank may consider it as the key variable to be influenced by means of its control of reserves. This analysis applies to RLA as well, although the chartered banks have more latitude here. Their day-to-day loans and holdings of treasury bills are not under the direct control of the Bank of Canada; however, a tightening of reserves can be used to induce the chartered banks to decrease their portfolios of the other liquid assets.

An increase in R, RLA, or TBN implies expanded demand for treasury bills; an increase in TB involves greater supply. The expected sign of the coefficient of a demand variable is negative and of a supply variable positive.

The estimated equation is:

$$\begin{aligned} CIS = \underset{(0.23)}{0.52} - \underset{(0.11)}{0.12} * R - \underset{(0.034)}{0.028} * RLA + \underset{(0.0018)}{0.0032} * TB \\ - \underset{(0.0017)}{0.0010} * TBN - \underset{(0.040)}{0.011} * Q1 - \underset{(0.051)}{0.076} * Q2 \\ - \underset{(0.049)}{0.071} * Q3 \qquad \text{(AOT)} \end{aligned}$$

$$p = 0.74 \quad DW = 1.11 \quad RSQ = 0.25 \quad RSQC = 0.45$$
$$RSQT(TBN) = 0.21$$

23. Long-term Interest Rate

The long-term interest rate is measured by the yield of a Government of Canada long-term bond selected so as to achieve consonance with a United States bond in terms of earliest redemption date and coupon rate. Just as the short-term interest rate depends on the variables R and RLA, so could the long-term rate. Instead it is made to depend on the short-term interest rate itself. On the one hand, CIS may be interpreted as a proxy for common factors R and RLA. On the other, a priori there should be a correlation between long- and short-term rates.

Special factors in the long-term market must be introduced. Net new issues of long-term marketable securities are a supply factor analogous to treasury bill offerings in the money market. All such issues are included in the variable; it is not limited to those of the government of Canada. It is assumed that the government long-term bond rate is indicative of the spectrum of rates in the entire long-term securities market. This assumption is not always true, but is reasonable for purposes of the model.

In 1958 the government became concerned because many of the huge bond issues of the Second World War would mature over the next few years, with a consequent decrease in the average term to maturity of its outstanding debt. It was decided to improve the situation by means of a tremendous financial operation undertaken over a short period of time. This was the famous "Conversion Loan" operation, which entailed the exchange of enormous quantities of newly issued long-term bonds in return for debt maturing over the next few years. As a matter of fact the average term to maturity of government of Canada securities increased by 65 percent over a period of three months! A discontinuous change of this magnitude is a strong force pushing interest rates upward.

Moreover, effects of this governmental action were not limited to the bond market. The Conversion Loan and its consequences constitute the principal reason why the government decided to change the withholding tax on transfer of investment income abroad and even to adopt an aggressive exchange fund policy under the floating rate system. The government's concern with the relationships among inflow of long-term capital, the exchange rate, and merchandise exports has been mentioned above (see equation 15). The withholding tax and exchange fund policy had the objective of lowering the exchange rate. An alternative would have been to usher in a period of lower long-term interest rates, thus operating directly on the capital inflow. But the Conversion Loan had the opposite effect on rates of interest![35]

35. This is not to deny that monetary, as distinct from debt management, policy also operated to keep interest rates high. Monetary policy is proxied by the variables R and RLA, which enter the determination of the long-term interest rate recursively through the inclusion of CIS in the relationship.

Moreover, the policies that the government adopted in view of the constraint imposed by the Conversion Loan unleashed forces of speculation in the foreign exchange market and the market was beset by uncertainties. Participants did not know what the government would do next. The government attempted to keep the dollar at an artificially low rate and its official reserves began to *decline* (rather than increase, as would occur under normal circumstances) because of fear on the part of the private sector of the market that the rate might fall even further.

In the first four months of 1962 reserves decreased so substantially that continuance of the government's policy became intolerable. The government then had two choices insofar as exchange rate policy was concerned. It could withdraw as an extraordinary trader from the foreign exchange market, or it could formally terminate the floating rate. Obviously, to initiate once again a drastic change in exchange fund policy would entail still further bewilderment over sharp changes in governmental action. The return to the fixed rate was thus made almost inevitable, and the Minister of Finance issued the following press release on May 2, 1962: "The Hon. Donald M. Fleming, Minister of Finance, announced tonight that the international exchange rate of the Canadian dollar is being stabilized, effective immediately, at 92½ cents in terms of U.S. currency."[36]

Consequences—both direct and ultimate—of the Conversion Loan, as well as general theoretical considerations, suggest that the following variable enter the relation explaining the long-term interest rate: the average term to maturity of government of Canada long-term marketable securities. Naturally perpetuals are excluded in order to obtain a finite measure. The variable is lagged half an observation period in the sense that it is measured at the beginning of the current quarter. This lag is introduced for three reasons. First, it is expected that by nature the long-term securities market is not as quickly adjustable as the money market. Second, as a matter of policy the Bank of Canada at times purchases government of Canada bonds and then resells them when it considers the market is prepared to take them at appropriate prices. In a similar vein dealers may purchase long-term securities

36. Office of the Minister of Finance, *Press Release*, May 2, 1962.

and wait to see what the market will bring. Third, in connection with the Conversion Loan the speculative effect on the market may take some time to show its greatest impact.

The long-term securities market is even more open to foreign influence than is the money market. Analogous to the variable TBN introduced in the equation referring to the latter market is the net inflow of portfolio capital. This includes trade in outstanding securities as well as net new issues. Canadian portfolio investment abroad enters the variable as a negative flow. This inclusion is not irrelevant, since the outflow represents a diversion of demand from domestic to foreign securities. The definition of portfolio investment is restricted to movements of bonds, debentures, and stocks. Other investments of a conventional portfolio nature cannot be included because of lack of information; but even if data were available, such flows would be excluded because of removal from the securities market to which the long-term interest rate applies.

The relation outlined is:

$$\begin{aligned} \text{CIL} = a_{23} + b_{23} * \text{CIS} + c_{23} * \text{ATM} + d_{23} * \text{S} + e_{23} * \text{PNIIC} \\ + f_{23} * \text{Q1} + g_{23} * \text{Q2} + h_{23} * \text{Q3} + E_{23} \end{aligned}$$

where CIL = long-term interest rate, percent per quarter

ATM = average term to maturity of government of Canada long-term marketable securities at beginning of quarter, in months

PNIIC = net inflow of portfolio capital, in millions of dollars

ATM is a predetermined variable in two respects. It is lagged and also is a policy variable because it is restricted to government of Canada securities. S is current endogenous because it includes securities other than those of the federal government. PNIIC is also current endogenous.

Expected signs of coefficients are as follows: $b_{23}, c_{23}, d_{23} > 0$, $e_{23} < 0$.

The estimated equation:

$$\begin{aligned} \text{CIL} = {} & \underset{(0.068)}{0.39} + \underset{(0.075)}{0.34} * \text{CIS} + \underset{(0.00079)}{0.0033} * \text{ATM} + \underset{(0.000098)}{0.000087} * \text{S} \end{aligned}$$

$$- \underset{(0.00025)}{0.000027} * PNIIC - \underset{(0.039)}{0.017} * Q1 - \underset{(0.043)}{0.014} * Q2$$

$$+ \underset{(0.035)}{0.013} * Q3 \qquad \text{(OT)}$$

$$DW = 0.59 \quad RSQ = 0.82 \quad RSQC = 0.85$$
$$RSQT(CIS) = 0.85 \quad RSQT(S) = 0.73$$
$$RSQT(PNIIC) = 0.63$$

24. Net New Issues of Non-federal Marketable Long-term Securities

A relation is needed to explain the endogenous component of the variable S. Federal bond issues are predetermined—a matter of policy. However, net new issues of corporate bonds and stocks are endogenous. Provincial and municipal bond issues are also in this category. They are not undertaken for any purpose other than financing of expenditure or refunding of old debt. Unlike federal bond issues, those of provinces and municipalities play no role, with respect to policy goals, in stabilizing the bond market or affecting interest rates. The relation explaining net new issues of non-federal securities is to be interpreted as a supply equation. This suggests an explanatory variable, namely, the long-term interest rate, as a measure of the prices at which securities can be sold.

Corporate issues of bonds and stocks constitute 53 percent of net new issues in the period 1951–1961, inclusive. Corporate need and availability of funds (from sources other than the securities market) must play a role in the relation. Profits plus capital consumption allowances and miscellaneous valuation adjustments minus direct taxes are a measure of the internal availability of funds. What is an indicator of need? The answer is: the amount that corporations intend to spend, specifically, expected expenditure to be financed non-currently. This expenditure will be covered by means of various sources of funds including the securities market. A proxy of expected expenditure is actual current-dollar investment in machinery, equipment, and non-residential construction. This has the advantage of relating to the same time interval as the measure of corporate liquidity. But it is not entirely satisfactory, because not all fixed capital formation (excluding residential construction) is performed by corporations. Furthermore, the assumption is that past investment spending is an indicator of planned future spending. Fortunately the measure of need for funds does not enter the model directly. Rather the appropriate explanatory variable is the ratio of corporate liquidity to current-dollar investment. This ratio form implies that the assumption stated above is not unreasonably restrictive. Both numerator and denominator are expressed in current dollars, and the ratio itself is lagged one quarter.

Net new issues of provincial and municipal bonds account for 46 percent of the variable over 1951–1961. The lower levels of government resorted more and more to the securities market during the period of the fluctuating rate, and a time trend enters the relation as a factor indicating the increase in government finance via the securities market. The time trend is an alternative to a variable analogous to the corporate ratio discussed above. Such a variable might be the ratio over all provincial and municipal governments of budgetary surplus or deficit to total expenditure, but this is unsatisfactory because the ratio does not give sufficient weight to the expansion of the role of lower-level governments—particularly provincial governments—in the Canadian economy. The time trend may be considered an index of this political or sociological phenomenon.

An explanatory variable which refers to all issues is that part of S which is predetermined, that is, net new issues of federal marketable long-term securities. Government of Canada bonds constitute a large part of the volume of securities traded. The fact that a large amount of government securities are issued may restrain issuance of private securities. It is true that to some extent this force works by increasing the long-term interest rate. But it may also have an independent effect, that is, an effect not reflected in the interest rate. CIL, because it refers to government of Canada bonds, may not be the appropriate interest rate for a relation explaining issues of other bonds; but *together with SG* it may be a good proxy. Moreover, it is not only interest rate but extent of available supply of funds which influences security offerings. Large issues by the government of Canada may be interpreted to imply less available funds (at the same given point of time) for other security issuers.[37] The non-federal security issuers may therefore hold back. Reciprocally, retirements of federal government securities increase the supply of funds.[38] Therefore net new issues are the relevant explanatory variable, and the relation is:

$$\text{SO} = a_{24} + b_{24} * \text{LIQ1} + c_{24} * \text{T} + d_{24} * \text{CIL} + e_{24} * \text{SG} + f_{24} * \text{Q1} + g_{24} * \text{Q2} + h_{24} * \text{Q3} + E_{24}$$

where SO = net new issues of non-federal long-term securities, in millions of dollars

LIQ1 = ratio of corporate liquidity to expenditure on new machinery, equipment, and non-residential construction, lagged one quarter

T = time trend, i if ith observation

SG = net new issues of government of Canada marketable long-term securities, in millions of dollars

LIQ1, T, and SG are predetermined variables. A priori considerations dictate that b_{24} be negative and c_{24} positive. A normal supply relationship implies that d_{24} is negative. A positive coefficient would indicate the necessity to lower bond prices in order to successfully place new issues in the market. The coefficient of SG is theoretically negative.

The estimated equation is:

$$\begin{aligned} \text{SO} = {} & \underset{(410.0)}{740.0} - \underset{(430.0)}{700.0} * \text{LIQ1} + \underset{(4.0)}{5.9} * \text{T} - \underset{(270.0)}{63.0} * \text{CIL} \\ & - \underset{(0.14)}{0.34} * \text{SG} + \underset{(60.0)}{160.0} * \text{Q1} + \underset{(65.0)}{210.0} * \text{Q2} \\ & - \underset{(49.0)}{3.8} * \text{Q3} \qquad \text{(AOT)} \end{aligned}$$

37. This statement may be inapplicable to the extent that the issues are taken up by the Bank of Canada.

38. This may not be true if the matured debt was held by the central bank.

$$p = 0.37 \quad DW = 1.84 \quad RSQ = 0.38 \quad RSQC = 0.42$$
$$RSQT(CIL) = 0.94$$

25. Earned Wage Income

Two relations determine the earned component of personal income and its distribution. The first explains wage, the second non-wage, income. Earned wage income consists of wages, salaries and supplementary labor income but excludes military pay and allowances. The theory adopted to explain earned wage income is that such income is a certain proportion of gross national expenditure, but this proportion varies both seasonally and cyclically. Naturally gross national expenditure is an explanatory variable. For consistency it excludes military pay and allowances. Both earned wage income and gross national expenditure are expressed in current dollars. In this respect the equation is of a monetary rather than real dimension. Neither of the variables is deflated because wage *income* is by nature a money flow. Moreover, wage bargaining is in money terms. Readjustment of wage rates according to a consumer price index is an insignificant—if not entirely absent—feature of wage contracts in Canada.

The proportion of the labor force that is employed is an explanatory variable that serves as a measure of the cycle. This cycle includes *all* workers while the dependent variable (earned wage income) by nature refers to *paid* workers only. There is no inconsistency; this is the only sensible way to include a variable relating to employment with respect to the labor force. Although the employed can be divided into paid and unpaid workers,[39] no such distinction can be made for the unemployed.

The uniform treatment of seasonality in the stochastic equations provides dummy seasonal variables. The basic explanatory variable and the measures of cycle and seasonality have been set forth; the equation is therefore:

$$YWC = a_{25} + b_{25} * YM + c_{25} * PEREMP + d_{25} * Q1 + e_{25} * Q2 + f_{25} * Q3 + E_{25}$$

39. The distinction between paid and unpaid workers is of importance for Canada. See equations 36 and 37.

where YWC = earned civilian wage income, in millions of dollars

YM = gross national expenditure excluding military pay and allowances, in millions of dollars

PEREMP = proportion of labor force employed

Both YM and PEREMP are current endogenous variables. It is naturally expected that the coefficient of YM is positive. On the other hand, the coefficient of PEREMP is theoretically negative. There are two reasons for this sign. First, profits fluctuate violently with the cycle. Wage income as a percentage of gross national product therefore varies inversely with the cycle. Wages are a sticky factor return in this respect. Second, as the percentage of the labor force employed increases—beyond a certain point, of course—relatively unskilled workers are hired. They naturally earn less on the average than those already employed. Providing other factors of production are not strained to the limit but remain accessible, in general output will not fall in proportion to the loss of productivity of the new workers. Both arguments imply that PEREMP be unlagged.

Equation 25 in estimated form is:

$$\begin{aligned}\text{YWC} = {} & \underset{(1500.0)}{4200.0} + \underset{(0.019)}{0.49} * \text{YM} - \underset{(1400.0)}{4400.0} * \text{PEREMP} \\ & + \underset{(67.0)}{79.0} * \text{Q1} + \underset{(37.0)}{42.0} * \text{Q2} - \underset{(45.0)}{230.0} * \text{Q3} \qquad \text{(OT)}\end{aligned}$$

$$\text{DW} = 1.74 \quad \text{RSQ} = 0.99 \quad \text{RSQC} = 0.99$$

$$\text{RSQT(YM)} = 0.99 \quad \text{RSQT(PEREMP)} = 0.95$$

26. Earned Non-wage Personal Income

The relation explaining earned non-wage personal income is:

$$\begin{aligned}\text{YNW} = {} & a_{26} + b_{26} * \text{YM} + c_{26} * \text{Q1} + d_{26} * \text{Q2} \\ & + e_{26} * \text{Q3} + E_{26}\end{aligned}$$

where YNW = earned non-wage personal income, in millions of dollars

This is an empirical relation as well as a structural one. As a structural equation it is not entirely satisfactory, but cannot be improved because of lack of information. The components of the dependent variable and the principal variable which would be used to explain each of them are listed in Table 3.

TABLE 3. Earned non-wage personal income.

Component	Explanatory variable
Net income of non-farm unincorporated business[a]	Gross national expenditure minus change in farm inventories
Net income received by farm operators from farm production[b]	Change in farm inventories
Dividends	Holdings of common and preference stocks
Interest	Holdings of savings deposits, bonds, etc.
Rental income	Disposable income

[a] This flow includes professional income. The designation "net" means net of expenses rather than net of taxes.

[b] Rental and interest income are excluded. The definition of farm production is in *National Accounts, Income and Expenditure, 1926–1956*, p. 116.

Data on personal holdings of interest- or dividend-bearing assets are fragmentary. Information concerning personal savings deposits in chartered banks and holdings of Canada Savings Bonds is complete. Approximate personal holdings of government of Canada marketable securities and provincial, municipal, corporate and other bonds can be constructed, but only on a year-end basis and not without including in the estimate all residual errors of estimation of the complete breakdown of holdings including non-personal holdings.[40] Annual data on personal holdings of stocks do not exist. Data on other interest-bearing asset holdings of persons are at best annual, at worst non-existent. Construction of an aggregate explanatory variable would require considerable interpolation and weighting of series by appropriate interest rates.

40. See, for example, Bank of Canada, *Statistical Summary Supplement, 1962*, pp. 60 and 100.

The task is not attempted.[41] As for disposable income, it is probably well proxied by gross national expenditure.

In estimated form equation 26 is:

$$\begin{aligned} YNW = {} & \underset{(96.0)}{410.0} + \underset{(0.012)}{0.11} * YM - \underset{(45.0)}{120.0} * Q1 + \underset{(45.0)}{73.0} * Q2 \\ & + \underset{(46.0)}{480.0} * Q3 \qquad \text{(OT)} \end{aligned}$$

$$DW = 1.64 \quad RSQ = 0.91 \quad RSQC = 0.91$$
$$RSQT(YM) = 0.99$$

27. Personal Expenditure on Consumer Non-durable Goods

For purposes of the model, consumption expenditure has a threefold breakdown: non-durable goods, durable goods, and services. Each component is explained by means of a stochastic equation of a uniform nature. Personal expenditure on each of the three categories is in constant-dollar form. Because the equations are similar in kind, they are discussed as one.

Not only disposable income but also its distribution affects expenditure on consumption. This theory is set forth in the traditional manner, namely, by including two income variables in the equation: disposable wage income and disposable non-wage income. Each income variable is deflated by the appropriate base-weighted price index of the equation in which it appears, that is, the price index of the objects of the expenditure under explanation.

Relative prices are probably not very significant when such broad categories of expenditure are under consideration. Rather, a greater degree of substitution occurs *within* each of the three sectors. Nevertheless, relative prices may be expected to have some intersectoral effect on grounds of the theory of consumer

41. To the argument that investment income should be taken as predetermined, it may be retorted that dividends are without doubt current endogenous. Regarding interest receipts the discussion of equation 17 is applicable.

behavior. The relative price variable is the ratio of the base-weighted price index of the component under explanation to a weighted average of the base-weighted price indexes of the other two components.

Liquid assets of the personal sector are given a role for two reasons: first, to represent the effects of disposable income in previous quarters. (The income variables in the equation refer to the current period.) The second function of a liquid assets variable is to serve in its own right as an influence on consumer expenditure, that is, to measure a variant of a "balances" effect. Liquid assets of the personal sector are measured by those assets for which data are available and for which all—or virtually all—holdings are contained in the personal sector. Unfortunately demand deposits of the chartered banks are not allocated between the personal and corporate sectors. However, personal savings deposits by definition belong to the personal sector. They are highly liquid. Although the chartered banks can legally enforce a notice period for withdrawing funds from a personal savings account, in practice withdrawal takes place on demand. Non-resident holdings of personal savings deposits are no doubt insignificant. A second kind of asset useful for the purpose at hand is Canada Savings Bonds. By law these bonds are restricted to individuals, they are redeemable on demand at any chartered bank, and they are not held by non-residents. The liquid assets variable is then the ratio of beginning-of-quarter public holdings of Canada Savings Bonds and personal savings deposits to the base-weighted price index (in the current quarter) of the expenditure component with which the equation deals.

With respect to the equations explaining expenditure on goods, stocks of the relevant commodities that are held by the personal sector would be an appropriate explanatory variable; however, no information on such stocks is available. The three consumer equations may now be stated (consecutively in symbolic and estimated forms).

$$\begin{aligned} \mathrm{CND} = {} & a_{27} + b_{27} * \mathrm{YDWND} + c_{27} * \mathrm{YDNWND} \\ & + d_{27} * \mathrm{PNDPO} + e_{27} * \mathrm{HLAND} + f_{27} * \mathrm{Q1} \\ & + g_{27} * \mathrm{Q2} + h_{27} * \mathrm{Q3} + E_{27} \end{aligned}$$

where CND = personal expenditure on consumer non-durable goods, in millions of constant (1957) dollars

YDWND = disposable wage income divided by base-weighted price index of consumer non-durable goods, in millions of deflated dollars

YDNWND = disposable non-wage income divided by base-weighted price index of consumer non-durable goods, in millions of deflated dollars

PNDPO = ratio of base-weighted price index of consumer non-durable goods to weighted average of base-weighted price indexes of consumer durable goods and services

HLAND = beginning-of-quarter public holdings of personal savings deposits and Canada Savings Bonds divided by base-weighted price index of consumer non-durable goods, in millions of deflated dollars

$$\begin{aligned} CND = {} & 10.0 + \underset{(430.0)}{0.37} * YDWND + 0.062 * YDNWND \\ & + \underset{(320.0)}{850.0} * PNDPO + \underset{(0.028)}{0.054} * HLAND \\ & - \underset{(21.0)}{580.0} * Q1 - \underset{(20.0)}{420.0} * Q2 - \underset{(23.0)}{460.0} * Q3 \qquad (OT) \end{aligned}$$

$$DW = 2.15 \quad RSQ = 0.99 \quad RSQC = 0.99$$

$$RSQT(PNDPO) = 0.99 \quad RSQT(HLAND) = 0.99$$

28. Personal Expenditure on Consumer Durable Goods

$$\begin{aligned} CD = {} & a_{28} + b_{28} * YDWD + c_{28} * YDNWD + d_{28} * PDPO \\ & + e_{28} * HLAD + f_{28} * Q1 + g_{28} * Q2 \\ & + h_{28} * Q3 + E_{28} \end{aligned}$$

where CD = personal expenditure on consumer durable goods, in millions of constant (1957) dollars

YDWD = disposable wage income divided by base-weighted price index of consumer durable goods, in millions of deflated dollars

YDNWD = disposable non-wage income divided by base-weighted price index of consumer durable goods, in millions of deflated dollars
PDPO = ratio of base-weighted price index of consumer durable goods to weighted average of base-weighted price indexes of consumer non-durable goods and services
HLAD = beginning-of-quarter public holdings of personal savings deposits and Canada Savings Bonds divided by base-weighted price index of consumer durable goods, in millions of deflated dollars

$$\begin{aligned} CD = &\underset{(2500.0)}{-6400.0} + 0.077 * YDWD + 0.015 * YDNWD \\ &+ \underset{(2000.0)}{5500.0} * PDPO + \underset{(0.062)}{0.14} * HLAD - \underset{(24.0)}{140.0} * Q1 \\ &+ \underset{(19.0)}{17.0} * Q2 - \underset{(27.0)}{35.0} * Q3 \qquad \text{(AOT)} \end{aligned}$$

$p = 0.53$ DW = 1.54 RSQ = 0.86 RSQC = 0.74
RSQT(PDPO) = 0.98 RSQT(HLAD) = 0.99

29. Personal Expenditure on Consumer Services

$$\begin{aligned} CS = &a_{29} + b_{29} * YDWS + c_{29} * YDNWS + d_{29} * PSPO \\ &+ e_{29} * HLAS + f_{29} * Q1 + g_{29} * Q2 \\ &+ h_{29} * Q3 + E_{29} \end{aligned}$$

where CS = personal expenditure on consumer services, in millions of constant (1957) dollars
YDWS = disposable wage income divided by base-weighted price index of consumer services, in millions of deflated dollars
YDNWS = disposable non-wage income divided by base-weighted price index of consumer services, in millions of deflated dollars
PSPO = ratio of base-weighted price index of consumer services to weighted average of base-weighted price indexes of consumer durable and non-durable goods

HLAS = beginning-of-quarter public holdings of personal savings deposits and Canada Savings Bonds divided by base-weighted price index of consumer services, in millions of deflated dollars

$$
\begin{aligned}
CS = & \underset{(260.0)}{-470.0} + 0.31 * YDWS + 0.038 * YDNWS \\
& + \underset{(460.0)}{580.0} * PSPO + \underset{(0.040)}{0.051} * HLAS - \underset{(18.0)}{24.0} * Q1 \\
& + \underset{(17.0)}{1.4} * Q2 - \underset{(22.0)}{120.0} * Q3 \qquad \text{(AOT)}
\end{aligned}
$$

$p = 0.54 \quad DW = 1.70 \quad RSQ = 0.93 \quad RSQC = 0.98$
$RSQT(PSPO) = 0.99 \quad RSQT(HLAS) = 0.99$

All variables in the consumer expenditure equations are current endogenous, with the exception of the seasonal factors. Coefficients of the income variables are theoretically positive, as are those of the liquid assets variables. On the other hand, coefficients of price ratios are expected to be negative. Furthermore, it is expected that the coefficient of wage income exceeds that of the corresponding non-wage income variable.

It should be noted that CND, CD, and CS include purchases by the entire personal sector rather than households alone. They are personal expenditure on consumer goods and services. Included as persons in the Canadian national accounts are private non-commercial institutions (such as hospitals, universities, and labor unions) private pension funds, and insurance companies (insofar as services to persons are performed). Naturally, treatment of these organizations as persons extends to the product side of the national accounts as well. Thus investment income of these institutions is included in personal income.[42] The fact that the consumer equations extend beyond households to incorporate the entire personal sector does not destroy the theories. Though

42. An outline and justification of the non-household component of the personal sector is found in *National Accounts, Income and Expenditure, 1926–1956*, pp. 123–124.

based on the theory of the individual consumer, the relations hold for all consumers (the personal sector). For example, non-commercial institutions receive income (net of intrasectoral transfer payments), say, from investments. They purchase goods and services, that is, they have operating expenses. Of course, their expenditure pattern differs from that of households. Ultimately for purposes of analysis what is desired is a breakdown of income and expenditure data into households (by size and income class), private non-commercial institutions (by type), private pension funds, and life insurance companies. Although a breakdown of revenue (income) is statistically possible, one of expenditure would be more difficult to achieve.

30. Residential Construction

The relation explaining constant-dollar new residential construction is similar to the consumer expenditure equations in the sense that it includes analogous explanatory variables. Disposable wage and non-wage income are added together to form a disposable income variable; beginning-of-quarter public holdings of personal savings deposits and Canada Savings Bonds also enter the relation. Both variables are deflated by the base-weighted price index of residential construction. The "pure" price variable is the ratio of the base-weighted price index of residential construction to a weighted average of the base-weighted price indexes of consumer goods and services. The variables discussed in this paragraph are demand factors on the part of the ultimate users of residential construction.

Financial factors are of considerable importance and are represented by two additional variables. The first is the interest differential between National Housing Act mortgages and the securities (bond) market. This differential is of great relevance to the chartered banks because by law they cannot originate mortgages except under the National Housing Act. It is true that other lenders have recourse to conventional as well as NHA mortgages. But the interest differential remains relevant: first, insofar as the rates on conventional mortgages are proxied by the

NHA interest rate; second, because in the event that lenders shift from the NHA to the conventional mortgage market not all prospective borrowers will make the switch, because conventional terms would be more unfavorable than NHA terms.

The National Housing Act of 1954 changed the structure of the non-conventional mortgage market. First, it permitted the chartered banks (and Quebec savings banks) to take up first mortgages, a practice which had previously been illegal. Second, for the first time a system of government-administered insurance on NHA mortgages was set up. It is true that lenders had received federal protection even before the Act. "But the protection to the lender against loss under the joint loan system was in the form of accumulated credits to the particular lending institutions which originated the loans and it attached to these institutions as originators rather than as owners of loans. The loss protection was not specific to the individual mortgages themselves and was not inherently transferrable with the mortgages."[43] It is clear that the system of insurance on mortgages themselves enhanced the liquidity and hence the attractiveness of these assets. Third, the practice of joint loans was abolished. Under this system the federal government was empowered to share mortgages with private lenders while protecting the latter against loss. However, the government did not restrict its right to enter the mortgage market directly and provide the totality of funds for individual mortgages. The new National Housing Act dates from March 22, 1954, and its importance to the relation is measured by means of a dummy variable which serves to alter the intercepts.

All explanatory variables (except the dummy factor) are lagged two quarters. This is a simplified lag structure. For precision, each explanatory variable should individually be given an appropriate lag. Because of prior knowledge of the new National Housing Act, the dummy variable follows the Act without a significant lag. Other influences are at work in the residential construction market but are not given an explicit role in the relation. Direct lending by the government is a policy variable.

43. Central Mortgage and Housing Corporation, *Submission to the Royal Commission on Banking and Finance* (Ottawa, 1962), p. 6.

Furthermore, the price of new houses is not the only market factor affecting demand. The borrower as distinct from lender interest rate,[44] the time allowed to repay the mortgage, the value of the mortgage in relation to the property which secures it, the maximum amount of the mortgage[45] are all relevant. An index incorporating all these factors can be constructed but is by nature arbitrary, therefore is not included in the relation, which remains:

$$\begin{aligned} RC = a_{30} &+ b_{30} * YDRC2 + c_{30} * HLARC2 \\ &+ d_{30} * PHCPI2 + e_{30} * DIR2 + f_{30} * ACT \\ &+ g_{30} * Q1 + h_{30} * Q2 + i_{30} * Q3 + E_{30} \end{aligned}$$

where RC = new residential construction, in millions of constant (1957) dollars

YDRC2 = disposable income divided by base-weighted price index of residential construction, in millions of deflated dollars, lagged two quarters.

HLARC2 = beginning-of-quarter public holdings of personal savings deposits and Canada Savings Bonds divided by base-weighted price index of residential construction, in millions of deflated dollars, lagged two quarters

PHCPI2 = ratio of base-weighted price index of residential construction to weighted average of base-weighted price indexes of consumer goods and services, lagged two quarters

DIR2 = lender interest rate on National Housing Act loans minus long-term interest rate in bond market, percent per quarter, lagged two quarters

ACT = 1 if second quarter 1954 or beyond, 0 otherwise

All explanatory variables in the relation are predetermined. Expected signs of coefficients are: $b_{30}, c_{30}, e_{30}, f_{30} > 0$, $d_{30} < 0$.

44. Under the system of joint loans, the government provided funds at a lower interest rate than did the private lender. The borrower was assessed an intermediate rate. With respect to insured mortgages the borrower's effective interest rate exceeds that of the lender because it is the former that is required to pay the insurance charges.

45. There is a legal maximum for insured mortgages. The terms of NHA loans are discontinuously altered at the discretion of the government subject to provisions of the Act.

The estimated equation is:

$$\begin{aligned} RC = {} & \underset{(480.0)}{430.0} + \underset{(0.029)}{0.038} * YDRC2 + \underset{(0.022)}{0.018} * HLARC2 \\ & - \underset{(590.0)}{470.0} * PHCPI2 + \underset{(63.0)}{130.0} * DIR2 + \underset{(28.0)}{27.0} * ACT \\ & - \underset{(21.0)}{140.0} * Q1 - \underset{(11.0)}{15.0} * Q2 + \underset{(11.0)}{14.0} * Q3 \qquad \text{(ALS)} \end{aligned}$$

$p = 0.64$ DW $= 1.14$ RSQ $= 0.89$ RSQC $= 0.75$

31. Non-residential Construction

The equation for residential construction has been set forth. Remaining components of business fixed capital formation are (1) non-residential construction and (2) machinery and equipment. Like other expenditure flows which serve as dependent variables, these series are expressed in constant dollars, and they are each explained by a stochastic equation. Though the forms of the two relationships are somewhat different, discussion of the equation explaining construction will be largely applicable to that explaining machinery and equipment.

Private capital formation depends on the liquidity of investors. Liquidity is more than profits or net income. Direct taxes are a negative element; and the fact that fixed investment is a gross rather than net concept implies that capital consumption allowances and miscellaneous valuation adjustments are also relevant parts of liquidity. Just as not only income but its distribution enters the explanation of consumer expenditure, so the distribution of liquidity is of relevance in business investment equations. The distinction made is that between corporate and other investors, and reflection of the associated theory takes place by including the respective disjoint measures of liquidity as explanatory variables.

The corporate liquidity measure has been discussed; it is the sum of profits, capital consumption allowances, miscellaneous valuation adjustments, and direct taxes (which are a negative flow). An analogous series represents the liquidity of non-corporate investors. The capital formation under consideration excludes that performed by the government sector; in fact non-corporate investors are limited to farm operators, other unincorporated businesses, and private non-commercial institutions. The liquidity variable is the sum of net received income of farm operators from farm production, net income of non-farm unincorporated businesses, capital consumption allowances and miscellaneous valuation adjustments of the three categories of investors; the negative flow is again taxes, but government transfer payments to farmers are a partial offset. A base-weighted price index of non-residential construction is required for purposes of deflating the liquidity variables. However, only current-weighted price indexes are available. There are two such indexes, one derived from seasonally adjusted, the other seasonally unadjusted data. They are the ratio of the current- to the constant-dollar measures (either seasonally adjusted or otherwise, as the case may be) of new non-residential construction. The better measure of a base-weighted price index is that derived from the *seasonally adjusted* data because: "Quarter-to-quarter changes in these indexes reflect not only pure price change, but also changing expenditure patterns within and between groups. For the unadjusted data, these changes in expenditure patterns are significant because of seasonal variation. The implicit price indexes based on the unadjusted data, therefore, should not be used for price analysis. In the case of the seasonally adjusted data, however, only small changes in expenditure patterns occur and the implicit price indexes usually provide a reasonable measure of price change."[46] The liquidity variables are lagged two quarters. This uniform lag is adopted for all fixed investment equations.

Quite apart from high current profits the rate of growth of the Canadian economy influences investment. Moreover, past sales are the crux of the acceleration theory of investment, and the theory adopted gives weight to both the liquidity and acceleration theories. Components of the activity variable are expenditure on consumer goods and services, gross fixed capital formation,

46. *National Accounts, Income and Expenditure by Quarters, 1947–61*, p. 99.

government expenditure on goods, and merchandise exports. Merchandise imports enter as a negative component. All elements are expressed in constant dollars. Change in inventories is excluded because such flows are induced as well as autonomous, and the autonomous part cannot be isolated. The change in inventories may represent a scarcity (or superfluity) of final demand. In this respect it is accounted for by the activity variable itself. On the other hand, it is true that a growing economy requires growth in its inventory stock. The change in farm inventories is relevant insofar as it affects the investment decisions of farm operators. However, this change is fully reflected in the net income of farm operators, which enters the non-corporate liquidity variable. Change in farm inventories is not a component of the activity variable because there is no spillover to non-farm investment due to the change itself. The fact that part of merchandise imports is included in inventories implies that there is some double counting involved in the subtraction of the totality of merchandise imports. This problem was encountered before (see equation 10); the information required for a satisfactory solution is not available. Net tourist receipts are added to the activity variable because expenditure on consumer services includes the item: net travel expenditure. "This net adjustment is necessary to include, in personal expenditure, the expenditures of Canadian residents in foreign countries, and to exclude the expenditures of non-residents in Canada."[47] However, the opposite treatment is required in the construction of a determinant of domestic investment.

Let A be the activity measure as outlined. Then the associated explanatory variable is not the activity level itself but the slope of the linear equation relating the natural logarithm of the activity level to time. The observations are the six preceding quarters and the dependent variable has the value 1 for the observation furthest in the past, 2 for the succeeding observation, and so on, until the value 6 for the most recent period. The slope is estimated by means of ordinary least squares. Interpretation of the resulting explanatory variable is best achieved by setting forth the pro-

47. *National Accounts, Income and Expenditure, 1926–1956*, p. 161.

cedure mathematically. Let t be the independent variable. Then the estimated regression equation is

$$\log A = a + b * t$$

Taking differentials,

$$dA/A = b * dt$$

Rearranging terms,

$$b = (dA/dt)/A$$

Therefore the variable in the limit is the rate of change of the activity measure as a proportion of its actual level. All observations of this variable are obtained by means of the moving regression. (Actually only the dependent variable moves. For reason of consistency the dependent variable possesses the same values for all regressions.) The variable enters the relation lagged two quarters.

The financing of investment requires more attention. Internal sources of funds have already entered the relation via the liquidity explanatory variables. The influence of external sources of funds is measured by the excess cash reserve ratio of the chartered banks. This variable is lagged two quarters.

Availability or non-availability of credit is more important as a stimulatory or depressive force on investment than are mere interest rates. Businessmen are *intent* on investing (either for autonomous reasons or because of the other explanatory variables in the equation), and higher interest charges will not dissuade them significantly. On the other hand, non-availability of credit might prevent them from carrying out their intent for lack of funds.

The excess cash reserve ratio is an index of availability of funds via the chartered banks since it measures the "looseness" of the banks, their unfilled capacity to make loans and buy securities. It also serves as a proxy for credit conditions in general, including the state of the securities market since government policy in the bond market is likely to be reflected in the excess reserve ratio of the chartered banks.

There exists the possibility of a relationship between residential and non-residential construction. In the nature of things there might be spillover effects from a change in the development of the one form of construction into the other. The National Housing Act ushered in a new structure of the residential construction market, and the increased intensity of residential building provided external economies for non-residential construction. Economies include development of a skilled labor force and sources of supply of materials. Of course, external diseconomies, such as bidding-up prices of materials, may also be applicable. This suggests that the dummy variable ACT enter the relation for non-residential as well as that for residential construction. The equation explaining non-residential construction is therefore:

$$\begin{aligned}\text{CNR} = a_{31} &+ b_{31} * \text{CPCC2} + c_{31} * \text{YUBC2} + d_{31} * \text{FSP2} \\ &+ e_{31} * \text{R2} + f_{31} * \text{ACT} + g_{31} * \text{Q1} \\ &+ h_{31} * \text{Q2} + i_{31} * \text{Q3} + E_{31}\end{aligned}$$

where CNR = new non-residential construction, in millions of constant (1957) dollars

CPCC2 = corporate profits, capital consumption allowances and miscellaneous valuation adjustments minus direct taxes divided by price index of non-residential construction, in millions of deflated dollars, lagged two quarters

YUBC2 = liquidity of non-corporate private investors divided by price index of non-residential construction, in millions of deflated dollars, lagged two quarters

FSP2 = slope of ordinary least squares regression of logarithm of constant-dollar sum of output of goods which constitute final sales, expenditure on consumer services and net tourist receipts on time (observations are six preceding quarters), lagged two quarters

R2 = excess cash reserve ratio of chartered banks, percent, lagged two quarters

All explanatory variables are predetermined, and coefficients of the non-seasonal variables are theoretically positive. It is assumed that the net external economies represented by ACT are positive rather than negative. With respect to the relative magnitude of coefficients, the expectation is that b_{31} exceeds c_{31}. Corporations have greater need and ability than non-corporate investors to undertake large capital formation projects which are not feasible on a small scale. Furthermore, the operations of corporations as a group have a larger capital intensity than those of non-corporate private investors.

The estimated equation is:

$$\begin{aligned} \text{CNR} = & \underset{(170.0)}{-57.0} + \underset{(0.16)}{0.39} * \text{CPCC2} + \underset{(0.070)}{0.18} * \text{YUBC2} \\ & + \underset{(2000.0)}{1900.0} * \text{FSP2} + \underset{(41.0)}{12.0} * \text{R2} + \underset{(48.0)}{100.0} * \text{ACT} \\ & - \underset{(44.0)}{260.0} * \text{Q1} - \underset{(23.0)}{23.0} * \text{Q2} + \underset{(43.0)}{210.0} * \text{Q3} \qquad \text{(ALS)} \end{aligned}$$

$$p = 0.55 \quad \text{DW} = 1.31 \quad \text{RSQ} = 0.84 \quad \text{RSQC} = 0.80$$

32. Machinery and Equipment

The equation explaining investment in new machinery and equipment has almost the same form as that explaining new non-residential construction. The problem of unavailability of a suitable base-weighted price index exists, and the same solution is adopted. The only substantial difference in the two relations is the omission of the variable to measure external economies arising from residential construction. The equation is:

$$\begin{aligned} \text{EM} = & a_{32} + b_{32} * \text{CPME2} + c_{32} * \text{YUBME2} + d_{32} * \text{FSP2} \\ & + e_{32} * \text{R2} + f_{32} * \text{Q1} + g_{32} * \text{Q2} + h_{32} * \text{Q3} + E_{32} \end{aligned}$$

where EM = new machinery and equipment, in millions of constant (1957) dollars

CPME2 = corporate profits, capital consumption allowances and miscellaneous valuation adjustments minus direct taxes divided by price index of new machinery and equipment, in millions of deflated dollars, lagged two quarters

YUBME2 = liquidity of non-corporate private investors divided by price index of new machinery and equipment, in millions of deflated dollars, lagged two quarters

CPME2 and YUBME2 are predetermined variables. A priori the coefficients b_{32}, c_{32}, d_{32}, and e_{32} are greater than zero.

The estimated equation:

$$\begin{aligned} EM = \underset{(90.0)}{79.0} &+ \underset{(0.068)}{0.34} * CPME2 + \underset{(0.043)}{0.085} * YUBME2 \\ &+ \underset{(1000.0)}{3900.0} * FSP2 + \underset{(24.0)}{6.0} * R2 - \underset{(28.0)}{8.4} * Q1 \\ &+ \underset{(14.0)}{180.0} * Q2 + \underset{(23.0)}{160.0} * Q3 \qquad \text{(ALS)} \end{aligned}$$

$p = 0.41 \quad DW = 1.62 \quad RSQ = 0.89 \quad RSQC = 0.85$

33. Change in Non-farm Business Inventories

Change in inventories is expressed in constant dollars. Farm inventories are excluded; they enter the subsequent relation. The change in inventories over a given period is partly autonomous and partly induced. Active forces are those that operate on desired inventories; passive factors are those influences that give rise to changes in inventories that are unplanned. The explanatory variables that induce changes in planned—as distinct from unplanned—inventories may be divided into those that are objective and those that are speculative.

There are two objective explanatory variables. The first is a stock-flow ratio. What is desired is the ratio of the total stock of non-farm business inventories to final sales, both expressed in constant dollars. However, the official series of the stock of all inventories is not available. The following variable, which has been discussed above (see equation 10), is used in place of the ideal measure: the ratio over all manufacturing industries of beginning-of-quarter inventories to the sum of shipments over the four preceding quarters. This relation is important for its own sake because manufacturing inventories are a large proportion of total non-farm inventories. Moreover, it serves as a proxy for other relevant stock-flow ratios, such as those at the wholesale and retail levels.

Availability of funds influences inventory decisions. The liquidity (adjusted profits or net income) of both corporate and non-corporate investors (excluding farm operators) is a measure of this factor. Liquidity of farm operators is excluded because investment only in *non-farm* inventories is under explanation. The measure is deflated by the overall wholesale price index and lagged one quarter. Both numerator and denominator of this variable require explanation. For precision, the distribution of liquidity should play a role just as it does in explaining fixed investment. In the case of inventory investment it is assumed that the coefficients of the hypothetical dual variables are indistinguishable. This is because inventory investment is by nature not subject to the discontinuities inherent in fixed investment projects and the superior capital intensity under which corporations operate is restricted to fixed investment. The wholesale price index is the selected measure of price because its components are the principal deflators of current-dollar inventories in the national accounts. Moreover, the wholesale price index is base-weighted, though the base period precedes the beginning of the period to which the model refers.

Two objective influences on planned change in inventories have been set forth. They are complemented by a factor operating on price speculation. This factor is the percentage change in the wholesale price index, lagged one quarter. The percentage rather than the absolute change is relevant because the whole price index—unlike the exchange rate, of which the *absolute* change affects speculation—is subject to a trend, which naturally tends to suppress variation in a first difference. But more important justifications center on the interpretation of the overall wholesale price index. "Though general wholesale price indexes have been calculated by many countries for years there is no precise answer to the question of what such an index measures. This is so because the index cannot be associated with any adequately definable value aggregate."[48] Speculation refers to a large number of individual prices, and it is better to express an overall price index which serves only as a proxy for these underlying prices—and which is moreover devoid of interpretation in itself—as a percentage rather than absolute change, thus removing the index analogy of a dimension.

The outcome of plans to change inventories is altered with events. The culprit is final sales of goods. This represents activity in its effect on the unplanned change in inventories, and the equation is then:

$$\text{BI} = a_{33} + b_{33} * \text{SMANI} + c_{33} * \text{YG} + d_{33} * \text{CPUBI1} + e_{33} * \text{CWPI1} + f_{33} * \text{Q1} + g_{33} * \text{Q2} + h_{33} * \text{Q3} + E_{33}$$

where BI = change in non-farm business inventories, in millions of constant (1957) dollars

CPUBI1 = liquidity of non-farm investors divided by wholesale price index, in millions of deflated dollars, lagged one quarter

CWPI1 = ratio of change in wholesale price index to index of the previous quarter, percent, lagged one quarter

CPUBI1 and CWPI1 are predetermined variables. The coefficient of SMANI is theoretically negative on the grounds that a large (small) ratio of stocks to sales induces a decrease (increase) in planned inventories. Also the coefficient of YG is expected to be less than zero. It is a measure of the cause of unplanned change in inventories. It is true that as the total output of the economy increases the needed (hence planned) inventory stock also increases. But this does not imply that c_{33} is positive. The size effect may decrease the magnitude of c_{33}, but YG is required to be lagged to give proper structural attention to its effect on *planned* inventories. Though a time trend or a variable analogous to FSP2 could be included, the coefficient of SMANI suffices to

48. Dominion Bureau of Statistics, *Prices & Price Indexes* (May 1962), p. 49.

give scope to the size effect. The level of economic activity does not have the important role it would require if the dependent variable were the *stock* of inventories rather than its first difference. It is expected that d_{33} is greater than zero; but the sign of e_{33} is a function of the type of expectations held by speculators and therefore cannot be a priori determined.

The estimated equation is:

$$\begin{aligned} BI = {} & \underset{(1100.0)}{1300.0} - \underset{(4800.0)}{2700.0} * SMANI - \underset{(0.15)}{0.26} * YG \\ & + \underset{(0.44)}{0.46} * CPUBI1 + \underset{(17.0)}{27.0} * CWPI1 - \underset{(190.0)}{65.0} * Q1 \\ & + \underset{(59.0)}{12.0} * Q2 - \underset{(47.0)}{17.0} * Q3 \end{aligned} \qquad \text{(AOT)}$$

$$p = 0.23 \quad DW = 1.70 \quad RSQ = 0.57 \quad RSQC = 0.56$$
$$RSQT(YG) = 0.97$$

34. Change in Farm Inventories

Change in farm inventories is explained quite differently from that in non-farm inventories, although both are expressed in constant dollars. Ideally the change in farm inventories should be explained by means of the following identity: change in inventories = additions minus depletions. Additions and depletions should be dependent variables in respective stochastic equations. Moreover, depletions can be divided into those due to foreign demand (that is, exports of agricultural products) and those due to domestic demand, with an equation for each. What is really required is a complete quarterly input-output analysis of the agricultural sector. But information for such treatment does not exist, and therefore the change in farm inventories is not one side of an identity; rather it is the dependent variable of a stochastic equation. Because of the nature of agricultural production the seasonal factors are of great significance. They measure, in part, factors of supply. Because of the importance of exports of agricultural produce, an index of activity in those countries which import Canadian farm products is a component of an explanatory variable on the demand side. The variable itself is lagged one quarter as an approximate weighted average of the proper lag for the United States (nil according to equation 3) and that for other countries (two quarters corresponding to equations 4, 5 and 6). The weight of the United States in the index is 38 percent; the respective weights are based on current-dollar imports of Canadian agricultural products over the period 1951–1960, inclusive.

In order to give attention to price as well as income determinants of demand the index of activity levels is divided by a base-weighted price index of exports of Canadian farm products. If the components of the change in farm inventories were individually explained, then other demand and price variables such as Canadian disposable (especially wage) income, the ratio of the price indexes of Canadian and competing farm products (for exports) and the ratio of the price index of food to other components of the consumer price index (for domestic demand) would explicitly appear. In view of the necessity of a direct stochastic determination of change in farm inventories, only a few explanatory variables enter the relation, which is:

$$\mathrm{FI} = a_{34} + b_{34} * \mathrm{FIP1} + c_{34} * \mathrm{Q1} + d_{34} * \mathrm{Q2} + e_{34} * \mathrm{Q3} + E_{34}$$

where FI = change in farm inventories and grain in commercial channels, in millions of constant (1957) dollars

FIP1 = index of production of importers of Canadian farm products divided by price index of exports of Canadian farm products, lagged one quarter

FIP1 is a predetermined variable. Because an increase (decrease) in exports of farm products—which event depends directly on FIP1—leads to a decrease (increase) in Canadian stocks of such commodities, the coefficient of FIP1 is theoretically negative.

The estimated relationship is:

$$FI = \underset{(91.0)}{-140.0} - \underset{(96.0)}{220.0} * FIP1 + \underset{(43.0)}{190.0} * Q1 + \underset{(44.0)}{310.0} * Q2$$

$$+ \underset{(44.0)}{910.0} * Q3 \qquad \text{(LS)}$$

$$DW = 2.29 \quad RSQ = 0.92$$

35. Labor Force

Characteristics of the labor sector are explained by means of five stochastic equations. The labor force itself depends primarily on the number of people of working age. Both variables are restricted to the non-institutional civilian population fourteen years of age and over. A second explanatory variable is the number of unemployed. This is a factor measuring the excess demand or supply position in the labor market. An excess demand for labor (small unemployment) leads to employers seeking out workers and improving terms (in relation to the ability of the workers they are able to obtain). Therefore potential workers are induced to enter the labor force. Other possible explanatory variables, which are not included in the relation, are the real wage rate and specific demographic factors. The real wage rate could be defined as the ratio of the average wage rate to the index of prices of consumer goods and services; but the unemployment variable suffices to measure its influence. Another reason for the exclusion is the fact that relatively unskilled workers tend to be hired as full employment is approached. This phenomenon might, in fact, lower the average wage rate. With respect to demographic factors the adult population itself is important. Certain features, such as the expanding entrance of women in the labor force, might be measured by means of a time trend, which is adopted in the British model of Klein and his associates.[49] However, working-age population is itself to a great extent subject to a trend.

49. KBHV, p. 85.

A technical matter is the use of unemployment in absolute terms as distinct from the percentage of the labor force employed. In equation 25 the percentage rather than absolute employment appears because the underlying theory is that YW is a certain (varying) proportion of YM and both variables are money flows; employment then, as a measure of the business cycle, should be in percentage terms. In the equation which determines the size of the labor force there is no problem of units, unlike the equation explaining earned wage income. The dependent and two explanatory variables discussed above are all in the same units. But apart from methodology it would matter little if PEREMP were used in place of unemployment, since the one variable would not be seriously removed from the mirror image of the other.

The labor force equation:

$$\begin{aligned}\text{FORCEM} = {} & a_{35} + b_{35} * \text{CADULTM} + c_{35} * \text{UNEMPM} \\ & + d_{35} * \text{Q1} + e_{35} * \text{Q2} + f_{35} * \text{Q3} + E_{35}\end{aligned}$$

where FORCEM = labor force, millions of persons
CADULTM = non-institutional adults, millions of persons
UNEMPM = unemployed people in labor force, millions of persons

CADULTM is taken as a predetermined variable; in a complete demographic-economic model it would be endogenous. UNEMPM is current endogenous. It is expected that b_{35} is positive and c_{35} negative.

In estimated form the equation is:

$$\begin{aligned}\text{FORCEM} = {} & \underset{(0.30)}{-0.92} + \underset{(0.028)}{0.62} * \text{CADULTM} \\ & - \underset{(0.099)}{0.091} * \text{UNEMPM} - \underset{(0.019)}{0.080} * \text{Q1} \\ & + \underset{(0.0077)}{0.023} * \text{Q2} + \underset{(0.0082)}{0.15} * \text{Q3} \qquad \text{(AOT)}\end{aligned}$$

$p = 0.82 \quad DW = 1.96 \quad RSQ = 0.98 \quad RSQC = 0.99$
$RSQT(UNEMPM) = 0.95$

36. Employment of Paid Workers

The distinction between paid and unpaid workers is important for Canada, as unpaid workers constitute 22 percent of the number of employed on the average over the years 1951–1961, inclusive. Paid workers are by definition earners of wage income. Employment is explained in terms of man-hours rather than number of workers, since the former is clearly a measure of greater precision. The dependent variable under consideration is limited to paid workers; employment of unpaid workers is explained in the subsequent equation. Employment depends on real gross national production. The activity variable is exclusive of military pay and allowances because the dependent variable refers only to civilian employment. Interest and dividends of the balance of payments do not enter the measure because they do not involve current employment of labor. This is a demand-for-labor equation, whereas equation 35 deals with the supply side. It can be interpreted as derived from an aggregate production function (or from several disaggregated functions). This suggests that another variable be included, namely, the ratio of the price of labor (wage rate) to an index of prices of other factors of production. However, this variable is not included because of the tremendous difficulty of constructing a suitable index of prices of inputs other than labor. The problems involved center around the heterogeneity of capital goods and the necessity to incorporate the factor of technology.

The first labor employment equation:

$$\text{EMPM} = a_{36} + b_{36} * \text{YR} + c_{36} * \text{Q1} + d_{36} * \text{Q2} + e_{36} * \text{Q3} + E_{36}$$

where EMPM = employment of paid workers, millions of man-hours

YR = gross national expenditure excluding military pay and allowances, in millions of constant (1957) dollars

YR is a current endogenous variable and its coefficient is theoretically positive.

The estimated equation is:

$$\underset{}{\text{EMPM}} = \underset{(64.0)}{740.0} + \underset{(0.0081)}{0.20} * \text{YR} + \underset{(21.0)}{76.0} * \text{Q1} + \underset{(21.0)}{50.0} * \text{Q2}$$
$$- \underset{(22.0)}{190.0} * \text{Q3} \qquad \text{(OT)}$$

$$\text{DW} = 2.10 \quad \text{RSQ} = 0.94 \quad \text{RSQC} = 0.95$$
$$\text{RSQT(YR)} = 0.99$$

37. Employment of Unpaid Workers

The second labor employment equation deals with unpaid workers, that is, those people who are at work and yet do not earn wage income. There are three categories by type of worker: (1) own-account or independent workers (such as in the professions) who have no paid employees, (2) employers, that is, those who own a business or farm or have a profession *and* employ workers, (3) unpaid family workers (a phenomenon especially applicable to farms). There is another breakdown of unpaid workers: by type of occupation. Unpaid workers in agriculture constituted 56 percent of the total number of unpaid workers on the average over the eleven full years in the period of interest. This proportion is of importance in interpreting coefficients of the relation.

Employment of unpaid workers is expressed in man-hours in conformity to the variable measuring employment of paid workers. Real output is again an explanatory variable. But it has two effects, which are partially offsetting. On the one hand, increase in activity leads to reduced employment of unpaid workers. The reason is a combination of factors: substitution of capital goods resulting from applications of technological advances, and the attractiveness of paid work as the level of economic activity increases. This analysis is especially applicable to unpaid workers on farms, but the second component of the combination stated above affects all unpaid family workers, even those engaged in non-farm occupations. On the other hand, certain classes of unpaid workers may increase in number as a result of greater economic activity. This applies mainly to the professions.

Another explanatory variable enters the relation. It is unemployment—the number of unemployed people in the economy. If the labor market is tight in the sense that it is difficult to obtain workers at prevailing wage rates, unpaid work will increase. This factor counteracts the depressing effect of output. In fact unemployment itself is a measure of activity (rather, counter-activity, since unemployment and output tend to move in opposite directions). Consider an increase in activity. Then UNEMPM (decreasing) is likely to have a positive effect on the work of employers and should isolate the positive effect on employment of family workers, allowing YR (increasing) to take up the negative effect. Then the equation is:

$$\text{EMPNM} = a_{37} + b_{37} * \text{YR} + c_{37} * \text{UNEMPM} + d_{37} * \text{Q1} + e_{37} * \text{Q2} + f_{37} * \text{Q3} + E_{37}$$

where EMPNM = employment of unpaid workers, millions of man-hours

It is expected that the coefficients of YR and UNEMPM are both negative. It may be noted parenthetically that the shift of employment from agriculture to non-agricultural occupations as economic activity rises is not expected to significantly depress the coefficient of YR in the relation determining employment of *paid* workers (equation 36), because only 2 percent of paid workers are engaged in agriculture (taking the usual average).

The estimated equation:

$$\text{EMPNM} = \underset{(47.0)}{1100.0} - \underset{(0.0076)}{0.040} * \text{YR} - \underset{(55.0)}{130.0} * \text{UNEMPM}$$

$$- \underset{(18.0)}{69.0} * \text{Q1} + \underset{(11.0)}{60.0} * \text{Q2} + \underset{(14.0)}{140.0} * \text{Q3} \quad (\text{OT})$$

$$\text{DW} = 1.82 \quad \text{RSQ} = 0.93 \quad \text{RSQC} = 0.94$$

$$\text{RSQT(YR)} = 0.99 \quad \text{RSQT(UNEMPM)} = 0.95$$

38. Number of Hours Worked per Paid Worker

There is a downward trend in the average number of working hours per paid worker per time period (quarter). This trend is due to social factors, an affluent economy, and development of the recreation sector. It expresses itself in union demands and also in employers "voluntarily" shortening the number of hours of work required per time period for a given wage. Therefore a time trend enters the relation explaining average working hours. A second explanatory variable is real output. This is included on the grounds that less time worked per employee (rather than laying off of workers) is the initial result of a slowdown in production. Similarly increases in output are produced by overtime work (or expansion of working hours to the normal level) as well as by hiring of additional workers.

The fact that real output has an upward trend should not be confused with the downward dummy trend variable. To make the distinction precise a measure of productivity is included in the relation. The variable is real gross national expenditure (excluding military pay and allowances) divided by the total number of man-hours worked (paid workers only). This will not only pick up the upward trend in real output (thus allowing T to exhibit a downward trend) but is an explanatory variable for its own sake. It is, in fact, increases in productivity which make possible the trend of a shorter "work week" (in this case "work quarter") without the consequence of a lower standard of living or contraction of the investment sector of the economy in order to keep up consumption.

The productivity variable is a result of the effect on output of all other influences (including technology and utilization of capital goods) as well as increase in the quality of (paid) labor. This is precisely the measure that is required. It is incorrect to limit the change in productivity to that due only to alteration in the quality of the labor force. The totality of increases in productivity—irrespective of cause—constitutes a superior variable for this equation. It is noted that output is divided by the number of man-hours of paid workers only. This is done in order to conform to the dependent variable (itself restricted to paid workers). It can be argued that paid and unpaid workers are to some extent substitutable. This is true; but other factors of production are also substitutable for paid workers. The substitution relationships between paid and unpaid work are factors in equations 36 and 37 above.

The inclusion of the productivity variable has several desirable consequences for the relation. The coefficient of YR has netted out of it the effect of a trend growth in output, and is now a "pure" measure of activity as it affects hours worked per paid worker. The trend influences at work to lower average hours worked are divided into two parts. The technological factors, such as increased automation, enter the relation via the productivity variable. Factors of labor-bargaining, habitual tendencies and those that are cultural and social are included in the time trend variable. This dichotomy does not imply a denial that the technological, other economic, social, political, and cultural factors are interrelated. It entails merely a separation of the *ability* to impose a shorter "work week" without grave consequences for the economy from the *demand* for greater leisure. Hence the relation:

$$\text{AHP} = a_{38} + b_{38} * \text{YR} + c_{38} * \text{T} + d_{38} * \text{PROD} + e_{38} * \text{Q1} + f_{38} * \text{Q2} + g_{38} * \text{Q3} + E_{38}$$

where AHP = number of hours worked per paid worker

PROD = gross national expenditure excluding military pay and allowances divided by man-hours of paid workers, in constant dollars per man-hour

PROD is a current endogenous variable. Theoretical values of coefficients are: b_{38} positive, c_{38} negative, and d_{38} negative.

The estimated equation:

$$\text{AHP} = \underset{(25.0)}{530.0} + \underset{(0.0061)}{0.0092} * \text{YR} - \underset{(0.31)}{0.97} * \text{T} - \underset{(15.0)}{18.0} * \text{PROD} + \underset{(3.4)}{11.0} * \text{Q1} + \underset{(2.2)}{9.6} * \text{Q2} - \underset{(4.0)}{13.0} * \text{Q3} \qquad \text{(OT)}$$

$$\text{DW} = 1.64 \quad \text{RSQ} = 0.86 \quad \text{RSQC} = 0.90$$

$$\text{RSQT(YR)} = 0.99 \quad \text{RSQT(PROD)} = 0.97$$

39. Number of Hours Worked per Unpaid Worker

The work quarter of the unpaid worker should move together with that of the paid worker, because the social and economic factors affecting average number of hours worked remain applicable and also because especially in family businesses or farms the employer works together with his employees and family help. A large proportion of unpaid work is in agriculture, and the seasonal factors should differ in this relation because of the nature of agricultural production. Because of the form of the stochastic equations, the intercept and seasonal influences are intertwined; but it may be expected that in general the longer "work week" in agriculture as distinct from other occupations in the peak season of agricultural activity is another reason for a separate relationship explaining the hours of unpaid work, and the equation is:

$$\text{AHN} = a_{39} + b_{39} * \text{AHP} + c_{39} * \text{Q1} + d_{39} * \text{Q2} + e_{39} * \text{Q3} + E_{39}$$

where AHN = number of hours worked per unpaid worker

The coefficient of AHP is expected to be positive.
In estimated form equation 39 is:

$$\underset{(150.0)}{\text{AHN} = 290.0} + \underset{(0.29)}{0.66} * \text{AHP} - \underset{(4.3)}{31.0} * \text{Q1} + \underset{(5.0)}{21.0} * \text{Q2} + \underset{(5.1)}{36.0} * \text{Q3} \qquad \text{(AJT)}$$

$p = 0.25$ DW = 2.19 RSQ = 0.87 RSQC = 0.80
RSQT(AHP) = 0.85

40. Price Index of Final Sales

The remaining stochastic equations explain indexes of prices. The model requires a price index of the principal constituents of final output for two reasons. First, this price measure is necessary in order to relate the real to the monetary flows of the national accounts. (See equation 72 in chapter III.) Second, it is used as an explanatory variable in equations explaining price indexes of disaggregative groups of commodities. The overall price index is that of consumer expenditure, net tourist receipts, business gross fixed investment, government expenditure on goods, government wages (excluding military pay and allowances) and merchandise exports, all net of merchandise imports.[50] Net tourist receipts are included because it is the price index of *Canadian* production that is under consideration.

The price index is endogenous, and requires to be determined. Ideally it should be a base-weighted price index. But this type of index exists only for consumer expenditure and foreign trade. The use of an approximation to a base-weighted index by means of the current-weighted price index based on seasonally adjusted national accounts flows is inapplicable, because the flows relating to government and foreign trade are not available in seasonally adjusted form. Therefore there is no recourse but to take the current-weighted price index defined by current- and constant-dollar flows of the national accounts. The fact that it is precisely this index which is required in order to link constant-dollar and current-dollar flows of the model is not a reason for its use. If a base-weighted price index were available, the requisite measure could be explained by an equation in which the explanatory variables were the corresponding base-weighted price index and seasonal factors. This technique is in fact used with respect to a disaggregative price index (in equation 49). Although the index here is current-weighted, there is hope that the seasonal factors in the relation will net out shifts in weighting patterns sufficiently, so that the dependent variable approaches a base-weighted framework in its interactions with the non-dummy explanatory variables.

The dependent variable of the relation here set forth is called the price index of final sales. There are two principal explanatory variables. Wage rates are an important determinant of prices.

50. Because the price index excludes change in inventories, the perennial problem of inability to allocate merchandise imports to inventories and final sales is present. See equations 10 and 31.

The average wage rate for the economy is expressed in index number form (to correspond with the dependent variable) and thus enters the relation. The openness of the Canadian economy entails external direct effects on prices and requires inclusion of an appropriate variable. A base-weighted price index of merchandise imports is constructed for this purpose. Its components are converted to Canadian currency by means of an index of the exchange rate, and they are the price indexes (themselves base-weighted) of the commodity classes of imports explained in equations 8 to 11, inclusive.

The price index in this relation consists of both lagged and unlagged components. The indexes of prices of consumer and investment goods are not lagged because the underlying commodities are final goods as are those of the dependent variable. On the other hand, the price indexes of industrial materials and fuels and lubricants are largely intermediate goods; the theory is that prices of such goods have a lagged effect on prices of final goods. It is noted that such treatment of import price indexes is consistent with the current or lagged status, as the case may be, of the explanatory price ratios in relations 8 to 11. But the lags[51] are of a different kind. In the earlier equations they refer to the lag of price ratios as affecting imports; here they relate to the effect of price indexes on an aggregate price index. However, the basic determinants of the time structures of the relationships are the natures of underlying commodity classes; this is true for both types of equations. The equation explaining the price index of final sales is therefore:

$$\begin{aligned} \text{PFS} = {} & a_{40} + b_{40} * \text{WR} + c_{40} * \text{PMGSR} + d_{40} * \text{Q1} \\ & + e_{40} * \text{Q2} + f_{40} * \text{Q3} + E_{40} \end{aligned}$$

where PFS = current-weighted price index of final sales, 1957 = 1

WR = index of aggregate wage rate, 1957 = 1

PMGSR = base-weighted price index of imports of merchandise including exchange rate variation, 1957 = 1

51. Here the word "lag" is used in an all-inclusive manner, that is, it may refer to a current relationship (nil lag).

WR and PMGSR are current endogenous variables and their coefficients are theoretically positive.

The estimated equation:

$$\begin{aligned} PFS = {} & \underset{(0.041)}{0.37} + \underset{(0.029)}{0.48} * WR + \underset{(0.050)}{0.16} * PMGSR + \underset{(0.0021)}{0.0058} * Q1 \\ & + \underset{(0.0024)}{0.0016} * Q2 - \underset{(0.0022)}{0.016} * Q3 \qquad \text{(AOT)} \end{aligned}$$

$$p = 0.62 \quad DW = 1.65 \quad RSQ = 0.93 \quad RSQC = 0.97$$
$$RSQT(WR) = 0.99 \quad RSQT(PMGSR) = 0.97$$

41. Price Index of Consumer Non-durable Goods

Discussion of the equation determining the base-weighted price index of consumer non-durable goods is relevant for several subsequent relations, but especially for equations explaining the price indexes of consumer durables and investment goods because the three equations stated have identical forms. The primary explanatory variable is the aggregate price index, namely, the price index of final sales. This is a measure of general influences on disaggregate price indexes, influences such as overall prices, wage rates, and prices of imports. This immediately suggests a variable which serves as a correction factor. The ratio of expenditure on consumer non-durables to final sales (the flows which compose PFS)—both measured in constant dollars—can indicate the extent to which the price index of consumer non-durable goods diverges from the price of final sales because of autonomous factors in its own market. In fact the ratio itself is a measure of the autonomy of the market for consumer non-durable goods in relation to that for all final products. Autonomy varies inversely with the ratio. The expenditure ratio serves another purpose. It is an indicator of demand conditions in the market for consumer non-durable goods relative to overall demand. Therefore its coefficient refers to the phenomenon of sectoral inflation.[52]

52. Equation 40 does not include a corresponding variable measuring demand-pull because the numerator of an analogous ratio is final sales themselves. Hence the resultant variable is identically unity and therefore excluded.

Two specific influences are included in the relation. The first is a stock-flow variable. It is the ratio of beginning-of-quarter inventories in non-durable consumer goods industries to the sum of shipments over the four preceding quarters. General problems in construction of such a variable have been discussed above.[53] It may be remarked that inventories at all stages of production are included in the ratio. The inventory-shipment ratio is a measure of the supply situation. If inventories are low (high) relative to shipments in the recent past, prices will (will not) rise with an increase in sales. In the latter situation orders can easily be fulfilled.

The second specific factor is the base-weighted price index of imports of non-durable consumer goods. The index is divided by the index of the spot exchange rate for purpose of conversion to Canadian currency. This variable is not lagged, because the imports considered are consumer goods themselves. They are final products able to be sold to consumers without further processing. The prices of imports that are not final goods also have an effect on the dependent variable. Imports of industrial materials are used in the production of domestically produced consumer goods. The variable PFS, as noted above, serves as a proxy for this and other influences. The prices of imports of industrial materials would affect the price index of consumer goods in a lagged manner; and a price index of the former class of commodities enters the relation explaining PFS with a one quarter lag. It is noteworthy that the role of PFS in proxying general and miscellaneous effects tends to introduce recursiveness into the model.

The explanatory variables of the equation explaining the price index of consumer durable goods are precisely analogous to those of the present relation, and so both equations may be written.

$$\begin{aligned} \text{PNDB} = {} & a_{41} + b_{41} * \text{SIND} + c_{41} * \text{PFS} + d_{41} * \text{CNDFS} \\ & + e_{41} * \text{PMNDR} + f_{41} * \text{Q1} + g_{41} * \text{Q2} \\ & + h_{41} * \text{Q3} + E_{41} \end{aligned}$$

53. See equation 10. Because the considered variable refers to a subset of all manufacturing industries, comments on deflation should be envisaged as appropriately modified.

where PNDB = base-weighted price index of consumer non-durable goods, 1957 = 1

SIND = ratio of beginning-of-quarter inventories in non-durable consumer goods industries to sum of shipments over preceding four quarters

CNDFS = ratio of expenditure on consumer non-durable goods to final sales

PMNDR = base-weighted price index of imports of consumer non-durable goods divided by index of spot exchange rate

SIND is a predetermined variable while CNDFS and PMNDR are current endogenous. Theoretical signs of coefficients are as follows: $b_{41} < 0$, $c_{41}, d_{41}, e_{41} > 0$.

Equation 41 in estimated form:

$$\begin{aligned} \text{PNDB} = {} & \underset{(0.17)}{0.066} + \underset{(0.33)}{0.56} * \text{SIND} + \underset{(0.082)}{0.48} * \text{PFS} \\ & + \underset{(0.28)}{0.44} * \text{CNDFS} + \underset{(0.072)}{0.21} * \text{PMNDR} \\ & + \underset{(0.0072)}{0.0098} * \text{Q1} + \underset{(0.0084)}{0.016} * \text{Q2} + \underset{(0.012)}{0.026} * \text{Q3} \quad \text{(AOT)} \end{aligned}$$

$$p = 0.71 \quad \text{DW} = 1.37 \quad \text{RSQ} = 0.68 \quad \text{RSQC} = 0.84$$
$$\text{RSQT(PFS)} = 0.99 \quad \text{RSQT(CNDFS)} = 0.87$$
$$\text{RSQT(PMNDR)} = 0.95$$

42. Price Index of Consumer Durable Goods

$$\begin{aligned} \text{PDB} = {} & a_{42} + b_{42} * \text{SID} + c_{42} * \text{PFS} + d_{42} * \text{CDFS} \\ & + e_{42} * \text{PMDR} + f_{42} * \text{Q1} + g_{42} * \text{Q2} \\ & + h_{42} * \text{Q3} + E_{42} \end{aligned}$$

where PDB = base-weighted price index of consumer durable goods, 1957 = 1

SID = ratio of beginning-of-quarter inventories in durable consumer goods industries to sum of shipments over preceding four quarters

CDFS = ratio of expenditure on consumer durable goods to final sales
PMDR = base-weighted price index of imports of consumer durable goods divided by index of spot exchange rate

SID is a predetermined variable; CDFS and PMDR are current endogenous. Expected signs of coefficients: $b_{42} < 0$, c_{42}, d_{42}, $e_{42} > 0$.

Equation 42 in estimated form:

$$\begin{aligned} \text{PDB} = {} & 1.0 + \underset{(0.0043)}{0.19} * \text{SID} + 0.027 * \text{PFS} - 1.4 * \text{CDFS} \\ & + 0.044 * \text{PMDR} - \underset{(0.0023)}{0.0024} * \text{Q1} + \underset{(0.0036)}{0.015} * \text{Q2} \\ & - \underset{(0.0027)}{0.014} * \text{Q3} \qquad \text{(AOT)} \end{aligned}$$

$p = 0.72$ DW = 1.43 RSQ = 0.55 RSQC = 0.41

43. Price Index of Investment Goods

The form of the equation explaining the (overall) price index of investment goods is identical to that for consumer goods. The only difference is due to the fact that no base-weighted price index of investment goods is available. As an approximation to such an index the implicit price index based on the seasonally adjusted current- and constant-dollar flows of business gross fixed capital formation is used.

$$\begin{aligned} \text{PFC} = {} & a_{43} + b_{43} * \text{SIK} + c_{43} * \text{PFS} + d_{43} * \text{FKFS} \\ & + e_{43} * \text{PMKR} + f_{43} * \text{Q1} + g_{43} * \text{Q2} \\ & + h_{43} * \text{Q3} + E_{43} \end{aligned}$$

where PFC = price index of investment goods, 1957 = 1
SIK = ratio of beginning-of-quarter inventories in investment goods industries to sum of shipments over preceding four quarters
FKFS = ratio of business gross fixed capital formation to final sales

PMKR = base-weighted price index of imports of investment goods divided by index of spot exchange rate

SIK is predetermined; FKFS and PMKR are current endogenous. Theoretical signs of coefficients are: $b_{43} < 0$, c_{43}, d_{43}, $e_{43} > 0$.

The equation is estimated as:

$$\begin{aligned}
\text{PFC} = & \underset{(0.090)}{-0.20} - \underset{(0.14)}{0.13} * \text{SIK} + \underset{(0.10)}{0.82} * \text{PFS} + \underset{(0.15)}{0.21} * \text{FKFS} \\
& + \underset{(0.071)}{0.36} * \text{PMKR} - \underset{(0.0028)}{0.00034} * \text{Q1} - \underset{(0.0061)}{0.0047} * \text{Q2} \\
& + \underset{(0.0046)}{0.00072} * \text{Q3} \qquad \text{(AOT)}
\end{aligned}$$

$$p = 0.43 \quad \text{DW} = 1.69 \quad \text{RSQ} = 0.98 \quad \text{RSQC} = 0.99$$
$$\text{RSQT(PFS)} = 0.99 \quad \text{RSQT(FKFS)} = 0.92$$
$$\text{RSQT(PMKR)} = 0.98$$

44. Base-weighted Price Index of Merchandise Exports

Three of the variables used to explain the base-weighted price index of merchandise exports are analogous to those appearing in the three preceding relations. The roles of the price index of final sales and the ratio of constant-dollar merchandise exports to final sales are adequately explained under equation 41 above. A third explanatory variable, the beginning-of-quarter inventories in export industries divided by the sum of shipments over the previous four quarters, requires some additional discussion. This variable refers not to all industries that export but only to those in which (1) a high proportion of production is exported and (2) fluctuations in activity are caused largely by export trade. Moreover, shipments refer to all shipments—both to domestic and foreign destinations; therefore shipments are not in general equal to exports. The assumption is that the inventory-shipment ratio for those industries producing largely for export is relevant either for its own sake, or as a proxy for the ideal stock-flow relation which applies to all exports.

Prices of imports do not directly enter this relation. It is true that such prices have an influence with respect to re-exports and with the part of exports that represents domestic value added to imported commodities. The factor of re-exports may be dismissed because the dependent variable is constructed from price and unit value movements of domestic exports only. An example of the second influence of import prices is the export of a manufactured commodity which is made in part from imported raw materials. But this situation by nature is not of importance for principal categories of Canadian exports, namely, food, forest products, and mining products. Of course, imports of goods and services pervade the economy as a whole—and PFS is a proxy for such influence. There are no *specific* import price indexes that are relevant. However, a special price variable does enter the relation. The price index of exports competitive to Canada is a factor for two reasons. First, some Canadian exports, such as wheat, have their prices influenced by international agreements. Exports competitive to Canada are by nature similar to Canadian exports, and the price index of the former serves as a measure of international prices to which part of Canadian exports tends to conform by agreement. The second reason is simply the competitiveness of world markets. Canadian exporters must adjust their prices to those of their competitors or suffer consequences in their volume of exports. On the other hand, if competitive prices rise, Canadian exporters can increase their profits by raising prices with little fear of decreases in their share of export markets. For conversion purposes the exchange rate is of importance in this matter, and the price index of competitive exports is divided by the spot exchange rate. The resulting variable is lagged one quarter, and the equation is:

$$\begin{aligned} \text{PXB} = a_{44} &+ b_{44} * \text{SIX} + c_{44} * \text{PFS} + d_{44} * \text{XFS} \\ &+ e_{44} * \text{PXO1} + f_{44} * \text{Q1} + g_{44} * \text{Q2} \\ &+ h_{44} * \text{Q3} + E_{44} \end{aligned}$$

where PXB = base-weighted price index of merchandise exports, 1957 = 1

SIX = ratio of beginning-of-quarter inventories in industries producing largely for export to sum of shipments over preceding four quarters
XFS = ratio of merchandise exports to final sales
PXO1 = price index of exports competitive to Canada divided by spot exchange rate, lagged one quarter

SIX and PXO1 are predetermined variables; XFS is current endogenous. It is expected that b_{44} is negative while c_{44}, d_{44}, and e_{44} are positive.

The estimated equation:

$$\begin{aligned} \text{PXB} = {} & \underset{(0.094)}{0.42} - \underset{(0.17)}{0.51} * \text{SIX} + \underset{(0.076)}{0.27} * \text{PFS} + \underset{(1.0)}{2.2} * \text{XFS} \\ & + \underset{(0.056)}{0.062} * \text{PXO1} - \underset{(0.0018)}{0.0018} * \text{Q1} - \underset{(0.0065)}{0.0097} * \text{Q2} \\ & + \underset{(0.0024)}{0.00083} * \text{Q3} \qquad \text{(AJT)} \end{aligned}$$

$$p = 0.78 \quad \text{DW} = 1.46 \quad \text{RSQ} = 0.74 \quad \text{RSQC} = 0.71$$
$$\text{RSQT(PFS)} = 0.99 \quad \text{RSQT(XFS)} = 0.62$$

45. Price Index of Industrial Materials

The equation explaining the price index of industrial materials contains three explanatory variables that correspond to variables in relations 41 to 43. There is an inventory-shipment ratio; but it is not restricted to a particular subclass of industries. The variable is measured over all manufacturing industries. Its numerator includes inventories of all kinds, namely, raw materials, goods in process, and finished products. This is because the definition of raw materials is not an absolute concept but rather is relative to the industry. The price index of final sales is an explanatory variable, but there is no variable comparable to, say, CNDFS as a correction factor or measure of sectoral inflation. The change in inventory stock is not an appropriate numerator. One reason is that this change can be positive, negative, or even zero. But such a procedure would be in any case unsound because industrial materials refer to the inter-industry level of the economy as much as to the final sales level. This fact does not exclude relating the price index of industrial materials to the overall price index. The latter retains its function as an indicator of general price and wage influences.

A specific price index of imports is relevant for this relation. It is the base-weighted price index of imports of industrial materials divided by the index of the spot exchange rate. This variable is current rather than lagged, because even though the imports are intermediate as distinct from final goods, the commodity content of the dependent variable is of the same nature. Hence the equation:

$$\text{PWIM} = a_{45} + b_{45} * \text{SMANI} + c_{45} * \text{PFS} + d_{45} * \text{PMIMR} + e_{45} * \text{Q1} + f_{45} * \text{Q2} + g_{45} * \text{Q3} + E_{45}$$

where PWIM = base-weighted price index of industrial materials, 1957 = 1

PMIMR = base-weighted price index of imports of industrial materials divided by index of spot exchange rate

PMIMR is a current endogenous variable. The coefficient of SMANI is theoretically negative while those of PFS and PMIMR are positive.

The estimated equation is:

$$\begin{aligned}\text{PWIM} = \underset{(0.12)}{0.52} - \underset{(0.30)}{0.27} * \text{SMANI} + \underset{(0.065)}{0.22} * \text{PFS} \\ + \underset{(0.037)}{0.31} * \text{PMIMR} - \underset{(0.0030)}{0.0011} * \text{Q1} + \underset{(0.0034)}{0.0020} * \text{Q2} \\ - \underset{(0.0030)}{0.00055} * \text{Q3} \qquad \text{(AOT)}\end{aligned}$$

$p = 0.58$ DW = 1.79 RSQ = 0.74 RSQC = 0.87
RSQT(PFS) = 0.99 RSQT(PMIMR) = 0.97

46. Price Index of Consumer Services

The price index of consumer services involves a relation substantially different from those used to explain other price indexes. Wage rates are by nature far more important in service than in goods industries. Therefore an index of wage rates in service occupations is included in the relation. It is desired to have the index include wage rates only in consumer service industries, but the available index pays some attention to business services as well.[54] The index of prices of final sales is another explanatory variable. It is a proxy for general price and wage influences, as in preceding equations. However, the ratio of expenditure on consumer services to final sales does not enter this relation. It affects the price index of consumer services but in a recursive manner, namely, by influencing the service industry wage rate (equation 47). Consumer services are largely endogenous to the economy; there are no direct external influences. On the other hand, if the price index of business services were to be explained, prices of such services—or associated wage rates—in the United States would constitute explanatory variables. These considerations lead to the following equation.

$$\text{PSB} = a_{46} + b_{46} * \text{WRS} + c_{46} * \text{PFS} + d_{46} * \text{Q1} + e_{46} * \text{Q2} + f_{46} * \text{Q3} + E_{46}$$

where PSB = base-weighted price index of consumer services, 1957 = 1

WRS = index of wage rate in consumer service industries, 1957 = 1

WRS is a current endogenous variable. The coefficients b_{46} and c_{46} are a priori positive.

54. To the extent that business services include categories—such as accountancy and law—on which the personal sector expends funds, their wage rates are relevant to determination of the price index of consumer services. In any event the influence of business services cannot be removed because of scarcity of information with respect to both the weight of business services in the overall service wage rate index and the wage rate index of business services itself.

The estimated equation is:

$$\underset{}{\text{PSB}} = \underset{(0.094)}{0.31} + \underset{(0.058)}{0.45} * \text{WRS} + \underset{(0.15)}{0.24} * \text{PFS} - \underset{(0.0019)}{0.0045} * \text{Q1}$$

$$- \underset{(0.0023)}{0.0016} * \text{Q2} + \underset{(0.0020)}{0.0066} * \text{Q3} \qquad \text{(AOT)}$$

$p = 0.62$ DW = 1.84 RSQ = 0.97 RSQC = 0.99
RSQT(WRS) = 0.99 RSQT(PFS) = 0.99

47. Wage Rate in Consumer Service Industries

Just as price indexes of specific industries or of particular commodities are dependent on the overall price index, so the wage rate in service industries is a function of the overall wage rate. Specific factors are difficult to isolate; but the fact that the service industry over time is an increasing portion of the economy should be relevant. The ratio of constant-dollar expenditure on consumer services to final sales is a factor indicating the demand for personal services, hence for labor in the consumer service industry; therefore it affects the service wage rate. Again this variable is a correction factor in the sense that it measures the demand for consumer services relative to the totality of final demand. However, it serves to alter the influence of an overall wage as distinct from price index. A technical matter is the addition of net tourist receipts to the numerator of the ratio. This is done because expenditure on consumer services includes net tourist *payments*. But in this case it is desired to include foreign expenditure in Canada and exclude Canadian expenditure abroad. This is in conformity with the definition of final sales. The equation is then:

$$\text{WRS} = a_{47} + b_{47} * \text{WR} + c_{47} * \text{SFS} + d_{47} * \text{Q1} + e_{47} * \text{Q2} + f_{47} * \text{Q3} + E_{47}$$

where SFS = ratio of expenditure on consumer services excluding net tourist payments to final sales

SFS is current endogenous and both its coefficient and that of WR are theoretically positive.

The estimated equation:

$$\begin{aligned} WRS = &-1.0 + 1.3 * WR + 3.5 * SFS - 0.095 * Q1 \\ &\quad (0.12)\ (0.041) \qquad (0.62) \qquad (0.020) \\ &- 0.040 * Q2 - 0.069 * Q3 \qquad \text{(AOT)} \\ &\quad (0.011) \qquad (0.0051) \end{aligned}$$

$$p = 0.54 \quad DW = 2.02 \quad RSQ = 0.98 \quad RSQC = 0.99$$

$$RSQT(WR) = 0.99 \quad RSQT(SFS) = 0.97$$

48. Price Index of Foreign Tourist Expenditure in Canada

The price index of foreign tourist expenditure in Canada is constructed as a weighted average of appropriate components of the price indexes of consumer non-durable goods and services. Therefore the main explanatory variable is a weighted average of the two latter price indexes; the weights are the totals of the component weights allocated to one or other of the principal price indexes. The dependent variable, the explanatory variable, and component indexes of the latter are all base-weighted. This is the ideal situation for price analysis, and the equation is:

$$\begin{aligned} PTC = &\ a_{48} + b_{48} * PNDS + c_{48} * Q1 + d_{48} * Q2 \\ &+ e_{48} * Q3 + E_{48} \end{aligned}$$

where PTC = base-weighted price index of foreign tourist expenditure in Canada, 1957 = 1

PNDS = base-weighted price index of consumer services and non-durable goods, 1957 = 1

PNDS is a current endogenous variable and its coefficient is theoretically positive.

The estimated equation is:

$$\begin{aligned} PTC = &\ 0.11 + 0.89 * PNDS - 0.0010 * Q1 - 0.0035 * Q2 \\ &\ (0.059)\ (0.059) \qquad (0.0015) \qquad (0.0017) \\ &- 0.0080 * Q3 \qquad \text{(AOT)} \\ &\quad (0.0015) \end{aligned}$$

$$p = 0.78 \quad DW = 1.87 \quad RSQ = 0.86 \quad RSQC = 0.98$$
$$RSQT(PNDS) = 0.99$$

49. Current-weighted Price Index of Merchandise Exports

The current-weighted price index of merchandise exports depends on the base-weighted index. Because changes in expenditure patterns (weights) under the current-weighted index are the causes of divergence between the two indexes and because these shifts are expected to be largely seasonal in nature, the seasonal dummy variables should be of importance.

$$\begin{aligned} PXC = {} & a_{49} + b_{49} * PXB + c_{49} * Q1 + d_{49} * Q2 \\ & + e_{49} * Q3 + E_{49} \end{aligned}$$

where PXC = current-weighted price index of merchandise exports, 1957 = 1

The coefficient of PXB is expected to be positive.

$$\begin{aligned} PXC = {} & \underset{(0.14)}{0.21} + \underset{(0.14)}{0.79} * PXB + \underset{(0.0035)}{0.0022} * Q1 + \underset{(0.0040)}{0.0022} * Q2 \\ & + \underset{(0.0035)}{0.0013} * Q3 \qquad \text{(AOT)} \end{aligned}$$

$$p = 0.63 \quad DW = 1.87 \quad RSQ = 0.46 \quad RSQC = 0.75$$
$$RSQT(PXB) = 0.94$$

50. Price Index of New Machinery, Equipment, and Nonresidential Construction

The price index of new machinery, equipment, and nonresidential construction is current-weighted; it is based on the current- and constant-dollar flows that are *not* seasonally adjusted. For purposes of price analysis it is desirable that the dependent variable be base-weighted. The fact that this price index is used to link the monetary and real flows of the underlying expenditures is not the reason why it remains current-weighted in this relation; for one could use a base-weighted price index here, and then explain the corresponding current-weighted price index by means of the technique used in equation 49. A base-weighted price index of new machinery, equipment, and non-residential construction is not available. It is possible here—unlike the case of the price index of final sales—to approximate a base-weighted price index by means of the current-weighted price index derived from the *seasonally adjusted* current- and constant-dollar expenditure flows. This is not done because of the nature of the principal explanatory variable in the relation. This is the price index of investment goods, itself not base-weighted but so approximated by means of appropriate seasonally adjusted real and monetary flows. (The price index of investment goods differs from the dependent variable in commodity content by including new residential construction.)

Because the explanatory price index is itself somewhat subject to weighting shifts (although it is hoped that those seasonally induced are largely removed), it is a superfluous correction to change the current-weighted states of the dependent price index from that based on the raw expenditure flows to that derived from corresponding seasonally adjusted series. The principal result of such a move would be to alter a component of the divergence in the two indexes, namely, that due to differing changes in weighting patterns. But it is the function of the seasonal variables to account for such changes in any event. On the other hand, were the explanatory variable free from weight changes (that is, were it a base-weighted index), there would be an incentive to construct the dependent variable in such a way that it approximated that status. Thus the following relationship is justified.

$$\begin{aligned} \mathrm{PMNRC} = {} & a_{50} + b_{50} * \mathrm{PFC} + c_{50} * \mathrm{Q1} + d_{50} * \mathrm{Q2} \\ & + e_{50} * \mathrm{Q3} + E_{50} \end{aligned}$$

where PMNRC = current-weighted price index of new machinery, equipment, and non-residential construction, 1957 = 1

It is expected that the coefficient of PFC is greater than zero. The estimated relationship:

$$\begin{aligned} PMNRC = {} & \underset{(0.020)}{-0.0047} + \underset{(0.020)}{1.0} * PFC + \underset{(0.0024)}{0.0056} * Q1 \\ & + \underset{(0.0027)}{0.0030} * Q2 - \underset{(0.0024)}{0.0024} * Q3 \qquad \text{(AOT)} \end{aligned}$$

$p = 0.38$ DW = 1.63 RSQ = 0.99 RSQC = 0.99
RSQT(PFC) = 0.99

III / Identities and the Complete Model

The stochastic equations were presented in chapter II. The first function of chapter III is to outline the non-stochastic relationships. Then the complete model is summarized, its salient features discussed, and its construction re-examined from a methodological standpoint.

Presentation of the identities (represented by the variables they define) is arranged as follows, where the enumeration is consecutive to that of the stochastic equations.

Exchange Rates

51. Index of spot exchange rate
52. Change in spot exchange rate
53. Product of W and change in spot exchange rate
54. Adjusted spot exchange rate
55. Forward exchange differential
56. Change in forward exchange differential

Balance of Payments

Current Account Balances

57. Balance of merchandise trade
58. Balance of non-merchandise current transactions

Capital Account

59. Balance of long-term capital
60. Net inflow of portfolio capital

Merchandise Trade

61. Imports of merchandise
62. Imports of merchandise from other countries

63. Balance of trade with the United States
64. Balance of trade with other countries
65. Foreign aid to "other countries"

Financial Sector

66. Differential of long-term interest rates
67. Net new issues of long-term marketable securities
68. Foreign corporate liquidity
69. Liquid assets variable for consumer non-durable goods
70. Liquid assets variable for consumer durable goods
71. Liquid assets variable for consumer services

Gross National Expenditure

72. Gross national expenditure in current dollars
73. Gross national expenditure in constant dollars
74. Output of goods constituting final sales

Investment

75. Business gross fixed capital formation
76. New machinery, equipment, and non-residential construction: current dollars
77. New machinery, equipment, and non-residential construction: constant dollars

Expenditure Ratios

78. Ratio of expenditure on consumer non-durable goods to final sales
79. Ratio of expenditure on consumer durable goods to final sales
80. Ratio of business gross fixed capital formation to final sales
81. Ratio of merchandise exports to final sales
82. Ratio of expenditure on consumer services to final sales

Disposable Income

83. Disposable wage income: non-durable goods
84. Disposable wage income: durable goods
85. Disposable wage income: services
86. Disposable non-wage income: non-durable goods
87. Disposable non-wage income: durable goods

88. Disposable non-wage income: services
89. Disposable income: imports of goods

Prices

90. Price ratio: non-durable consumer goods
91. Price ratio: durable consumer goods
92. Price ratio: consumer services
93. Price variable: imports of consumer goods
94. Price variable: imports of investment goods
95. Price index of imports of consumer non-durable goods
96. Price index of imports of consumer durable goods
97. Price index of imports of investment goods
98. Price index of imports of industrial materials
99. Price index of imports of merchandise
100. Price index of consumer services and non-durable goods
101. Price ratio: tourist expenditures
102. Wage rate index

Labor

103. Proportion of labor force employed
104. Unemployment
105. Productivity

51. Index of Spot Exchange Rate

$$RSI = RS/1.0430$$

where RSI = index of spot exchange rate, 1957 = 1

The constant is the factor required to convert the spot exchange rate to the time base desired. It is the average value of the rate over the four quarters of 1957.

52. Change in Spot Exchange Rate

$$CRS = RS - RS1$$

where RS1 = spot exchange rate, number of United States dollars per Canadian dollar, lagged one quarter

RS1 is a lagged endogenous variable, therefore predetermined.

53. Product of W and Change in Spot Exchange Rate

$$WCRS = W * CRS$$

Construction of the predetermined dummy variable W assures that WCRS is identical to CRS from the first quarter of 1961 onward but nil in earlier quarters.

54. Adjusted Spot Exchange Rate

$$RSA = [(1 + USIS/100)/(1 + CIS/100)] * RS$$

Identities 54 to 56 are outlined above. (See equation 2 in chapter II.) The United States treasury bill rate (USIS) is a predetermined variable.

55. Forward Exchange Differential

$$RFD = RF - RSA$$

56. Change in Forward Exchange Differential

$$CRFD = RFD - RFD1$$

RFD1 is a lagged endogenous, hence predetermined, variable.

57. Balance of Merchandise Trade

$$\begin{aligned} BM = {} & XUS * PXC + XB * PXC + XWEJ * PXC \\ & + XO * PXC + XC * PXC + GOLDM * RSI \\ & - GMC * (PGMCC/RSI) - GMI * (PGMIC/RSI) \\ & - GMIM * (PGMIMC/RSI) \\ & - GMFL * (PGMFLC/RSI) - CGRK * PXCL \\ & - GMR * (PGMR/RSI) - OCO - OCBE \end{aligned}$$

where XC = exports of merchandise to communist countries, in millions of constant (1957) dollars

GOLDM = exports of non-monetary gold, in millions of constant (1957) dollars

PGMCC = current-weighted price index of imports of consumer goods, 1957 = 1

PGMIC = current-weighted price index of imports of investment goods, 1957 = 1
PGMIMC = current-weighted price index of imports of industrial materials, 1957 = 1
PGMFLC = current-weighted price index of imports of fuels and lubricants, 1957 = 1
CGRK = re-imports of Canadian goods, in millions of constant (1957) dollars
PXCL = current-weighted price index of re-imports of Canadian goods, 1957 = 1
GMR = residual merchandise imports, in millions of constant (1957) dollars
PGMR = current-weighted price index of residual merchandise imports, 1957 = 1
OCO = official contributions to "other countries," in millions of dollars
OCBE = official contributions exclusive of those to "other countries," in millions of dollars

Throughout the model price indexes expressed in foreign currency are converted to Canadian dollars by means of a multiplicative factor, namely, the index of the spot exchange rate. This superficially involves treating the price index as if it referred to only one underlying commodity. In fact every component price relative of the index must be envisaged as converted to Canadian currency. Does it follow that the result of this process yields a multiplicative exchange rate factor for the total index? This result seems intuitively reasonable for base-weighted price indexes, but not necessarily so for those that are current-weighted. There are five such composite current-weighted price indexes in equation 57. It is necessary to prove that the conversion method is legitimate. For completeness the result will be established for both Laspeyeres and Paasche indexes.

The proof begins with a given import price index. This is the apparent (or domestic) index in the sense that exchange rate variation is included, that is, the index is expressed in Canadian currency. It is desired to establish the relationship between the apparent price index and the corresponding one in foreign currency. Basic notation is set forth above. (See equation 3 in chapter II.) For simplicity both time and weight base are taken to be the year 1957.

Case 1: Laspeyeres Index

The apparent price index is:

$$\frac{\sum p_n q_o}{\sum p_o q_o}$$

$$= \frac{\sum \frac{p_n}{p_o} * p_o q_o}{\sum p_o q_o}$$

$$= \sum \left(\frac{p_n}{p_o}\right) * \left(\frac{p_o q_o}{\sum p_o q_o}\right) \qquad \text{(i)}$$

where $\frac{p_n}{p_o}$ is a typical domestic price relative and $\frac{p_o q_o}{\sum p_o q_o}$ the corresponding weight. Denote exogenous prices by capital letters. Then (i) equals

$$\sum \left(\frac{P_n/\mathrm{RSI}_n}{P_o/\mathrm{RSI}_o}\right) * \frac{(P_o/\mathrm{RSI}_o)q_o}{\sum (P_o/\mathrm{RSI}_o)q_o}$$

$$= \sum \left(\frac{P_n/\mathrm{RSI}_n}{P_o}\right) * \frac{P_o q_o}{\sum P_o q_o} \qquad \text{since } \mathrm{RSI}_o = 1$$

$$= \frac{1}{\mathrm{RSI}_n} \sum \left(\frac{P_n}{P_o}\right) * \frac{P_o q_o}{\sum P_o q_o}$$

where $\sum \left(\frac{P_n}{P_o}\right) * \frac{P_o q_o}{\sum P_o q_o}$ is the price index in foreign currency.

Case 2: Paasche Index

The apparent price index is:

$$\frac{\sum p_n q_n}{\sum p_o q_n}$$

$$= \frac{\sum p_n q_n}{\sum \left(\frac{p_o}{p_n}\right) * p_n q_n} \qquad \text{(ii)}$$

where $\frac{p_o}{p_n}$ is the inverse of a typical domestic price relative and p_nq_n the corresponding value.

(ii) equals:

$$\frac{\sum(P_n/\mathrm{RSI}_n)q_n}{\sum \frac{(P_o/\mathrm{RSI}_o)}{(P_n/\mathrm{RSI}_n)} * (P_n/\mathrm{RSI}_n)q_n}$$

$$= \frac{\sum(P_n/\mathrm{RSI}_n)q_n}{\sum \frac{(P_o/\mathrm{RSI}_o)}{P_n} * P_nq_n} \quad \text{by cancellation}$$

$$= \frac{1}{\mathrm{RSI}_n} \frac{\sum P_nq_n}{\sum \left(\frac{P_o}{P_n}\right) * P_nq_n} \quad \text{since } \mathrm{RSI}_o = 1$$

and $\frac{\sum P_nq_n}{\sum \left(\frac{P_o}{P_n}\right) * P_nq_n}$ is the price index in foreign currency.

The model takes the import price indexes PGMCC, PGMIC, PGMIMC, and PGMFLC as predetermined. It has now been proved that they are exogenous in the sense that they are net of all exchange rate variation. However, strictly speaking, a current-weighted import price index is not predetermined even if its component price relatives are exogenous both because they exclude exchange rate variation and because foreign prices are not endogenous to the model. The reason is that the weights of (inverses of) price relatives are current imports of the underlying commodities. True, these imports are expressed in foreign rather than domestic currency. However, the volume flows might be endogenous variables in a disaggregative model. The present model does not attempt to explain component flows of the adopted import classifications; nor do the associated price indexes (or relatives) enter the model as variables. Therefore the predetermined nature of the current-weighted indexes is valid.

The exogeneity of constant-dollar exports to communist

countries has been justified above. (See equation 6 in chapter II.) It is noted from the identity that current-dollar export flows are deflated by a unique price index irrespective of destination. This procedure is imprecise insofar as the commodity compositions of these flows differ. Were the export categories by commodity class rather than area of destination, there would be no justification for a unique overall deflator. The import flows in this equation are classified in the former manner and therefore possess specific price indexes for purposes of deflation.

Non-monetary exports of gold are not included in merchandise exports arranged by area. Their deflator is based on the official United States price of gold adjusted for the exchange rate. Because there was no alteration in the United States gold price over the period of interest, constant-dollar exports are obtained as the ratio of the current-dollar flow to the spot exchange rate index. *Real* exports of gold are taken as a predetermined variable.

Although re-exports of merchandise are not given special attention—these flows are included in XUS, XB, WXEJ, XO, and XC—re-imports are removed from the commodity classes of imports and constitute a special variable. Re-imports are defined as imports of Canadian goods that were recorded as merchandise exports any time over the preceding five years. Included in this category are such diverse items as airplanes temporarily abroad for purposes of aerial photography, special farm machinery that works up and down the United States border in accordance with the season of the year, and defective merchandise returned. Deflation of the current-dollar series is a problem, because the goods were originally exported over a long time span. It is assumed that the mean lag involved is rather short, partly because of the seasonally induced machinery movements and partly because defective merchandise exports are likely to be returned with reasonable promptness. These and other forces which indicate a relatively short lag are re-enforced, as always, by the preponderant position of the United States as regards origin of imports. Because the goods involved represent past exports, the deflator is based on the current-weighted price index of Canadian exports (PXC). It is the average value of this index over the preceding four quarters. Re-imports in constant dollars are treated exogenously; because of its lagged nature the price index also is a predetermined variable.

The sum of current-dollar consumer goods, investment goods, industrial materials, fuels and lubricants, and re-imports does not equal the balance of payments definition of merchandise imports. There are two components of a divergence. The first are those merchandise items which enter none of the five commodity classes. But even given the addition of this component, the adjusted sum is not identical to the total merchandise import flow which is required to enter this identity. Although the balance of payments item is constructed from the same basic source as that used to obtain the commodity class variables, the former flow includes certain adjustments to commodity trade statistics which cannot be applied to the latter variables because of unavailability of information. "The object of most of these remaining adjustments is to record the transactions at the most relevant time for balance of payments purposes rather than to reflect the transactions at the time they may have been recorded in custom documents. Thus data covering aircraft, ships and defense purchases are usually included on the basis of progress payments rather than shipments, and wheat movements are based largely on statistics of clearances rather than customs entries."[1] These adjustments are desirable for purposes of the model because the balance of merchandise trade is a variable that enters the equation explaining the exchange rate. The sum of the two components constituting the divergence from the appropriate total current-dollar flow of imports is an unexplained residual movement. In any quarter this residual may be positive or negative. An appropriate deflator for the item is not available. As an alternative the current-weighted price index of total merchandise imports (exclusive of re-imports and residual imports) divided by the exchange rate index is used. PGMR is a predetermined variable—as are other Paasche price indexes of

1. *The Canadian Balance of International Payments, 1960*, p. 19. The wheat movements, of course, refer to exports rather than imports.

imports—because the weights of its component indexes are import flows that the model does not explain and the indexes themselves are not recognized as variables.

Government grants—OCO and OCBE—represent a debit entry in the balance of payments made to correspond to merchandise exports forwarded abroad as official donations. Government donations of goods do not give rise to demand for Canadian dollars in the foreign exchange market. The exports are offset by the donation itself; therefore the foreign exchange market is bypassed, and the balance of merchandise must include official grants as a negative flow in order to remove those exports which do not entail demand for Canadian dollars. A similar treatment of private donations of goods—both to and from Canadian residents—is not required because these flows are excluded from the merchandise trade variables themselves. A minor part of official donations represents technical assistance as distinct from commodity transfers; but because division into a twofold flow cannot be performed on the basis of available information, the totality of official contributions is treated as the debit equivalent of donations of goods. Official grants are the results of government policy and therefore predetermined variables.

58. Balance of Non-merchandise Current Transactions

$$
\begin{aligned}
BS = & -TRN * PTRN - FRSN * PFRSN \\
& - OTHERN * POTHN - GT * PGT - DIVP \\
& + DIVR - PINT1 - CINTN - FIM
\end{aligned}
$$

where PTRN = price index of net travel payments

PFRSN = price index of net freight and shipping payments

POTHN = price index of net payments for business services and miscellaneous transactions

GT = net government current payments, in millions of constant (1957) dollars

PGT = price index of net government current payments, 1957 = 1

PINT1 = net payments of interest, in millions of dollars, lagged one quarter

FIM = net payments of inheritances and migrants' funds, in millions of dollars

The balance of non-merchandise current transactions is an explanatory variable in the determination of the spot exchange rate. It includes not only services but also investment income and other transfers.

PTRN, PFRSN, and POTHN are implicit price indexes of net payments for their underlying services. Because the three variables are constructed analogously, it suffices to explain only the first. It is necessary to recall the procedure by which the variable TRN was obtained and the associated notation. (See equation 12 in chapter II.) Now, what the identity requires is net tourist payments in current dollars; the variable TRN is net deflated payments. Therefore consider division of the current- by the constant-dollar flow. The quotient is PTRN. In symbols

$$\text{PTRN} = (P_c - R_c)/\text{TRN} = (P_c - R_c)/(P_c/(P_p/r) - R_c/P_r) \tag{ii}$$

This mixture of symbols is not an identity in the model. It rather indicates the method of construction of the variable PTRN. In fact PTRN is considered a predetermined variable. This treatment requires some discussion. TRN is current endogenous in the model. But $(P_c - R_c)$, that is, net travel payments in current dollars, is not a variable. Nor are the gross flows which compose it. As far as the model is concerned, P_c and R_c are symbols without meaning. Were $(P_c - R_c)$ a variable, there would be no need for the further variable PTRN. But the former would clearly be a current endogenous flow. Moreover, the denominator of the right-hand side of the illustration above includes two variables which are current endogenous in the model, namely, the price index of tourist expenditure in Canada (P_r) and the exchange rate index (r). In spite of its inherent endogeneity PTRN is considered predetermined, because explanation of its components would involve expanding the model to explain net *current-dollar* tourist payments. Similarly current-dollar flows of the other services would have to be explained stochastically. Explanation of these items would entail still other new variables, many of which would be of a current endogenous nature. The model might expand to a significant extent; and moreover it is not desired to give disproportionate treatment to individual items of the service account, which are in general small relative to those of the merchandise account.

The implicit price indexes involve a further problem. If TRN is zero, PTRN has no corresponding value; it is undefined. A zero value of TRN implies

$$P_c/(P_p/r) = R_c/P_r$$

a possible event, but highly unlikely since it depends on special combinations of values of five component items. In fact the sample of observations is such that PTRN, PFRSN, and POTHN are well defined throughout the period of interest. In the nature of things PTRN, PFRSN, or POTHN would be undefined only because the respective underlying five components were not measured with sufficient precision. Given finer measures the implicit price index might be very large but still finite. This is not a logically necessary state of affairs but one based on empirical experience. Nevertheless, even though the implicit price indexes are well defined for the sample period of the present model, an expanded model would omit these variables and explain the current-dollar service flows stochastically.

Net government current payments exclude merchandise transactions, mutual aid to North Atlantic Treaty Organization countries (insofar as this is not included under merchandise transactions), servicing of government debt, and official donations. The underlying gross payments and receipts are largely connected with military expenditure, but a diverse group of miscellaneous transactions is also included. Both payments and receipts are deflated by the current-weighted price index (PGT) of (Canadian) government expenditure based on the current- and constant-dollar national accounts. Because a current-weighted index rather than an approximation to a base-weighted one is desired, the underlying national accounts flows are not seasonally adjusted. This deflator is a priori reasonable for gross *payments* if it is assumed that the flow reflects the composition of total government expenditure. As for receipts, they are largely expenditure by the United States government for military facilities (such as radar installations) *in Canada* as well as recompense for training of European air personnel *in Canada*. Hence there is reason to believe that such expenditure corresponds to Canadian government defense expenditure, and the deflator is again legitimate. Naturally a current-weighted price index of government defense expenditure would constitute an even better deflator. Both the constant-dollar flow of government current transactions and its price index are taken as predetermined variables. Actually the price index of government expenditure depends on prices in the private sector of the economy, and were it not used solely as a proxy for a price index of a minor part of Canadian and foreign government expenditure, it would be explained stochastically.

Because CINTN is the *change* in net payments of interest, the predetermined variable PINT1 (net payments in the preceding quarter) must enter the relation in order to yield *current* net payments. The latter is a predetermined variable.

Net payments of inheritances and migrants' funds might be considered endogenous. Transfers with respect to inheritances are legitimately predetermined, but migrants' funds depend on migration to and from Canada. Nevertheless the net flow is taken as predetermined. If it were endogenous, migration of people would constitute an explanatory variable. But then if migrants' funds were endogenous, ipso facto so is migration itself. Migration would depend on many factors including relative economic conditions at home and abroad, immigration laws, prior migration by relatives and friends, and personal whim. Once again it is not desired to expand the model in a particular direction, and the net transfers under consideration therefore remain predetermined.

59. Balance of Long-term Capital

$$\text{BLK} = \text{DIC} + \text{PNIR} + \text{PTOS} + \text{OLK} - \text{DLGC}$$

where OLK = balance of other long-term capital movements, in millions of dollars

DLGC = drawings on government of Canada loans, in millions of dollars

The balance of other long-term capital movements is net capital imports from those long-term capital movements which can be statistically isolated and which are not included in the other four components of BLK. Its constituent items are Canadian direct investment abroad, repayments of government of Canada loans, and subscriptions to international financial agencies. The total net flow is a predetermined variable. Canadian direct investment abroad is not a current endogenous variable because it is not concentrated in any one area in such a way that it plays a significantly important role in that area's economy. Therefore no external explanatory variable could enter an appropriate stochastic relation. Moreover, it is not a flow of sufficient magnitude relative to other long-term capital movements to warrant individual explanation. An interesting feature is the apparent sensitivity of this item to release from exchange control. Canadian direct investment abroad nearly quadrupled in 1952 compared to the flow in 1951. But these figures exaggerate the importance of exchange control. "The increase in 1952 was no doubt partly due to the termination of exchange control, but in the main it reflected some large transactions of a special character."[2] Nevertheless, were this capital movement an endogenous variable, the dummy variable FA would have to be included in its equation in order to lower the intercept in the four quarters during which exchange control was in effect.

DLGC enters negatively in the relation because, although a capital outflow, its movements are taken as positive. It is a predetermined variable.

60. Net Inflow of Portfolio Capital

$$\text{PNIIC} = \text{PNIR} + \text{PTOS}$$

61. Imports of Merchandise

$$\text{GM} = \text{GMC} + \text{GMI} + \text{GMIM} + \text{GMFL} + \text{GMR} + \text{CGRK}$$

2. Dominion Bureau of Statistics, *The Canadian Balance of International Payments in the Post-War Years, 1946–1952*, p. 42.

This equation represents a breakdown of imports by commodity class as distinct from area of destination.

62. Imports of Merchandise from Other Countries

$$\begin{aligned} GMO = {} & [GMC * (PGMCC/RSI) + GMI * (PGMIC/RSI) \\ & + GMIM * (PGMIMC/RSI) \\ & + GMFL * (PGMFLC/RSI) + CGRK * PXCL \\ & + GMR * (PGMR/RSI) \\ & - GMUS * (PGMUS/RSI)]/(PGMO/RSI) \end{aligned}$$

where GMO = imports of merchandise from countries other than the United States, in millions of constant (1957) dollars
PGMUS = price index of imports from the United States, 1957 = 1
PGMO = price index of imports from other countries, 1957 = 1

Given the addition of a predetermined variable PGMUS (the price index used to obtain GMUS from current-dollar imports originating in the United States), the model contains all the variables required to construct the difference between total imports and imports from the United States, *both in current dollars;* that is, current-dollar imports from countries other than the United States. This is the overall numerator of the right-hand side of equation 62. It is deflated by a price index of imports from these countries, the index itself adjusted for exchange rate variation. Ideally PGMO should be a Paasche index, with the weights referring not to overall price indexes of individual countries and hence defined as current-dollar imports *by country* but rather referring to *commodity* classes whence the individual country price indexes were derived. In fact such refinement is not statistically possible, and the pseudo current-weighting, that is, by country of origin only, is not performed. PGMO remains consistent with PGMUS in this respect. Regions of the United States may be interpreted analogously to individual countries; and no such treatment of regional price indexes occurs in the construction of PGMUS.

It should be noted that the following is *not* a valid identity:

$$\text{GMO} + \text{GMUS} = \text{GMC} + \text{GMI} + \text{GMIM} + \text{GMFL} + \text{GMR} + \text{CGRK}$$

Definition of GMO by means of this relation would mean asymmetrical deflation of current-dollar flows. Just as imports from the United States have a specific deflator, so should imports of other origin. The degree of freedom lost in the construction of total merchandise imports by both commodity class and country refers to a current- as distinct from a constant-dollar flow. The reason is that its own appropriate deflator is assigned to each component of total merchandise imports, whether the breakdown is by commodity class or by area.

63. Balance of Trade with the United States

$$\text{BMTUS} = \text{GMUS} - \text{XUS} - \text{GOLDM}$$

Equations 63 and 64—the balance of trade identities—refer to all commodity movements rather than merchandise trade only. Each equation contains an item other than the appropriate merchandise flows by area. It is statistically impossible to allocate exports of non-monetary gold to the United States and other countries. However, there is good reason to believe that the bulk of the movement is to the United States. "The principal market for Canadian gold has been the United States and a leading factor influencing the price of gold for decades has been the official purchases of the United States."[3] Therefore GOLDM is treated as if it represented exports to the United States alone. Gold is a merchandise export like any other. It requires transportation. Therefore it is included in the equation. Because their sole function in the model is to serve as indicators of commodity flows for the purpose of explaining freight and shipping expenditures, the balance of trade variables should for precision include an adjustment factor to correct for the alterations in raw trade statistics for the purpose of timing flows to correspond to pay-

3. *The Canadian Balance of International Payments, 1960*, p. 72.

ments rather than commodity movements. However, the requisite information is not available.

64. Balance of Trade with Other Countries

BMTO = GMO − XB − XWEJ − XO − XC − XNATO

where XNATO = exports of goods as mutual aid to NATO countries, in millions of constant (1957) dollars

Mutual aid to countries of the North Atlantic Treaty Organization consists of provision by the Canadian government of goods (military equipment and supplies), services (such as training of NATO air force personnel in Canada), and funds (contributions to joint military installations and budgets of NATO). The goods component of this category of transactions is excluded from merchandise exports, and the services and capital transfers do not affect net government current payments. There is no need to include these unilateral transfers of goods and services in the variables that explain the spot exchange rate because by nature they represent both debits and credits in the balance of payments, hence do not involve demand for Canadian dollars. The transfers of funds do increase the supply of Canadian dollars; but they cannot be isolated from the service component. Shipments of goods affect net freight and shipping payments. No part is sent to the United States; hence the associated variable is a component flow of the balance of trade with other countries. The current-dollar series is deflated by the price index of (merchandise) exports of iron and steel and their products. This is a base-weighted index; the weights to construct a Paasche index do not exist. But it is a reasonable assumption that the bulk of the value of the shipments is composed of aircraft, vessels, military vehicles, spare parts of these items, and miscellaneous weapons. For these items the commodity nature of the deflator is applicable. However, insofar as munitions and explosives are included in the aid, a price index of chemicals would be given a role were quantitative details of the shipments known. XNATO is a predetermined variable; it is under control of the government.

65. Foreign Aid to "Other Countries"

$$OCDPXB = (OCO + DLGC)/PXB$$

"Other countries" designates those to which the variable XO refers. A small portion of official contributions is allocable to Britain and the OECD area. This flow constitutes the variable OCBE and is hence excluded from OCO. No such division of DLGC need be made, because foreign aid in the form of loans is limited to India and Ceylon in the period under study.

66. Differential of Long-term Interest Rates

$$DIL = CIL - USIL$$

where USIL = United States long-term interest rate, percent per quarter

The United States long-term interest rate is an exogenous variable. It is constructed together with the Canadian long-term rate so as to obtain comparable series.

67. Net New Issues of Long-term Marketable Securities

$$S = SO + SG$$

68. Foreign Corporate Liquidity

$$SIF = SIFUD/RSI$$

where SIFUD = index of liquidity of corporations in the United States and United Kingdom, 1957 = 1

69. Liquid Assets Variable for Consumer Non-durable Goods

$$HLAND = HLA/PNDB$$

where HLA = beginning-of-quarter public holdings of personal savings deposits and Canada Savings Bonds, in millions of dollars

HLA is a predetermined variable.

70. Liquid Assets Variable for Consumer Durable Goods

$$HLAD = HLA/PDB$$

71. Liquid Assets Variable for Consumer Services

$$HLAS = HLA/PSB$$

72. Gross National Expenditure in Current Dollars

$$\begin{aligned} YM = {} & (CND + CD + CS - TRN + ACE + GDI + GG \\ & + GWASR + XUS + XB + XWEJ + XO + XC \\ & - GM) * PFS + GOLDM * RSI \\ & + GOLDOR * RSI + CINVM - FRSN * PFRSN \\ & - OTHERN * POTHN - GT * PGT + DIVR \\ & - DIVP - PINT1 - CINTN - OCO - OCBE \end{aligned}$$

where ACE = adjustment for consumer expenditure, in millions of constant (1957) dollars
GG = government expenditure on goods, in millions of constant (1957) dollars
GWASR = government civilian wages, in millions of constant (1957) dollars
GOLDOR = gold output added to official reserves, in millions of constant (1957) dollars
CINVM = change in inventories, in millions of dollars

This equation is a principal link between real and monetary expenditure flows. The bracketed terms which multiply PFS are constant-dollar flows of the expenditure items to which PFS refers. Some of these variables require explanation. ACE is a predetermined variable which serves only as a correction factor based on the following considerations. The published constant-dollar national accounts do not have a unique weight base throughout the period under study. A weighting scheme based on 1949 prices applies until the end of 1955, and one based on 1957 prices thereafter. But there is a unique time base, namely, the year 1957. The process of converting the 1949-weighted series to a 1957 time base involves ratios of the differently-weighted price indexes in an overlapping period, and therefore implies that components of any aggregate flow will not in general sum to the total flow, since the overall series is independently converted. An adjusting entry must be added to the sum of the components in order to obtain the independently converted aggregate flow. This adjustment factor may be positive or negative and in itself has no economic significance. Therefore such items are taken as predetermined variables.[4] The adjustment for consumer expenditure enters the bracketed sum in equation 72 because *all* the component series of such expenditure are present, that is, it is desired to include the overall flow.[5]

The model divides constant-dollar government expenditure into two flows, namely, civilian wages and salaries (GWASR) and expenditure on goods (GG). "Expenditure on goods" is in reality a residual item. It includes all government expenditure on goods and services other than civilian wages and salaries and military pay and allowances. The constant-dollar flow of the latter item is extraneous to the model. Thus, in addition to expenditure on goods, GG includes foreign aid in the form of technical assistance (an insignificant flow), government expenditure on services according to the balance of payments, and imputed rent on government-owned buildings.[6] The pure component of government expenditure on goods cannot be isolated because of lack of information; but GG is a good proxy to the ideal variable desired. It is reasonable to assume that expenditure on goods constitutes an overwhelming proportion of the flow represented in GG.

4. Details on adjustment factors are found in *National Accounts, Income and Expenditure, 1926–1956*, p. 179 and *National Accounts, Income and Expenditure by Quarters, 1947–61*, p. 100.

5. One might wonder why no adjustment terms appear when total merchandise exports or imports are considered as, for example, in equation 57. Methodologically the reason is that the balance of payments variables are derived not from the national accounts publications but from other sources. However, such entries do not appear even in the official national accounts, because constant-dollar component flows of exports and imports are not published. Analogous remarks apply to government expenditure.

6. *National Accounts, Income and Expenditure, 1926–1956*, pp. 108–109 and 162.

GWASR and GG are predetermined variables. This treatment requires justification because the variable YWC includes government wages as well as wage income of the private sector of the economy, and YWC is current endogenous. The explanation is that "real" government expenditure is exogenous but current-dollar expenditure is endogenous. With respect to wages the government determines that a certain amount of work be done ("real" wages). What it pays to have this work performed depends partly on wages for corresponding work in the private sector of the economy. In simplified terms the theory is that the number of civil servants is exogenous—a matter of government policy—but the average wage rate is jointly determined. A similar argument applies to expenditure on goods. The government determines to purchase a certain "real" amount of goods; the money cost is endogenous insofar as the goods are purchased from the private sector of the economy. However, current-dollar purchases from abroad are endogenous on a lower level because foreign prices are predetermined; the sole endogeneity is due to variations in the exchange rate which alter Canadian dollar prices. A further remark on government expenditure is warranted. Government is defined to include provincial and municipal as well as federal governments. An expanded model would separate these three levels and treat some or possibly all of provincial and municipal expenditures as endogenous.[7]

GOLDOR is that part of gold production which is sold to the Exchange Fund Account as distinct from that part exported. Because GOLDOR is analogous to GOLDM, it too is a predetermined variable.

CINVM includes the current-dollar change in both farm and non-farm business inventories. The alternative of multiplying the current endogenous constant-dollar change in inventories by an

7. However, there would exist tremendous problems in constructing the relevant variables. Separation of municipal from provincial wages is difficult to accomplish; in fact the division is not published. Moreover, the flows, especially those representing expenditure on goods, would need to be deflated individually because the composition of expenditure differs among the three levels of government. An obvious example is the importance of military expenditure in the federal government.

implicit price index (itself taken either as predetermined or jointly determined) is methodologically unsound for non-farm inventories because: "The deflators for inventory book values, however, cover varying time periods, in accordance with assumptions made in regard to turnover periods and accounting methods. Some deflators of inventory book values may include price indexes for the preceding twenty-four months, others for the preceding month only. The deflators for all other components of Gross National Expenditure are based on the average of prices for the time period being deflated, in the case of annual deflation, twelve months, in the case of quarterly deflation, three months."[8] The current-dollar change in inventories is a predetermined variable. An expanded model would alter this classification.

Official contributions are part of government expenditure on goods. They must be subtracted from the net flow of the other components of gross national expenditure because foreign aid represents a donation to foreigners. No Canadian resident obtains the transfer. Therefore it must be excluded from the total receipts of national output which are to be allocated (according to equation 25) between recipients of wage income and all other domestic claimants.

73. Gross National Expenditure in Constant Dollars

$$\begin{aligned} \mathrm{YR} = {} & \mathrm{CND} + \mathrm{CD} + \mathrm{CS} - \mathrm{TRN} + \mathrm{ACE} + \mathrm{GDI} + \mathrm{BI} \\ & + \mathrm{FI} + \mathrm{AINV} + \mathrm{GG} + \mathrm{GWASR} + \mathrm{XUS} + \mathrm{XB} \\ & + \mathrm{XWEJ} + \mathrm{XO} + \mathrm{XC} + \mathrm{GOLDM} + \mathrm{GOLDOR} \\ & - \mathrm{GM} - \mathrm{FRSN} - \mathrm{OTHERN} - \mathrm{GT} \end{aligned}$$

where AINV = adjustment for change in inventories, in millions of constant (1957) dollars

8. *National Accounts, Income and Expenditure, 1926–1956*, p. 184. It is true that re-imports are deflated by the price index of exports in previous quarters. However, the deflator is uniform for all observation units with respect to both commodity nature and time pattern.

Merchandise exports of goods which represent official contributions are not (negative) components of YR because they remain part of *output* as distinct from *income* (where "income" connotes income disposable to Canadian residents).

74. Output of Goods Constituting Final Sales

$$YG = CND + CD + GDI + GG + XUS + XB + XWEJ + XO + XC + GOLDM + GOLDOR - GM$$

There is no reason to exclude those merchandise exports which are foreign aid, because of the nature of the stochastic equations (10 and 33) in which YG is an explanatory variable. Donations of goods do not exclude the fact that these goods are part of component flows of Canadian *output* and *expenditure*. Thus whether official grants of goods are included or excluded in an aggregate variable depends on the purpose which this variable serves, that is, depends on the structure of the stochastic equation (or equations) in which this variable is included.

75. Business Gross Fixed Capital Formation

$$GDI = RC + CNR + EM + AGDI$$

where AGDI = adjustment for business gross fixed capital formation, in millions of constant (1957) dollars

76. New Machinery, Equipment, and Non-residential Construction: Current Dollars

$$MNRCC = CME * PMNRC$$

77. New Machinery, Equipment, and Non-residential Construction: Constant Dollars

$$CME = CNR + EM$$

78. Ratio of Expenditure on Consumer Non-durable Goods to Final Sales

$$CNDFS = CND/(CND + CD + CS - TRN + ACE + GDI + GG + GWASR + XUS + XB + XWEJ + XO + XC - GM)$$

It is noted that the denominator of the right-hand side of equation 78 is identical to the constant-dollar flows for which PFS serves as a measure of price. Merchandise exports which are foreign aid are not excluded from these flows because the concern—referring to stochastic equation 41—centers on composition of Canadian output as distinct from allocation of income to Canadian recipients. With respect to equation 72, foreign aid is subtracted not from the aggregate flow which multiplies PFS but from the totality of all other components of current-dollar gross national expenditure. Were the former procedure employed, there would be a flaw in the use of CNDFS and analogous variables to correct for the influence of PFS in stochastic equations 41 to 44, because then the denominators of these variables and the underlying constant-dollar flows which compose PFS would differ. However, the primary reason for including all merchandise exports in the aggregate flow to which PFS refers is the fact that the index is designed to price Canadian *output* irrespective of its disposition.

79. Ratio of Expenditure on Consumer Durable Goods to Final Sales

$$CDFS = CD/(CND + CD + CS - TRN + ACE + GDI + GG + GWASR + XUS + XB + XWEJ + XO + XC - GM)$$

80. Ratio of Business Gross Fixed Capital Formation to Final Sales

$$FKFS = GDI/(CND + CD + CS - TRN + ACE + GDI + GG + GWASR + XUS + XB + XWEJ + XO + XC - GM)$$

81. Ratio of Merchandise Exports to Final Sales

$$XFS = (XUS + XB + XWEJ + XO + XC)/(CND + CD + CS - TRN + ACE + GDI + GG + GWASR + XUS + XB + XWEJ + XO + XC - GM)$$

82. Ratio of Expenditure on Consumer Services to Final Sales

$$SFS = (CS - TRN)/(CND + CD + CS - TRN + ACE + GDI + GG + GWASR + XUS + XB + XWEJ + XO + XC - GM)$$

83. Disposable Wage Income: Non-durable Goods

The *earned* components of personal income are explained stochastically. Earned wage income (YWC) and non-wage income (YNW) are dependent variables in equations 25 and 26, respectively. However, variables used to explain purchases of consumer goods refer to *disposable* as distinct from earned income. Moreover, military pay and allowances are legitimately part of wage income for purposes of explaining expenditures on consumer goods, but they are excluded from the variable YWC. The second problem is easily solved. Military pay and allowances are considered a predetermined variable[9] and are added to *civilian* wage income (YWC) to form a joint civilian and military flow of earned wage income. The first problem, namely, the transition from

9. One might object on the grounds that although constant-dollar military wage expenditure, that is, the number of military personnel and their distribution by rank, is exogenous, the current-dollar flow is not, because the wage structure of the military establishment bears some relation to civilian wage rates. This statement is to some extent reasonable, but the nature of military service increases the autonomy of the structure of wage rates as compared to that of the government civilian labor force. Two factors contribute to this situation: (1) contracts for military service are of longer duration than most civilian labor contracts and (2) non-monetary aspects are extremely important elements in evaluating the attractiveness of a military career. A third factor, namely, the existence of compulsory military service, is inapplicable to Canada.

earned to disposable income concepts, requires careful treatment. The difference between earned and disposable income is composed of transfer payments from corporations and government (positive flows) and personal direct taxes (negative flows). Because wage and non-wage disposable income are components of disjoint variables, it is necessary that the transfer payments and taxes be allocated between the two income categories. This is by no means a simple matter, since taxation data refer to all income; there is no official breakdown—legal or statistical—of personal income tax payments into components of income on which the tax was paid. For purposes of the model an allocation of personal income taxes is made on the basis of the relative proportions of wage and non-wage personal income; the weights are current in the sense that they refer only to the quarter under consideration. Other direct taxes and transfer payments in general can be allocated with considerably less arbitrariness on two bases: the underlying theory that non-wage disposable income entails a larger propensity to save than wage income and the related fact that, for the great majority of recipients of important categories of transfer payments, wages constitute the overwhelming portion of their earned income flow.

Both wage and non-wage disposable income are obtained from earned income by subtracting the net outflow of funds via direct taxes and transfer payments. These transfers are referred to as "net direct taxes" and are predetermined variables in the present model. An expanded model would distinguish the various categories of direct taxes and transfer payments and explain their flows stochastically on the basis of taxation rates, structure of the population (for family allowances and old age pensions), unemployment, current-dollar income and expenditure flows, and other variables. (Of course, some taxes and transfer payments might continue to be treated as exogenous.) The fact that the model deals only with *net* flows of a large variety of unilateral government transactions implies that a predetermined classification is not unreasonable. If component flows were required to enter the model, endogeneity would be in order.

On the basis of the above discussion the identities relating to disposable income variables are stated.

$$YDWND = (YWC + YMILIT - TW)/PNDB$$

where YMILIT = military pay and allowances, in millions of dollars
TW = net direct taxes on wage income, in millions of dollars

84. Disposable Wage Income: Durable Goods

$$YDWD = (YWC + YMILIT - TW)/PDB$$

85. Disposable Wage Income: Services

$$YDWS = (YWC + YMILIT - TW)/PSB$$

86. Disposable Non-wage Income: Non-durable Goods

$$YDNWND = (YNW - TNW)/PNDB$$

where TNW = net direct taxes on non-wage personal income, in millions of dollars

87. Disposable Non-wage Income: Durable Goods

$$YDNWD = (YNW - TNW)/PDB$$

88. Disposable Non-wage Income: Services

$$YDNWS = (YNW - TNW)/PSB$$

89. Disposable Income: Imports of Goods

$$YDMC = (YWC + YMILIT + YNW - TW - TNW)/(PGMCB/RSI)$$

where PGMCB = base-weighted price index of imports of consumer goods, 1957 = 1

PGMCB is an exogenous variable. Import price indexes are constructed net of exchange rate variation; they are taken as predetermined variables. This designation would not constitute reasonable treatment if Canadian demand were a factor of great significance in the output of the group of foreign commodities that underlies any import price index. However, this reservation does not apply—partly because the United States is the principal supplier of Canadian imports. Exports to Canada constitute only a minute part of United States output.[10]

90. Price Ratio: Non-durable Consumer Goods

$$PNDPO = PNDB/(WDND * PDB + WSND * PSB)$$

where WDND = weight of durable goods in PNDPO
WSND = weight of services in PDNPO

The price indexes of consumer goods and services, namely, PNDB, PDB, and PSB, do not have a unique weight base throughout the period the model covers. For the last five quarters of the observation period weights of the year 1957 apply; for all other quarters the weights refer to 1949. (This does not exclude the fact that the price indexes remain on a 1957 *time* base for all observations.) Precision requires that the dual weighting pattern apply to joint indexes constructed from PNDB, PDB, and PSB. Therefore the weights of PDB and PSB in the denominator of PNDPO are not constants; the combination part of a weight for the final five quarters of the observation period differs from the corresponding item in the earlier quarters. The weights represent not only coefficients of combination but also linking factors (because of the dual weighting pattern), and are non-endogenous variables.

10. In the years 1951–1961, inclusive, exports to Canada were 19 percent of total United States merchandise exports; however, total merchandise exports constituted only 4 percent of U.S. gross national expenditure. Hence Canadian imports of merchandise represent less than 1 percent of total U.S. output. (These figures are derived from U.S. Department of Commerce, *Business Statistics, 1963, Biennial Edition*, pp. 3, 13, 110, and 112.)

91. Price Ratio: Durable Consumer Goods

$$PDPO = PDB/(WNDD * PNDB + WSD * PSB)$$

where WNDD = weight of non-durable goods in PDPO
WSD = weight of services in PDPO

92. Price Ratio: Consumer Services

$$PSPO = PSB/(WNDS * PNDB + WDS * PDB)$$

where WNDS = weight of non-durable goods in PSPO
WDS = weight of durable goods in PSPO

93. Price Variable: Imports of Consumer Goods

$$PMCRPD = (PGMCB/RSI)/PDPCG$$

where PDPCG = price index of domestically produced consumer goods, 1957 = 1

PDPCG is a current endogenous variable.

94. Price Variable: Imports of Investment Goods

$$PMIRPD = (PGMIB/RSI)/PDPIG$$

where PGMIB = base-weighted price index of imports of investment goods, 1957 = 1
PDPIG = price index of domestically produced investment goods, 1957 = 1

PGMIB is a predetermined variable, as are all price indexes of imports. PDPIG is current endogenous.

95. Price Index of Imports of Consumer Non-durable Goods

$$PMNDR = PMND/RSI$$

where PMND = base-weighted price index of imports of consumer non-durable goods, 1957 = 1

96. Price Index of Imports of Consumer Durable Goods

$$PMDR = PMD/RSI$$

where PMD = base-weighted price index of imports of consumer durable goods, 1957 = 1

97. Price Index of Imports of Investment Goods

$$PMKR = PGMIB/RSI$$

98. Price Index of Imports of Industrial Materials

$$PMIMR = PGMIMB/RSI$$

where PGMIMB = base-weighted price index of imports of industrial materials, 1957 = 1

99. Price Index of Imports of Merchandise

$$PMGSR = PFLIM1 + 0.313 * (PGMIB/RSI) + 0.303 * (PGMCB/RSI)$$

where PFLIM1 = base-weighted price index of imports of industrial materials, fuels and lubricants divided by index of spot exchange rate, lagged one quarter

PMGSR is a weighted average of four base-weighted import price indexes (including exchange rate variation), but two of the indexes are lagged. (See equation 40 in chapter II.) It is superfluous to introduce two predetermined variables, namely, the price index of imports of industrial materials and that of fuels and lubricants, both converted to Canadian currency and lagged one quarter, in a situation in which the two indexes times their respective weights can be summed to produce a single predetermined variable. It is clear that the resulting (lagged) price index, though base-weighted, is not on a 1957 time base even though its component price indexes are on such a base. The explanation is that the component weights sum to less than unity.

100. Price Index of Consumer Services and Non-durable Goods

$$PNDS = 0.6 * PNDB + 0.4 * PSB$$

101. Price Ratio: Tourist Expenditures

$$PTR = (PTA/RSI)/PTC$$

where PTA = base-weighted price index of Canadian tourist expenditure abroad, 1957 = 1

PTA is an exogenous variable. It is a weighted average of various United States consumer price indexes.

102. Wage Rate Index

$$WR = (YWC/EMPM)/1.6576$$

Wage income (YWC) is measured in millions of dollars; employment (EMPM) of workers that receive wages is expressed in millions of man-hours. Therefore YWC divided by EMPM yields the average wage rate, expressed in dollars per man-hour. In order to obtain an index the average wage rate is itself divided by its average value over the four quarters of 1957. This approach of determining the wage rate is to be distinguished from the inclusion of the wage rate itself as a dependent variable in a stochastic equation. The advantage of this alternative procedure is that it allows a more precise measure of the wage rate, that is, the variable may refer to earnings over a shorter unit time period than the quarter-year. But the method lacks two advantages of the approach adopted for this study. The first is the inclusion of the *totality* of wage income and the *totality* of man-hours worked in the construction of the wage rate. Measures of wage rates based on periods shorter than a quarter-year entail incomplete coverage. (This is not a logically necessary fact but one based on observation.) Therefore in a second dimension of precision, namely, inclusion of all relevant data, the "identity approach" is superior to the "stochastic procedure." The further advantage of the adopted method is the fact that it acknowledges the interdependence of the three variables: total wage income, man-hours employed, and the average wage rate. Even if the average wage rate is constructed over a period of less duration than a quarter, if it is the true rate in the sense that it entails complete coverage, then the identity above applies, though the observation period differs from the quarter year. Because the model of this study is in fact based on quarterly observations, the identity approach (equation 102) is the appropriate means of introducing the average wage rate into the system.

103. Proportion of Labor Force Employed

$$\text{PEREMP} = (\text{EMPM}/\text{AHP} + \text{EMPNM}/\text{AHN})/\text{FORCEM}$$

EMPM and EMPNM are millions of man-hours of employment, while AHP and AHN represent the average number of hours worked per man. Then EMPM/AHP and EMPNM/AHN are employment of paid and unpaid workers, respectively, expressed in millions of persons. FORCEM has the same unit of measurement; therefore the identity is valid.

104. Unemployment

$$\text{UNEMPM} = \text{FORCEM} - \text{EMPM}/\text{AHP} - \text{EMPNM}/\text{AHN}$$

Equation 104 is a rearrangement of the terms in 103. The explanation of equation 103 assures as well that UNEMPM possesses the proper dimension unit, that is, millions of persons.

105. Productivity

$$\text{PROD} = \text{YR}/\text{EMPM}$$

YR is measured in millions of (constant) dollars, EMPM in millions of man-hours; therefore PROD is expressed as the number of (constant) dollars of output per man-hour.

SEMI-IDENTITIES

The distinguishing feature of a stochastic equation is that it includes both parameters and an error term. An identity is an equation that possesses neither parameters nor an error term. The model of the present study involves a third type of equation, namely, a relation that includes parameters but is devoid of an error factor. Such a relation belongs to one of two subclasses. First, it can have the interpretation of a *behavioral* equation in which no stochasticity appears. For this interpretation to be valid the dependent variable must be measured independent of the explanatory variables. The non-stochastic behavioral relation is not part of econometric study because of the present state of economic knowledge. Sufficient information to produce *exact* behavioral relationships does not exist. It may be hoped that as economic theory and econometrics develop, this goal of ultimate precision will eventually be reached. However, it can be maintained that human behavior is inherently stochastic, and hence the objective is not only impossible to attain but also harmful to research because it may distort its advance from a productive to a barren direction. It is the second type of semi-identity which enters the model. This relation is in fact an identity in the sense that the left-hand side variable is *defined* as the right-hand side of the equation. However, the equation does contain parameters. Were these parameters unconstrained, the dependent (left-hand side) variable would be unmeasurable. Therefore it is necessary that the parameters of the semi-identity be functions of parameters that belong to stochastic equations of the model. In special cases a parameter of a semi-identity will *equal* a parameter of the stochastic part of the model, or it may differ by some known multiplicative or additive factor. In general cases the parameter of the semi-identity will depend not only on external parameters but also on variables. Both the special and general case are illustrated in the three semi-identities which complete the model.

106. Price Index of Domestically Produced Consumer Goods

$$\text{PDPCG} = 0.629 * [(\text{PNDB} - e_{41} * \text{PMNDR})/a_{106}] + 0.371 * [(\text{PDB} - e_{42} * \text{PMDR})/b_{106}]$$

This variable is explained in chapter II under equation 8. The coefficient a_{106} is the average value of (PNDB $-$ e_{41} * PMNDR) over the four quarters of 1957. An analogous remark applies to b_{106}.

Replacing symbolic parameters by estimates, equation 106 becomes

$$\text{PDPCG} = 0.629 * [(\text{PNDB} - 0.21 * \text{PMNDR})/0.79] + 0.371 * [(\text{PDB} - 0.044 * \text{PMDR})/0.96]$$

107. Price Index of Domestically Produced Investment Goods

$$\text{PDPIG} = (\text{PFC} - e_{43} * \text{PMKR})/a_{107}$$

PDPIG is discussed under equation 9. The average value of (PFC $-$ e_{43} * PMKR) over the four quarters of 1957 is defined as a_{107}.

The equation in estimated form:

$$\text{PDPIG} = (\text{PFC} - 0.36 * \text{PMKR})/0.64$$

108. Price Index of Domestically Produced Industrial Materials

$$\text{PDPIM} = (\text{PWIM} - d_{45} * \text{PMIMR})/a_{108}$$

where PDPIM = price index of domestically produced industrial materials, 1957 = 1

PDPIM is discussed under equation 10. The average value of (PFC $-$ d_{45} * PMIMR) over the four quarters of 1957 is defined as a_{108}.

The estimated equation:

$$\text{PDPIM} = (\text{PWIM} - 0.31 * \text{PMIMR})/0.69$$

CHAPTER III

SUMMARY OF THE MODEL

The model is a set of 108 relationships which are arranged as in Table 4.

TABLE 4. Equations by type.

Type	Equations	Total number
Stochastic equation	1 to 50	50
Identity	51 to 105	55
Semi-identity	106 to 108	3

Variables of the model are again named and identified, but according to the following outline:

A. Expenditure Flows
   1. Aggregate expenditure
   2. Consumption
   3. Fixed investment
   4. Inventories
   5. Government
   6. Merchandise exports
   7. Merchandise imports
   8. Balances of merchandise trade
   9. Gold
   10. Services

B. Income Flows
   1. Total personal income
   2. Personal wage income
   3. Personal non-wage income
   4. Liquidity of investors

C. Balance of Payments
   1. Investment income
   2. Inheritances and migrants' funds
   3. Foreign aid

4. Long-term capital
5. Short-term capital
6. Official reserves

D. Financial Variables
   1. Personal liquid assets
   2. Security issues
   3. Reserve ratios of banks

E. Exchange Rates
   1. Spot exchange rate
   2. Forward exchange rate

F. Interest Rates
   1. Short-term interest rates
   2. Long-term interest rates

G. Prices
   1. Aggregate price
   2. Consumer goods and services
   3. Investment goods
   4. Intermediate goods
   5. Merchandise exports
   6. Merchandise imports
   7. Services

H. Labor
   1. Labor force
   2. Employment
   3. Wage rates

I. Foreign Output

J. Inventory-Sales Ratios

K. Merchant Marine

L. Weights

M. Dummy Variables

Allocation of variables to the above classifications is sometimes arbitrary because a variable may include components which belong to different categories. However, consistent treatment applies to all variables of a given type. Under each of the economic categories variables are arranged according to an econometric classification, namely:

a. current endogenous

b. lagged endogenous

c. current exogenous

d. lagged exogenous

The endogenous-exogenous breakdown of *current* variables is apparent from the model itself. With respect to *lagged* variables, the procedure of minimizing the exogenous subset by limiting its elements to those whose current value actually appears in the model is not followed. Instead the endogenous-exogenous allocation is based on the judgment of the model-builder as to whether the current value of a lagged variable would have been explained had it entered the model. Application of the economic-econometric classification scheme to all the variables of the model yields the following tabulation. Current endogenous variables are followed by a number which refers to the equation that explains the variable under consideration.

A. *Expenditure Flows*

1. *Aggregate expenditure*

a. *current endogenous*

YR = gross national expenditure excluding military pay and allowances, in millions of constant dollars (73)

PROD = gross national expenditure excluding military pay and allowances divided by man-hours of paid workers, in constant dollars per man-hour (105)

YG = output of goods which constitute final sales, in millions of constant dollars (74)

YM = gross national expenditure excluding military pay and allowances, in millions of dollars (72)

b. *lagged endogenous*

YGFL1 = output of goods constituting final sales plus personal expenditure on services, in millions of constant dollars, lagged one quarter

FSP2 = slope of ordinary least squares regression of logarithm of constant-dollar sum of output of goods which constitute final sales, expenditure on consumer services and net tourist receipts on time (observations are six preceding quarters), lagged two quarters

2. *Consumption*

a. *current endogenous*

CND = personal expenditure on consumer non-durable goods, in millions of constant dollars (27)

CD = personal expenditure on consumer durable goods, in millions of constant dollars (28)

CS = personal expenditure on consumer services, in millions of constant dollars (29)

TRN = net travel payments, in millions of constant dollars (12)

CNDFS = ratio of expenditure on consumer non-durable goods to final sales (78)

CDFS = ratio of expenditure on consumer durable goods to final sales (79)

SFS = ratio of expenditure on consumer services excluding net tourist payments to final sales (82)

c. *current exogenous*

ACE = adjustment for consumer expenditure, in millions of constant dollars

3. *Fixed investment*

a. *current endogenous*

GDI = business gross fixed capital formation, in millions of constant dollars (75)

CME = new machinery, equipment, and non-residential construction, in millions of constant dollars (77)

MNRCC = new machinery, equipment, and non-residential construction, in millions of dollars (76)

RC = new residential construction, in millions of constant dollars (30)

CNR = new non-residential construction, in millions of constant dollars (31)

EM = new machinery and equipment, in millions of constant dollars (32)

FKFS = ratio of business gross fixed capital formation to final sales (80)

c. *current exogenous*

AGDI = adjustment for business gross fixed capital formation, in millions of constant dollars

4. *Inventories*

a. *current endogenous*

BI = change in non-farm business inventories, in millions of constant dollars (33)

FI = change in farm inventories and grain in commercial channels, in millions of constant dollars (34)

c. *current exogenous*

CINVM = change in inventories, in millions of dollars

AINV = adjustment for change in inventories, in millions of constant dollars

5. *Government*

c. *current exogenous*

GG = government expenditure on goods, in millions of constant dollars

GWASR = government civilian wages, in millions of constant dollars

YMILIT = military pay and allowances, in millions of dollars

GT = net government current payments, in millions of constant dollars

6. *Merchandise exports*

a. *current endogenous*

XUS = exports of merchandise to the United States, in millions of constant dollars (3)

XB = exports of merchandise to the United Kingdom, in millions of constant dollars (4)

XWEJ = exports of merchandise to OECD countries and Japan, in millions of constant dollars (5)

XO = exports of merchandise to "other countries," in millions of constant dollars (6)

XFS = ratio of merchandise exports to final sales (81)

c. *current exogenous*

XC = exports of merchandise to communist countries, in millions of constant dollars

XNATO = exports of goods as mutual aid to NATO countries, in millions of constant dollars

7. *Merchandise imports*

a. *current endogenous*

GMUS = imports of merchandise from the United States, in millions of constant dollars (7)

GMO = imports of merchandise from countries other than the United States, in millions of constant dollars (62)

GM = total imports of merchandise, in millions of constant dollars (61)

GMC = imports of consumer goods, in millions of constant dollars (8)

GMI = imports of investment goods, in millions of constant dollars (9)

GMIM = imports of industrial materials, in millions of constant dollars (10)

GMFL = imports of fuels and lubricants, in millions of constant dollars (11)

c. *current exogenous*

CGRK = re-imports of Canadian goods, in millions of constant dollars

GMR = residual merchandise imports, in millions of constant dollars

8. *Balances of merchandise trade*

a. *current endogenous*

BM = balance of merchandise trade, in millions of dollars (57)

BMTUS = imports from the United States minus exports to the United States, in millions of constant dollars (63)

BMTO = imports from other countries minus exports to other countries, in millions of constant dollars (64)

9. *Gold*

c. *current exogenous*

GOLDM = exports of non-monetary gold, in millions of constant dollars

GOLDOR = gold output added to official reserves, in millions of constant dollars

10. *Services*

a. *current endogenous*

BS = balance of non-merchandise current transactions, in millions of dollars (58)

FRSN = net freight and shipping payments, in millions of constant dollars (13)

OTHERN = net payments for business services and miscellaneous transactions, in millions of constant dollars (14)

B. *Income Flows*

1. *Total personal income*

a. *current endogenous*

YDMC = disposable income divided by base-weighted price index of imports of consumer goods itself divided by the index of the spot exchange rate, in millions of deflated dollars (89)

b. *lagged endogenous*

RYD1 = ratio of index of Canadian disposable income deflated by the price index of Canadian tourist expenditure abroad itself divided by the index of the spot exchange rate to index of disposable income abroad deflated by the price index of tourist expenditure in Canada, lagged one quarter

YDRC2 = disposable income divided by base-weighted price index of residential construction, in millions of deflated dollars, lagged two quarters

2. *Personal wage income*

a. *current endogenous*

YWC = earned civilian wage income, in millions of dollars (25)

YDWND = disposable wage income divided by base-weighted price index of consumer non-durable goods, in millions of deflated dollars (83)

YDWD = disposable wage income divided by base-weighted price index of consumer durable goods, in millions of deflated dollars (84)

YDWS = disposable wage income divided by base-weighted price index of consumer services, in millions of deflated dollars (85)

c. *current exogenous*

TW = net direct taxes on wage income, in millions of dollars

3. *Personal non-wage income*

a. *current endogenous*

YNW = earned non-wage personal income, in millions of dollars (26)

YDNWND = disposable non-wage income divided by base-weighted price index of consumer non-durable goods, in millions of deflated dollars (86)

YDNWD = disposable non-wage income divided by base-weighted price index of consumer durable goods, in millions of deflated dollars (87)

YDNWS = disposable non-wage income divided by base-weighted price index of consumer services, in millions of deflated dollars (88)

c. *current exogenous*

TNW = net direct taxes on non-wage personal income, in millions of dollars

4. *Liquidity of investors*

a. *current endogenous*

SIF = index of liquidity of corporations in the United States and United Kingdom divided by index of spot exchange rate (68)

b. *lagged endogenous*

CPC1 = corporate profits, capital consumption allowances and miscellaneous valuation adjustments minus direct taxes, in millions of dollars, lagged one quarter

LIQ1 = ratio of corporate liquidity to expenditure on new machinery, equipment, and non-residential construction, lagged one quarter

CPUBI1 = liquidity of non-farm investors divided by wholesale price index, in millions of deflated dollars, lagged one quarter

CPCC2 = corporate profits, capital consumption allowances and miscellaneous valuation adjustments minus direct taxes divided by price index of non-residential construction, in millions of deflated dollars, lagged two quarters

CPME2 = corporate profits, capital consumption allowances and miscellaneous valuation adjustments minus direct taxes divided by price index of new machinery and equipment, in millions of deflated dollars, lagged two quarters

YUBC2 = liquidity of non-corporate private investors divided by price index of non-residential construction, in millions of deflated dollars, lagged two quarters

YUBME2 = liquidity of non-corporate private investors divided by price index of new machinery and equipment, in millions of deflated dollars, lagged two quarters

c. *current exogenous*

SIFUD = index of liquidity of corporations in the United States and United Kingdom, 1957 = 1

C. *Balance of Payments*

1. *Investment income*

a. *current endogenous*

DIVP = payments of dividends, in millions of dollars (15)

DIVR = receipts of dividends, in millions of dollars (16)

CINTN = change in net payments of interest, in millions of dollars (17)

b. *lagged endogenous*

PINT1 = net payments of interest, in millions of dollars, lagged one quarter

2. *Inheritances and migrants' funds*

c. *current exogenous*

FIM = net payments of inheritances and migrants' funds, in millions of dollars

3. *Foreign aid*

a. *current endogenous*

OCDPXB = drawings on government of Canada loans plus official contributions to "other countries," divided by base-weighted index of export prices, in millions of deflated dollars (65)

c. *current exogenous*

OCO = official contributions to "other countries," in millions of dollars

OCBE = official contributions exclusive of those to "other countries," in millions of dollars

4. *Long-term capital*

a. *current endogenous*

BLK = balance of long-term capital, in millions of dollars (59)

PNIIC = net inflow of portfolio capital, in millions of dollars (60)

DIC = direct investment in Canada, in millions of dollars (18)

PNIR = net inflow of portfolio capital via new issues and retirements of Canadian and foreign securities, in millions of dollars (19)

PTOS = net inflow of portfolio capital via trade in outstanding Canadian and foreign securities, in millions of dollars (20)

b. *lagged endogenous*

BNI2 = net balance of new issues of bonds and debentures, the gross flows weighted by Canadian and American long-term interest rates, in millions of dollars, lagged two quarters

BRTO1 = net balance of retirements and trade in outstanding issues of bonds and debentures, in millions of dollars, lagged one quarter

c. *current exogenous*

OLK = balance of other long-term capital movements, in millions of dollars

DLGC = drawings on government of Canada loans, in millions of dollars

d. *lagged exogenous*

SDINP = beginning-of-quarter ratio of stock of foreign direct investment in Canada to Canadian direct investment abroad

SOFIC2 = direct investment and portfolio investment on which dividends are received, invested in Canada at beginning of quarter, in millions of dollars, lagged two quarters

SOCIA2 = direct investment and portfolio investment on which dividends are received, Canadian investment abroad at beginning of quarter, in millions of dollars, lagged two quarters

5. *Short-term capital*

a. *current endogenous*

TBN = balance of transactions in Canadian treasury bills and United States treasury bills and certificates, in millions of dollars (21)

6. *Official reserves*

c. *current exogenous*

OR = change in official reserves due to exchange market operations, in millions of dollars

d. *lagged exogenous*

OINT1 = change in official holdings of United States dollars, weighted by United States treasury bill rate, in millions of dollars, lagged one quarter

RESB2 = beginning-of-quarter ratio of British official reserves to overseas sterling holdings, lagged two quarters

D. *Financial Variables*

1. *Personal liquid assets*

a. *current endogenous*

HLAND = beginning-of-quarter public holdings of personal savings deposits and Canada Savings Bonds divided by base-weighted price index of consumer nondurable goods, in millions of deflated dollars (69)

HLAD = beginning-of-quarter public holdings of personal savings deposits and Canada Savings Bonds divided by base-weighted price index of consumer durable goods, in millions of deflated dollars (70)

HLAS = beginning-of-quarter public holdings of personal savings deposits and Canada Savings Bonds divided by base-weighted price index of consumer services, in millions of deflated dollars (71)

b. *lagged endogenous*

HLARC2 = beginning-of-quarter public holdings of personal savings deposits and Canada Savings Bonds divided by base-weighted price index of residential construction, in millions of deflated dollars, lagged two quarters

d. *lagged exogenous*

HLA = beginning-of-quarter public holdings of personal savings deposits and Canada Savings Bonds, in millions of dollars

2. *Security issues*

a. *current endogenous*

S = net new issues of Canadian long-term marketable securities, in millions of dollars (67)

SO = net new issues of non-federal long-term securities, in millions of dollars (24)

c. *current exogenous*

SG = net new issues of government of Canada marketable long-term securities, in millions of dollars.

TB = government of Canada three-month treasury bills sold at tender, in millions of dollars

d. *lagged exogenous*

ATM = average term to maturity of government of Canada long-term marketable securities at beginning of quarter, in months

3. *Reserve ratios of banks*

c. *current exogenous*

R = excess cash reserve ratio of chartered banks, percent

RLA = excess liquid assets ratio of chartered banks, percent

d. *lagged exogenous*

R2 = excess cash reserve ratio of chartered banks, percent, lagged two quarters

E. *Exchange Rates*

1. *Spot exchange rate*

a. *current endogenous*

RS = spot exchange rate, number of United States dollars per Canadian dollar (1)

RSI = index of spot exchange rate, 1957 = 1 (51)

RSA = spot exchange rate adjusted for United States and Canadian short-term interest rates, number of United States dollars per Canadian dollar (54)

CRS = change in spot exchange rate, number of United States dollars per Canadian dollar (52)

WCRS = change in spot exchange rate if first quarter 1961 or beyond, 0 otherwise (53)

b. *lagged endogenous*

RS1 = spot exchange rate, number of United States dollars per Canadian dollar, lagged one quarter

2. *Forward exchange rate*

a. *current endogenous*

RF = ninety-day forward exchange rate, number of United States dollars per Canadian dollar (2)

RFD = forward exchange differential, number of United States dollars per Canadian dollar (55)

CRFD = change in forward exchange differential, number of United States dollars per Canadian dollar (56)

b. *lagged endogenous*

RFD1 = forward exchange differential, number of United States dollars per Canadian dollar, lagged one quarter

F. *Interest Rates*

1. *Short-term interest rates*

a. *current endogenous*

CIS = interest rate on government of Canada three-month treasury bills, percent per quarter (22)

c. *current exogenous*

USIS = interest rate on United States three-month treasury bills, percent per quarter

2. *Long-term interest rates*

a. *current endogenous*

CIL = long-term interest rate, percent per quarter (23)

DIL = Canadian long-term interest rate minus American long-term interest rate, percent per quarter (66)

b. *lagged endogenous*

DIR2 = lender interest rate on National Housing Act loans minus long-term interest rate in bond market, percent per quarter, lagged two quarters

c. *current exogenous*

USIL = United States long-term interest rate, percent per quarter

G. *Prices*

1. *Aggregate price*

a. *current endogenous*

PFS = current weighted price index of final sales, 1957 = 1 (40)

2. *Consumer goods and services*

a. *current endogenous*

PNDB = base-weighted price index of consumer non-durable goods, 1957 = 1 (41)

PDB = base-weighted price index of consumer durable goods, 1957 = 1 (42)

PSB = base-weighted price index of consumer services, 1957 = 1 (46)

PNDPO = ratio of base-weighted price index of consumer non-durable goods to weighted average of base-weighted price indexes of consumer durable goods and services (90)

PDPO = ratio of base-weighted price index of consumer durable goods to weighted average of base-weighted price indexes of consumer non-durable goods and services (91)

PSPO = ratio of base-weighted price index of consumer services to weighted average of base-weighted price indexes of consumer durable and non-durable goods (92)

PNDS = base-weighted price index of consumer services and non-durable goods, 1957 = 1 (100)

PMCRPD = ratio of base-weighted price index of imports of consumer goods divided by index of spot exchange rate to price index of domestically produced consumer goods (93)

PDPCG = price index of domestically produced consumer goods, 1957 = 1 (106)

PTR = ratio of price index of Canadian tourist expenditure abroad divided by index of spot exchange rate to price index of tourist expenditure in Canada (101)

PTC = base-weighted price index of foreign tourist expenditure in Canada, 1957 = 1 (48)

c. *current exogenous*

PTRN = price index of net travel payments

PTA = base-weighted price index of Canadian tourist expenditure abroad, 1957 = 1

3. *Investment goods*

a. *current endogenous*

PFC = price index of investment goods, 1957 = 1 (43)

PMNRC = current-weighted price index of new machinery, equipment, and non-residential construction, 1957 = 1 (50)

PMIRPD = ratio of base-weighted price index of imports of investment goods divided by index of spot exchange rate to price index of domestically produced investment goods (94)

PDPIG = price index of domestically produced investment goods, 1957 = 1 (107)

b. *lagged endogenous*

PHCPI2 = ratio of base-weighted price index of residential construction to weighted average of base-weighted price indexes of consumer goods and services, lagged two quarters

4. *Intermediate goods*

a. *current endogenous*

PWIM = base-weighted price index of industrial materials, 1957 = 1 (45)

PDPIM = price index of domestically produced industrial materials, 1957 = 1 (108)

b. *lagged endogenous*

CWPI1 = ratio of change in wholesale price index to index of the previous quarter, percent, lagged one quarter

PIMPD1 = ratio of base-weighted price index of imports of industrial materials divided by index of spot exchange rate to price index of domestically produced industrial materials, lagged one quarter

PFLPD1 = ratio of base-weighted price index of imports of fuels and lubricants divided by index of spot exchange rate to price index of domestically produced fuels and lubricants, lagged one quarter

5. *Merchandise exports*

a. *current endogenous*

PXB = base-weighted price index of merchandise exports, 1957 = 1 (44)

PXC = current-weighted price index of merchandise exports, 1957 = 1 (49)

b. *lagged endogenous*

PXRPO1 = ratio of product of base-weighted price index of Canadian exports and spot exchange rate to price index of exports competitive to Canada, lagged one quarter

PXRPO2 = ratio of product of base-weighted price index of Canadian exports and spot exchange rate to price index of exports competitive to Canada, lagged two quarters

PXO1 = price index of exports competitive to Canada divided by spot exchange rate, lagged one quarter

6. *Merchandise imports*

a. *current endogenous*

PMGSR = base-weighted price index of imports of merchandise including exchange rate variation, 1957 = 1 (99)

PMNDR = base-weighted price index of imports of consumer non-durable goods divided by index of spot exchange rate (95)

PMDR = base-weighted price index of imports of consumer durable goods divided by index of spot exchange rate (96)

PMKR = base-weighted price index of imports of investment goods divided by index of spot exchange rate (97)

PMIMR = base-weighted price index of imports of industrial materials divided by index of spot exchange rate (98)

b. *lagged endogenous*

PXCL = current-weighted price index of re-imports of Canadian goods, 1957 = 1

PFLIM1 = base-weighted price index of imports of industrial materials, fuels and lubricants divided by index of spot exchange rate, lagged one quarter

c. *current exogenous*

PGMUS = price index of imports from the United States, 1957 = 1

PGMO = price index of imports from other countries, 1957 = 1

PGMCB = base-weighted price index of imports of consumer goods, 1957 = 1

PGMCC = current-weighted price index of imports of consumer goods, 1957 = 1

PMND = base-weighted price index of imports of consumer non-durable goods, 1957 = 1

PMD = base-weighted price index of imports of consumer durable goods, 1957 = 1

PGMIB = base-weighted price index of imports of investment goods, 1957 = 1

PGMIC = current-weighted price index of imports of investment goods, 1957 = 1

PGMIMB = base-weighted price index of imports of industrial materials, 1957 = 1

PGMIMC = current-weighted price index of imports of industrial materials, 1957 = 1

PGMFLC = current-weighted price index of imports of fuels and lubricants, 1957 = 1

PGMR = current-weighted price index of residual merchandise imports, 1957 = 1

d. *lagged exogenous*

PMUSP1 = ratio of price index of United States exports to price index of exports of other countries exporting to Canada, lagged one quarter

7. *Services*

c. *current exogenous*

PFRSN = price index of net freight and shipping payments

POTHN = price index of net payments for business services and miscellaneous transactions

PGT = price index of net government current payments, 1957 = 1

H. *Labor*

1. *Labor force*

a. *current endogenous*

FORCEM = labor force, millions of persons (35)

c. *current exogenous*

CADULTM = non-institutional adults, millions of persons

2. *Employment*

a. *current endogenous*

EMPM = employment of paid workers, millions of man-hours (36)

EMPNM = employment of unpaid workers, millions of man-hours (37)

PEREMP = proportion of labor force employed (103)

UNEMPM = unemployed people in labor force, millions of persons (104)

AHP = number of hours worked per paid worker (38)

AHN = number of hours worked per unpaid worker (39)

3. *Wage rates*

a. *current endogenous*

WR = index of aggregate wage rate, 1957 = 1 (102)

WRS = index of wage rate in consumer service industries, 1957 = 1 (47)

I. *Foreign Output*

b. *lagged endogenous*

FIP1 = index of production of importers of Canadian farm products divided by price index of exports of Canadian farm products, lagged one quarter

c. *current exogenous*

USIP = index of industrial production of the United States, 1957 = 1

d. *lagged exogenous*

BIP2 = index of industrial production of the United Kingdom, 1957 = 1, lagged two quarters

WEJIP2 = index of production in OECD countries and Japan, 1957 = 1, lagged two quarters

OIP2 = index of production in "other countries," 1957 = 1, lagged two quarters

J. *Inventory-Sales Ratios*

b. *lagged endogenous*

SMANI = ratio of beginning-of-quarter inventories in all manufacturing industries to sum of shipments over preceding four quarters

SIND = ratio of beginning-of-quarter inventories in non-durable consumer goods industries to sum of shipments over preceding four quarters

SID = ratio of beginning-of-quarter inventories in durable consumer goods industries to sum of shipments over preceding four quarters

SIK = ratio of beginning-of-quarter inventories in investment goods industries to sum of shipments over preceding four quarters

SIX = ratio of beginning-of-quarter inventories in industries producing largely for export to sum of shipments over preceding four quarters

SFL = ratio of beginning-of-quarter inventories of fuels and lubricants to sum of sales over preceding four quarters

K. *Merchant Marine*

c. *current exogenous*

CMARIN = Canadian ocean-going merchant fleet, in thousands of gross tons

L. *Weights*

c. *current exogenous*

WDND = weight of durable goods in PNDPO

WSND = weight of services in PNDPO

WNDD = weight of non-durable goods in PDPO

WSD = weight of services in PDPO

WNDS = weight of non-durable goods in PSPO

WDS = weight of durable goods in PSPO

M. *Dummy Variables*

c. *current exogenous*

Q1 = 1 if first quarter, 0 otherwise

Q2 = 1 if second quarter, 0 otherwise

Q3 = 1 if third quarter, 0 otherwise

FA = 1 if 1951, 0 otherwise

ACT = 1 if second quarter 1954 or beyond, 0 otherwise

FIA = 1 if third quarter 1954 or beyond, 0 otherwise

W = 1 if first quarter 1961 or beyond, 0 otherwise

T = time trend, i if ith observation

The number of variables in each econometric classification is tabulated in Table 5.

TABLE 5. Variables by category.

	Current	Lagged	Total
Endogenous	108	34	142
Exogenous	63	12	75
Total	171	46	217

A simpler arrangement is based on the fact that the current endogenous variables are determined by the set of relationships constituting the model while variables in the three remaining categories are predetermined. The outline is as in Table 6.

TABLE 6. Variables by type.

Type	Number
Determined	108
Predetermined	109
Total	217

The set of relationships that constitutes the model was presented in a systematic manner but without reference to methodological considerations. Variables of the model were then tabulated according to an economic classificatory scheme which seemed to indicate that conventional methodology of macro-economic model-building might constitute the basis of the present study.

It is now appropriate to fulfill a promise made at the beginning of chapter II, namely, to show that the structure of the model outlined above is in fact an application of the methodological framework outlined in chapter I.

The conventional process of macro-model construction centers on component flows of the national accounts. The basic aim is one of income-output determination. On the basis of only the foregoing exposition the following interpretation of the present study is irrefutable: the model is simply an extension of the conventional income-determination model to include relationships with the outside world—a necessary procedure for the case of an open economy. Merchandise exports are examined by area of destination while imports are considered both by commodity class and place of origin. A novel feature is the attention paid to the service and investment income accounts of the balance of payments. The relationships between capital flows and financial markets enter the model; this is one aspect of a second direction of expansion of the income-determination system—to the financial sector. There is a third path of extension—the enveloping of the labor sector of the economy. Attention is paid to labor both as a factor of production and a recipient of income; a feature is the division of workers into those that receive wages and those that receive other forms of income (such as that earned in a profession) or represent unpaid (family) assistance to a business or farm. An unorthodox aspect is the omission of a production function. This does not mean that the model determines only the aggregate demand for output; supply factors do enter through relations explaining prices and underlie price variables themselves. Consequently the accurate statement is that the model determines not only the demand for output but also aggregate output itself, that is, the actual production of the economy. What the system does *not* explain is how technology and employment of the various factors of production *interact* to produce the determinate output. An analogy may be made to a (final) commodity market in which pure competition prevails. Suppose both the demand function and the price are known for a given period. On the basis of that information the amount of the commodity exchanged is determinate. Assume the amount of the commodity sold is identical to the amount produced in that period. Then the given information suffices to determine output itself, but it does not explain how the technology and combination of factors operated to produce that output.

The above summary of salient features of the model is certainly correct; but adoption and extension of the income determination schema *as a methodological framework* play no role in construction of the system. The procedure followed in actual formulation of the model is outlined in chapter I. Results of this procedure are illustrated by means of the enclosed diagram. The object of the model is to explain not the national accounts income and/or expenditure flows but rather the spot exchange rate. This is the principal variable of the system. No other variable is included in the model unless it either directly or indirectly serves to explain the exchange rate. Therefore this procedure implies an ordering arrangement of all the variables of the system. The ranking is a reflection of the degree to which a variable is removed from direct explanation of the spot exchange rate. Because the methodology of construction of the model tends to require the inclusion of new variables, the focus of attention in the ordering scheme is on the current endogenous variables, that is, those which are not taken as predetermined but must themselves be explained by means of relationships included in the system. Because it is not desired to produce a model that is incomplete, the end of the process involves the same number of relationships as there are determined variables.

Now the process by means of which the model was generated may be illustrated by means of Diagram I. The spot exchange rate (RS) alone occupies the first row of the diagram. It is the first-order variable. This variable is current endogenous. (If it were not a determined variable, the adopted methodology would not permit the construction of a model.) In order that the spot exchange rate be *directly* explained, equation 1 is selected as a relationship of the model. If all the explanatory variables of this equation were predetermined, construction of the model would be completed. However, four of these variables, namely, BM, BS,

DIAGRAM I. Ordering structure of the determined variables.

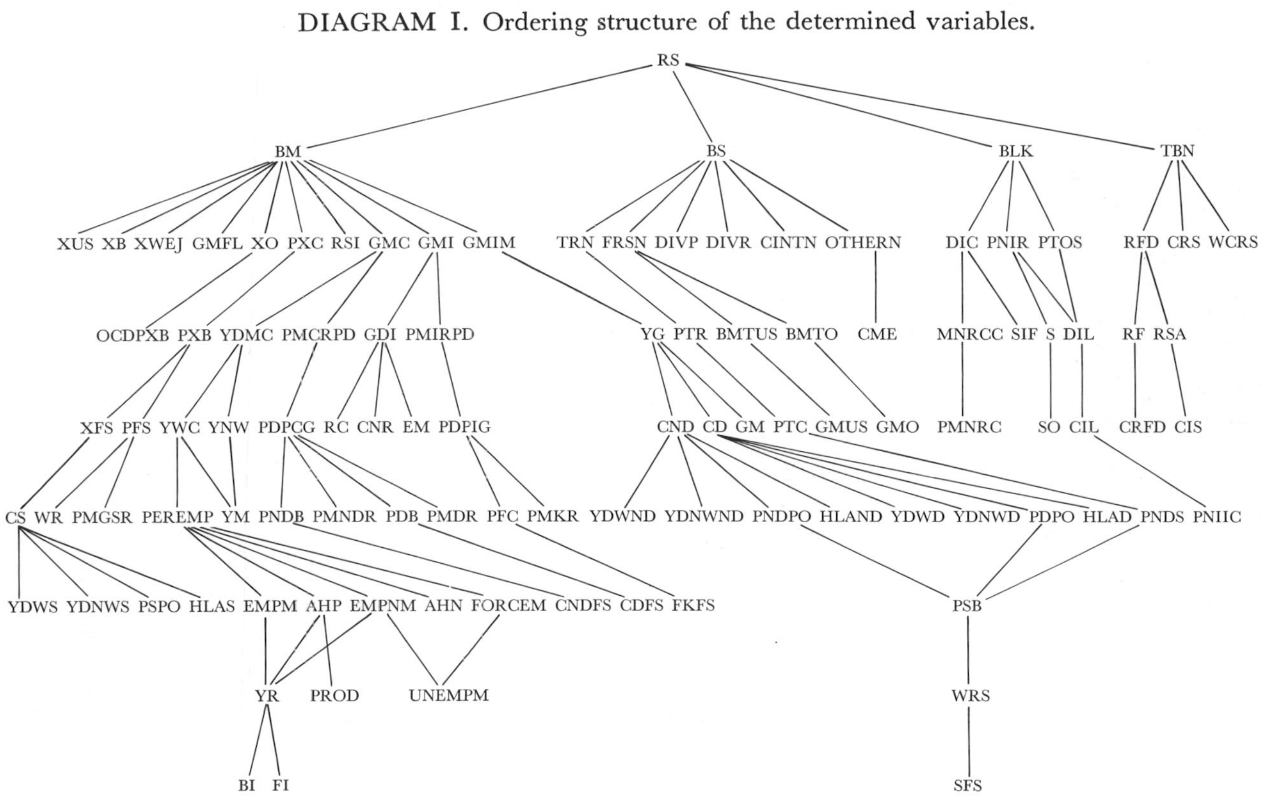

BLK, and TBN, are themselves determined variables. This group of variables constitutes the second-order subset of current endogenous variables.

It is now required that further relationships enter the model in order that these second-order variables be explained. BM is "explained" by dividing it into components which themselves are to be explained or taken as predetermined; this is equation 57. Other relations are selected to explain BS, BLK, and TBN. Those current endogenous variables—excluding first- and second-order variables—which enter the relationships adopted to explain the second-order variables, themselves constitute the third-order subset of determined variables. Further relationships must be selected so that this subset is directly explained. Those current endogenous variables of these relationships which are not included in the first-, second-, or third-order subsets of variables constitute the fourth-order subset of determined variables.

Generation of the model proceeds in this manner until a subset, say, the *N*th-order subset, of determined variables is reached such that the relationships adopted to explain this subset include no variables exclusive of predetermined variables and determined variables of orders 1 to *N*, inclusive. It is seen in the diagram that this stage is reached at the ninth order: the variables BI, FI, and SFS do not require higher-order current endogenous variables for their explanation.

Now, if each stage in the generation of the model involved the addition of new relationships in a number *equal* to the number of elements of the subset of determined variables under consideration, the model is complete not only methodologically (in the sense that no ordering subset of current endogenous variables is unexplained) but also mathematically (in the sense that the number of equations thus far included in the model is equal to the number of current endogenous variables). However, the model is not yet econometrically complete because there exist three current endogenous variables which enter the model but which are not included in the subsets of variables illustrated in the diagram described above. It is necessary to remember that price indexes of three categories of domestically produced goods, namely, consumer goods, investment goods, and industrial materials, are constructed by correcting an appropriate overall price index for the price index of imports of the goods under consideration. In the case of consumer and investment goods, the price indexes of domestically produced commodities are explained by means of two of the three semi-identities of the model, namely, equations 106 and 107. It is noted from rows four and five of the diagram that these price indexes methodologically enter the model because the price ratios of which they are respective components, that is, the variables PMCRPD and PMIRPD, are themselves current as distinct from lagged endogenous variables. With respect to industrial materials, however, the corresponding variable (PIMPD1) is lagged. Nevertheless this price ratio cannot exist unless the price index of domestically produced industrial materials itself exists.

The price index of domestically produced industrial materials is not independently measured; rather it is constructed by means of the third semi-identity, namely, equation 108. This relation involves three current endogenous variables which are not included in the above ordering schema of that category of variables. They are PDPIM, PWIM, and PMIMR. In order to explain them, three relationships are added to the model—equations 45, 98, and 108. These relationships include no current endogenous variables other than those in the ordering schema and the three extraneous ones. The argument that the three relationships and their associated variables should not be included in the model because PIMPD1, the endogenous variable which they help to construct, is *lagged* is not a valid position because both equations 45 and 108 contain *parameters* of the model. The crux of the matter is that PIMPD1 involves the parameters of equation 45 (the relation explaining PWIM). Therefore equation 45 must enter the system. But this equation includes the current endogenous variable PMIMR, which must be explained in order that the number of current endogenous variables should not exceed the number of relationships—hence equation 98. Finally the variable PDPIM—the component (in lagged form) of PIMPD1 which causes the phenomenon under discussion—is explained (by equation 108) because, like equation 45, it is not independent of the parameters of the system. (It involves a parameter of equation 45 itself.) Inclusion of the three relationships and their associated variables completes the model in an econometric sense and does not destroy the mathematical completeness. Methodological completeness does not apply to the entire set of determined variables but only to two subsets, namely, the 105 current endogenous variables illustrated in Diagram I and the three variables contained in Diagram II.

DIAGRAM II. Ordering structure of extraneous determined variables.

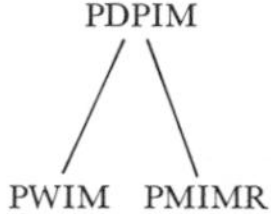

The two subsets are linked by means of the *lagged* endogenous variable PIMPD1. Were this variable *current*, the model would be methodologically complete as a unit. If PIMPD1 were current, the only alteration in the model (apart from the elimination of the lag in PIMPD1) would be the addition of the following identity:

$$\text{PIMPD1} = (\text{PGMIMB}/\text{RSI})/\text{PDPIM}$$

and PIMPD1 would enter the first diagram as a fourth-order variable (explaining GMIM).

There is a fourth concept of completeness, namely, dynamic completeness, which the model fails to possess. Dynamic completeness is required for analysis of the system by means of difference equations. Its criterion is that *all* endogenous variables are explained. This means that inclusion of a lagged endogenous variable in the model implies that its current value is included as well. Only two of the lagged endogenous variables, namely, RS1 and RFD1, meet this criterion.

IV / Impact Multipliers

Although all parameters of the model have been estimated, structural estimation alone does not suffice for the deduction of policy implications of a simultaneous equation model. Thus it is not in general valid that the true effect (in the current period) of a predetermined variable upon a current endogenous variable is identical to its direct effect on that variable. This would imply that a predetermined variable has a nil impact on a determined variable if it does not enter the equation explaining that variable, a result which clearly is not generally true. In fact the impact of a given predetermined variable upon a given current endogenous variable can be obtained only by tracing out the effects via all current endogenous variables of the system. Ultimately (although not in the structural sense) the set of current endogenous variables is a function of the set of predetermined variables, and the "obvious" way to explicitly obtain this dependence is to move (using legitimate algebraic operations) from the estimated structural system to the "*ex post* reduced form,"[1] that is, to explicitly obtain a functional relationship for each current endogenous variable such that the independent variables are all predetermined. Then differentiating each function (expressed as an equation with the determined variable on the left-hand side) with respect to each predetermined variable *in turn* yields the matrix of impact multipliers.

This procedure is of no difficulty providing the structural system is linear; for then the reduced form is itself linear and the multipliers are constants. However, if the model is non-linear the

1. Henceforth the term "reduced form" refers to the "*ex post* reduced form."

reduced form may be difficult to obtain; furthermore, some impact multipliers may be not constants but rather functions of the determined and predetermined variables. Thus there are two problems: (1) solution for the reduced form, and (2) interpretation of non-constant multipliers.

The model developed in this study is classified as non-linear. It is true that the 50 stochastic equations are linear in their coefficients. However, 39 identities are non-linear in the variables. Therefore the problems outlined above exist, and it is necessary to seek a solution.

The adopted procedure is that developed by Goldberger,[2] the approach itself based on suggestions originally expounded by Klein.[1]

Let the ith structural equation be written in functional notation as $F_i(E_1, \ldots, E_{108}, P_1, \ldots, P_{109}) = 0$, where E_i is the ith determined and P_j the jth predetermined variable. Then

$$dE = C * dP$$

where $C = -A^{-1} * B$

$$\text{and} \qquad \mathrm{d}E = \begin{bmatrix} \mathrm{d}E_1 \\ \vdots \\ \mathrm{d}E_{108} \end{bmatrix} \qquad \mathrm{d}P = \begin{bmatrix} \mathrm{d}P_1 \\ \vdots \\ \mathrm{d}P_{109} \end{bmatrix}$$

$$A = \begin{bmatrix} \partial F_1/\partial E_1 & \ldots & \partial F_1/\partial E_{108} \\ \vdots & & \vdots \\ \partial F_{108}/\partial E_1 & \ldots & \partial F_{108}/\partial E_{108} \end{bmatrix}$$

$$B = \begin{bmatrix} \partial F_1/\partial P_1 & \ldots & \partial F_1/\partial P_{109} \\ \vdots & & \vdots \\ \partial F_{108}/\partial P_1 & \ldots & \partial F_{108}/\partial P_{109} \end{bmatrix}$$

The impact of E_i upon P_j is the (i, j) element of the matrix C. Call this the impact multiplier of E_i with respect to P_j and denote it by $\partial E_i/\partial P_j$.

2. Arthur S. Goldberger, *Impact Multipliers and Dynamic Properties of the Klein-Goldberger Model* (Amsterdam, 1959), pp. 18–21.

3. Lawrence R. Klein, *A Textbook of Econometrics* (Evanston, 1956), pp. 120–121.

It is noted that this procedure does not yield the *ex post* reduced form; the multipliers are indeed obtained, but not by the "obvious" route. In fact it is the decision to solve for *changes* in the determined variables rather than for the variables themselves that reduces the problem from solution of a non-linear set of simultaneous equations to that of a linear one. However, the structural system itself remains non-linear;[4] thus not all the elements of A and B reduce from partial to ordinary derivatives. Hence before the matrix C can be computed it is necessary to evaluate the partials at a particular point. Let that point be $(\bar{E}_1, \ldots, \bar{E}_{108}, \bar{P}_1, \ldots, \bar{P}_{109})$, where $\bar{E}_i$, $\bar{P}_j$ are the means of E_i and P_j, respectively, these means calculated over the period the model covers, that is, from the first quarter of 1951 to the first quarter of 1962, inclusive. Clearly, "when the point . . . is chosen to correspond to the observed means of the variables over the sample period, the resultant values of the reduced form coefficients may be considered to be average values."[5]

The full matrix of impact multipliers has dimension 108 $\times$109. However, not all the multipliers are of interest. The important part of the matrix is arranged in Table 7. Note that the truncated matrix C' (rather than C itself) is listed, that is, columns refer to determined and rows to predetermined variables. The tabulated matrix has 108 columns; thus all current endogenous variables are included. However, there are only 43 rows; just that number of predetermined variables are of interest. Only those variables in one of the following classifications are included: (1) policy instruments, (2) foreign variables, (3) autonomous variables.

The policy variables in the model are listed beside the appropriate fields of operation as follows:

Fiscal policy: GG, GWASR, YMILIT, TW, TNW

Monetary policy: R, R2, RLA

Debt management policy: SG, TB, ATM

4. The Goldberger procedure can be interpreted as a particular linearization of the system. However, that interpretation is eschewed for pedagogical and methodological reasons.

5. Goldberger, *Impact Multipliers*, p. 20.

Exchange fund policy: OR, FA, W

Housing policy: ACT

Foreign aid policy: XNATO, OCO, OCBE, DLGC

Policy instruments are those variables which the model considers to be under full control of the Canadian government. XNATO is included on these grounds, even though it is probably a matter of foreign policy alone with little economic policy basis.

The foreign variables, arranged according to economic category, are given below.

Production: USIP, BIP2, WEJIP2, OIP2

Prices: PTA, PGMUS, PGMO, PGMCB, PMND, PMD, PGMIB, PGMIMB, PGMFLC, PMUSP1

Interest Rates: USIS, USIL

Liquidity: SIFUD, RESB2

Not all import price indexes are included in the chosen set of foreign variables. Only one index for each commodity class is selected. For the purpose of analysis a base-weighted price index is preferred to a corresponding current-weighted index. Hence PGMCB, PGMIB, and PGMIMB are included in lieu of PGMCC, PGMIC, and PGMIMC, respectively. However, PGMFLC has no base-weighted analogue as a pure variable in the model; therefore it must be used in spite of the undesirable weighting property.

Autonomous variables are classified and listed as follows.

Investment: SDINP, SOFIC2, SOCIA2

Savings: HLA

Population: CADULTM

Merchant Fleet: CMARIN

Autonomous variables are (1) variables that grow independently of the economic system or (2) variables that are stocks. Changes in stocks may be endogenous.

To illustrate the use of impact multipliers, four examples with policy implications are considered.

1. *Fiscal policy*

Suppose it is desired to compare the effectiveness of a decrease in direct taxes on wage income with an increase in government expenditure on goods, where the goal is stimulation of real income, measured by YR.

$$\frac{\partial YR/\partial GG}{-\partial YR/\partial TW} = \frac{1.1}{0.55} = 2$$

Therefore government *constant-dollar* expenditure on goods creates twice as much real income as is caused by a reduction in personal direct *monetary* taxes of the same nominal amount.

2. *Exchange fund policy*

An increase in reserves (decrease in OR) lowers the spot exchange rate (RS) predominantly because of its direct effect in the foreign exchange market (although its impact is less than its direct effect—see variable 64 in this chapter). A fall in the long-term interest rate (CIL) due to an increase in excess cash reserves of the banking system (R) reduces the exchange rate largely by reducing the balance of long-term capital (BLK). What are the relative strengths of these effects?

$$\frac{\partial RS/\partial R}{-\partial RS/\partial OR} = \frac{0.0023}{0.000033} = 700$$

An increase in the excess cash reserve ratio of one tenth of a percentage point induces the same decrease in the exchange rate as a 70 million dollar increase in official reserves of gold and U.S. dollars.

3. *Monetary policy*

Suppose an increase in USIL; this has a positive impact on CIL. How does this compare with the effect of a decrease in R?

$$\frac{\partial CIL/\partial USIL}{-\partial CIL/\partial R} = \frac{0.0016}{0.039} = 0.041$$

TABLE 7. Impact multipliers[a]

	1 YR	2 PROD	3 YG	4 YM	5 CND
GG	1.1	0.15E3	1.2	1.3	0.18
GWASR	1.4	0.20E3	0.31	1.2	0.18
YMILIT	0.55	0.79E4	0.31	0.44	0.39
XNATO	0.40E1	0.58E5	0.45E2	0.31E1	0.37E2
TW	−0.55	−0.79E4	−0.31	−0.44	−0.39
TNW	−0.96E2	−0.14E5	0.23E1	0.10	−0.45E1
SIFUD	−2.4	−0.34E3	−5.1	110.0	11.0
OCO	0.16	0.23E4	0.25	−2.8	−0.25
OCBE	0.13	0.18E4	0.21	−2.9	−0.26
DLGC	0.59E1	0.85E5	0.94E1	−1.2	−0.12
SDINP	−24.0	−0.34E2	−1.6	−33.0	−3.4
SOFIC2	0.31E3	0.45E7	0.50E3	−0.60E2	−0.50E3
SOCIA2	−0.87E2	−0.13E5	−0.14E1	0.17	0.14E1
OR	−0.11E1	−0.16E5	−0.24E1	0.51	0.51E1
RESB2	81.0	0.12E1	86.0	220.0	25.0
HLA	0.18	0.26E4	0.15	0.20	0.76E1
SG	−0.50E2	−0.71E6	−0.11E1	0.22	0.22E1
TB	−0.22E1	−0.32E5	−0.47E1	0.99	0.99E1
ATM	−0.69E1	−1.00E5	−0.15	3.1	0.31
R	0.79	0.11E3	1.7	−36.0	−3.6
RLA	0.19	0.27E4	0.40	−8.4	−0.84
R2	14.0	0.21E2	17.0	14.0	2.1
USIS	0.21	0.30E4	0.44	−9.4	−0.94
USIL	21.0	0.30E2	45.0	−950.0	−95.0
PTA	170.0	0.24E1	−11.0	200.0	6.7
PGMUS	35.0	0.50E2	3.9	27.0	3.2
PGMO	15.0	0.21E2	1.7	11.0	1.4
PGMCB	610.0	0.87E1	660.0	2400.0	220.0
PMND	−840.0	−0.12	−830.0	−990.0	−360.0
PMD	110.0	0.15E1	120.0	130.0	13.0
PGMIB	−690.0	−0.99E1	−740.0	−620.0	−140.0
PGMIMB	0.0	0.0	0.0	0.0	0.0
PGMFLC	−1.8	−0.26E3	7.2	−170.0	−17.0
PMUSP1	−4.4	−0.63E3	−0.49	−3.4	−0.40
CADULTM	−110.0	−0.15E1	−160.0	790.0	140.0
USIP	730.0	0.11	790.0	2000.0	230.0
BIP2	240.0	0.34E1	260.0	640.0	75.0
WEJIP2	150.0	0.22E1	160.0	410.0	48.0
OIP2	73.0	0.10E1	78.0	190.0	23.0
CMARIN	0.27E1	0.39E5	0.31E2	0.21E1	0.25E2
FA	4.4	0.64E3	9.5	−200.0	−20.0
ACT	100.0	0.15E1	120.0	97.0	15.0
W	14.0	0.20E2	30.0	−630.0	−63.0

[a] The table employs a version of exponential format. Thus 0.xx*En* implies *n* decimal places to the right of the decimal. For example, 0.35E2 would be read as 0.0035.

	6 CD	7 CS	8 TRN	9 CNDFS	10 CDFS
GG	0.10	0.16	−0.45E2	−0.36E4	0.28E6
GWASR	0.18	0.18	−0.94E2	−0.42E4	0.95E5
YMILIT	0.32E1	0.32	0.18E3	0.24E4	−0.21E5
XNATO	0.23E2	0.34E2	−0.30E4	0.13E6	0.22E6
TW	−0.32E1	−0.32	−0.18E3	−0.24E4	0.21E5
TNW	−0.87E2	−0.27E1	0.14E2	−0.57E5	−0.11E5
SIFUD	−13.0	3.7	2.3	0.16E2	−0.16E2
OCO	0.41	−0.72E1	−0.44E1	−0.42E4	0.53E4
OCBE	0.41	−0.78E1	−0.45E1	−0.42E4	0.53E4
DLGC	0.15	−0.39E1	−0.27E1	−0.20E4	0.19E4
SDINP	0.67	−2.4	−0.16	−0.28E3	0.13E3
SOFIC2	0.91E3	−0.14E3	−0.78E4	−0.85E7	0.12E6
SOCIA2	−0.25E1	0.39E2	0.22E2	0.24E5	−0.32E5
OR	−0.60E1	0.18E1	0.11E1	0.75E5	−0.78E5
RESB2	−5.5	16.0	2.1	−0.10E2	−0.17E2
HLA	0.86E1	0.68E1	−0.12E4	0.58E6	0.93E5
SG	−0.26E1	0.78E2	0.47E2	0.33E5	−0.34E5
TB	−0.12	0.35E1	0.21E1	0.15E4	−0.15E4
ATM	−0.37	0.11	0.66E1	0.46E4	−0.48E4
R	4.2	−1.3	−0.75	−0.53E3	0.55E3
RLA	0.99	−0.30	−0.18	−0.12E3	0.13E3
R2	1.9	2.1	−0.14	−0.57E3	0.62E4
USIS	1.1	−0.33	−0.20	−0.14E3	0.14E3
USIL	110.0	−33.0	−20.0	−0.14E1	0.15E1
PTA	−11.0	−14.0	−190.0	−0.64E2	−0.31E2
PGMUS	2.0	3.0	−0.27E1	0.12E3	0.20E3
PGMO	0.86	1.3	−0.11E1	0.50E4	0.83E4
PGMCB	−200.0	120.0	26.0	−0.40E2	−0.34E1
PMND	−520.0	−200.0	23.0	−0.19E2	−0.59E1
PMD	120.0	15.0	−0.45	−0.43E2	0.14E1
PGMIB	−170.0	−120.0	2.5	0.19E1	−0.14E1
PGMIMB	0.0	0.0	0.0	0.0	0.0
PGMFLC	19.0	−6.2	−3.5	−0.24E2	0.25E2
PMUSP1	−0.26	−0.38	0.33E2	−0.12E4	−0.25E4
CADULTM	−290.0	35.0	21.0	0.25E1	−0.37E1
USIP	−50.0	150.0	19.0	−0.94E2	−0.16E1
BIP2	−16.0	49.0	6.2	−0.30E2	−0.51E2
WEJIP2	−10.0	31.0	4.0	−0.19E2	−0.33E2
OIP2	−4.9	15.0	1.9	−0.92E3	−0.16E2
CMARIN	0.16E2	0.23E2	−0.21E4	0.96E7	0.16E6
FA	23.0	−7.0	−4.2	−0.29E2	0.31E2
ACT	14.0	15.0	−1.0	−0.40E2	0.45E3
W	74.0	−22.0	−13.0	−0.93E2	0.97E2

(continued on next page)

TABLE 7. Impact multipliers[a] (continued)

	11 SFS	12 GDI	13 CME	14 MNRCC	15 RC
GG	−0.20E4	0.0	0.0	0.33E2	0.0
GWASR	−0.20E4	0.0	0.0	−0.28E1	0.0
YMILIT	0.24E4	0.0	0.0	−0.92E2	0.0
XNATO	0.22E6	0.0	0.0	−0.11E2	0.0
TW	−0.24E4	0.0	0.0	0.92E2	0.0
TNW	−0.36E5	0.0	0.0	0.37E2	0.0
SIFUD	0.31E3	0.0	0.0	3.1	0.0
OCO	−0.10E4	0.0	0.0	−0.15	0.0
OCBE	−1.0E5	0.0	0.0	−0.15	0.0
DLGC	−0.42E5	0.0	0.0	−0.37E1	0.0
SDINP	−0.18E3	0.0	0.0	−0.15	0.0
SOFIC2	−0.22E7	0.0	0.0	−0.35E3	0.0
SOCIA2	0.61E6	0.0	0.0	0.97E2	0.0
OR	0.15E5	0.0	0.0	0.15E1	0.0
RESB2	−0.12E2	0.0	0.0	3.6	0.0
HLA	0.23E5	0.0	0.0	−0.75E3	0.0
SG	0.64E6	0.0	0.0	0.66E2	0.0
TB	0.28E5	0.0	0.0	0.29E1	0.0
ATM	0.90E5	0.0	0.0	0.92E1	0.0
R	−0.10E3	0.0	0.0	−1.1	0.0
RLA	−0.24E4	0.0	0.0	−0.25	0.0
R2	−0.30E3	18.0	18.0	18.0	0.0
USIS	−0.27E4	0.0	0.0	−0.28	0.0
USIL	−0.27E2	0.0	0.0	−28.0	0.0
PTA	0.19E1	0.0	0.0	−2.4	0.0
PGMUS	0.19E3	0.0	0.0	−0.95	0.0
PGMO	0.80E4	0.0	0.0	−0.40	0.0
PGMCB	−0.10E1	0.0	0.0	120.0	0.0
PMND	0.21E2	0.0	0.0	0.18	0.0
PMD	−0.22E2	0.0	0.0	0.45	0.0
PGMIB	0.98E2	0.0	0.0	510.0	0.0
PGMIMB	0.0	0.0	0.0	0.0	0.0
PGMFLC	−0.50E3	0.0	0.0	−4.7	0.0
PMUSP1	−0.22E4	0.0	0.0	0.12	0.0
CADULTM	0.65E2	0.0	0.0	120.0	0.0
USIP	−0.11E1	0.0	0.0	33.0	0.0
BIP2	−0.35E2	0.0	0.0	11.0	0.0
WEJIP2	−0.22E2	0.0	0.0	6.8	0.0
OIP2	−0.11E2	0.0	0.0	3.2	0.0
CMARIN	0.15E6	0.0	0.0	−0.74E3	0.0
FA	−0.57E3	0.0	0.0	−5.9	0.0
ACT	−0.21E2	130.0	100.0	100.0	27.0
W	−0.18E2	0.0	0.0	−19.0	0.0

[a] The table employs a version of exponential format. Thus 0.xx*En* implies *n* decimal places to the right of the decimal. For example, 0.35E2 would be read as 0.0035.

	16 CNR	17 EM	18 FKFS	19 BI	20 FI
GG	0.0	0.0	−0.36E4	−0.31	0.0
GWASR	0.0	0.0	−0.40E4	−0.80E1	0.0
YMILIT	0.0	0.0	−0.17E4	−0.79E1	0.0
XNATO	0.0	0.0	−0.21E6	−0.12E2	0.0
TW	0.0	0.0	0.17E4	0.79E1	0.0
TNW	0.0	0.0	0.15E6	−0.58E2	0.0
SIFUD	0.0	0.0	0.96E4	1.3	0.0
OCO	0.0	0.0	−0.58E5	−0.63E1	0.0
OCBE	0.0	0.0	−0.48E5	−0.55E1	0.0
DLGC	0.0	0.0	−0.22E5	−0.24E1	0.0
SDINP	0.0	0.0	0.10E3	0.41	0.0
SOFIC2	0.0	0.0	−0.12E7	−0.13E3	0.0
SOCIA2	0.0	0.0	0.33E6	0.36E2	0.0
OR	0.0	0.0	0.46E6	0.62E2	0.0
RESB2	0.0	0.0	−0.27E2	−22.0	0.0
HLA	0.0	0.0	−0.59E5	−0.39E1	0.0
SG	0.0	0.0	0.20E6	0.27E2	0.0
TB	0.0	0.0	0.89E6	0.12E1	0.0
ATM	0.0	0.0	0.28E5	0.38E1	0.0
R	0.0	0.0	−0.32E4	−0.43	0.0
RLA	0.0	0.0	−0.76E5	−0.10	0.0
R2	12.0	6.0	0.19E2	−4.4	0.0
USIS	0.0	0.0	−0.84E5	−0.11	0.0
USIL	0.0	0.0	−0.85E3	−12.0	0.0
PTA	0.0	0.0	−0.45E2	2.8	0.0
PGMUS	0.0	0.0	−0.18E3	−1.0	0.0
PGMO	0.0	0.0	−0.77E4	−0.43	0.0
PGMCB	0.0	0.0	−0.20E1	−170.0	0.0
PMND	0.0	0.0	0.28E1	210.0	0.0
PMD	0.0	0.0	−0.37E2	−31.0	0.0
PGMIB	0.0	0.0	0.23E1	190.0	0.0
PGMIMB	0.0	0.0	0.0	0.0	0.0
PGMFLC	0.0	0.0	−0.12E3	−1.8	0.0
PMUSP1	0.0	0.0	0.22E4	0.13	0.0
CADULTM	0.0	0.0	0.40E2	42.0	0.0
USIP	0.0	0.0	−0.25E1	−200.0	0.0
BIP2	0.0	0.0	−0.80E2	−66.0	0.0
WEJIP2	0.0	0.0	−0.51E2	−42.0	0.0
OIP2	0.0	0.0	−0.24E2	−20.0	0.0
CMARIN	0.0	0.0	−0.15E6	−0.79E3	0.0
FA	0.0	0.0	−0.18E3	−2.4	0.0
ACT	100.0	0.0	0.13E1	−31.0	0.0
W	0.0	0.0	−0.56E3	−7.7	0.0

(continued on next page)

TABLE 7. Impact multipliers[a] (continued)

	21 XUS	22 XB	23 XWEJ	24 XO	25 XFS
GG	0.0	0.0	0.0	0.17E4	−0.29E4
GWASR	0.0	0.0	0.0	0.21E4	−0.32E4
YMILIT	0.0	0.0	0.0	0.88E5	−0.13E4
XNATO	0.0	0.0	0.0	0.16E6	−0.16E6
TW	0.0	0.0	0.0	−0.88E5	0.13E4
TNW	0.0	0.0	0.0	−0.53E6	0.11E6
SIFUD	0.0	0.0	0.0	−0.49E3	0.75E4
OCO	0.0	0.0	0.0	0.29E1	−0.75E6
OCBE	0.0	0.0	0.0	0.16E4	−0.38E5
DLGC	0.0	0.0	0.0	0.29E1	0.21E5
SDINP	0.0	0.0	0.0	−0.23E4	0.81E4
SOFIC2	0.0	0.0	0.0	0.34E7	−0.92E8
SOCIA2	0.0	0.0	0.0	−0.95E6	0.26E6
OR	0.0	0.0	0.0	−0.24E5	0.36E6
RESB2	0.0	76.0	0.0	−0.54E2	0.81E2
HLA	0.0	0.0	0.0	0.28E5	−0.46E5
SG	0.0	0.0	0.0	−0.10E5	0.15E6
TB	0.0	0.0	0.0	−0.46E5	0.69E6
ATM	0.0	0.0	0.0	−0.14E4	0.22E5
R	0.0	0.0	0.0	0.17E3	−0.25E4
RLA	0.0	0.0	0.0	0.39E4	−0.59E5
R2	0.0	0.0	0.0	0.25E3	−0.40E3
USIS	0.0	0.0	0.0	0.44E4	−0.66E5
USIL	0.0	0.0	0.0	0.44E2	−0.67E3
PTA	0.0	0.0	0.0	0.21E2	−0.35E2
PGMUS	0.0	0.0	0.0	0.14E3	−0.14E3
PGMO	0.0	0.0	0.0	0.61E4	−0.61E4
PGMCB	0.0	0.0	0.0	−0.13E2	−0.16E1
PMND	0.0	0.0	0.0	−0.13E1	0.22E1
PMD	0.0	0.0	0.0	0.17E2	−0.29E2
PGMIB	0.0	0.0	0.0	−0.16E1	0.18E1
PGMIMB	0.0	0.0	0.0	0.0	0.0
PGMFLC	0.0	0.0	0.0	0.74E3	−0.93E4
PMUSP1	0.0	0.0	0.0	−0.15E4	0.15E4
CADULTM	0.0	0.0	0.0	−0.11E1	0.31E2
USIP	700.0	0.0	0.0	−0.50E1	0.74E1
BIP2	0.0	230.0	0.0	−0.16E1	0.24E1
WEJIP2	0.0	0.0	140.0	−0.10E1	0.15E1
OIP2	0.0	0.0	0.0	69.0	0.73E2
CMARIN	0.0	0.0	0.0	0.11E6	−0.11E6
FA	0.0	0.0	0.0	0.93E3	−0.14E3
ACT	0.0	0.0	0.0	0.18E2	−0.28E2
W	0.0	0.0	0.0	0.29E2	−0.44E3

[a]The table employs a version of exponential format. Thus 0.xx*En* implies *n* decimal places to the right of the decimal. For example, 0.35E2 would be read as 0.0035.

	26 GMUS	27 GMO	28 GM	29 GMC	30 GMI
GG	0.57E1	0.28E1	0.85E1	0.32E1	0.62E2
GWASR	0.37E1	0.18E1	0.56E1	0.17E1	0.27E1
YMILIT	0.74E1	0.36E1	0.11	0.84E1	0.15E1
XNATO	0.10E2	0.49E3	0.15E2	0.93E3	0.41E3
TW	−0.74E1	−0.36E1	−0.11	−0.84E1	−0.15E1
TNW	−0.51E1	−0.25E1	−0.76E1	−0.70E1	−0.72E2
SIFUD	2.1	1.2	3.2	11.0	−7.4
OCO	−0.35E1	−0.21E1	−0.53E1	−0.22	0.16
OCBE	−0.38E1	−0.23E1	−0.57E1	−0.22	0.16
DLGC	−0.23E1	−0.14E1	−0.35E1	−0.13	0.87E1
SDINP	−0.76	−0.39	−1.1	−1.5	0.42
SOFIC2	−0.62E4	−0.38E4	−0.92E4	−0.40E3	0.29E3
SOCIA2	0.17E2	0.10E2	0.26E2	0.11E1	−0.81E2
OR	0.10E1	0.59E2	0.15E1	0.51E1	−0.35E1
RESB2	6.7	3.6	10.0	14.0	−7.5
HLA	0.76E2	0.38E2	0.11E1	0.37E2	0.18E2
SG	0.44E2	0.26E2	0.66E2	0.23E1	−0.15E1
TB	0.20E1	0.11E1	0.29E1	0.99E1	−0.68E1
ATM	0.62E1	0.36E1	0.92E1	0.31	−0.22
R	−0.70	−0.42	−1.1	−3.6	2.5
RLA	−0.18	−0.98E1	−0.25	−0.85	0.58
R2	3.5	1.6	5.2	0.52E1	4.5
USIS	−0.19	−0.11	−0.28	−0.94	0.65
USIL	−19.0	−11.0	−28.0	−96.0	66.0
PTA	4.7	2.3	7.0	8.4	−0.99
PGMUS	0.88	−870.0	1.3	0.81	0.36
PGMO	0.37	−370.0	0.56	0.34	0.15
PGMCB	−430.0	−210.0	−640.0	−550.0	−120.0
PMND	−38.0	−19.0	−57.0	−19.0	−5.8
PMD	4.4	2.2	6.5	1.3	0.42
PGMIB	290.0	130.0	430.0	−24.0	490.0
PGMIMB	0.0	0.0	0.0	0.0	0.0
PGMFLC	−3.4	140.0	−5.1	−17.0	11.0
PMUSP1	−410.0	410.0	−0.17	−0.10	−0.45E1
CADULTM	9.2	6.5	14.0	100.0	−81.0
USIP	61.0	32.0	92.0	130.0	−69.0
BIP2	20.0	11.0	30.0	42.0	−22.0
WEJIP2	13.0	6.7	19.0	27.0	−14.0
OIP2	6.0	3.2	9.1	13.0	−6.8
CMARIN	0.69E3	0.34E3	0.10E2	0.63E3	0.28E3
FA	−3.9	−2.3	−5.9	−20.0	14.0
ACT	24.0	11.0	37.0	0.25	32.0
W	−12.0	−7.3	−19.0	−64.0	44.0

(continued on next page)

TABLE 7. Impact multipliers[a] (continued)

	31 GMIM	32 GMFL	33 BM	34 BMTUS	35 BMTO
GG	0.47E1	0.0	−0.16	0.57E1	0.28E1
GWASR	0.12E1	0.0	−0.14	0.37E1	0.18E1
YMILIT	0.12E1	0.0	−0.15	0.74E1	0.36E1
XNATO	0.18E3	0.0	−0.15E2	0.10E2	−1.0
TW	−0.12E1	0.0	0.15	−0.74E1	−0.36E1
TNW	0.88E3	0.0	0.85E1	−0.51E1	−0.25E1
SIFUD	−0.20	0.0	6.7	2.1	1.2
OCO	0.97E2	0.0	−1.1	−0.35E1	−0.50E1
OCBE	0.84E2	0.0	−1.1	−0.38E1	−0.23E1
DLGC	0.37E2	0.0	−0.46E1	−0.23E1	−0.43E1
SDINP	−0.62E1	0.0	0.72	−0.76	−0.39
SOFIC2	0.20E4	0.0	−0.10E3	−0.62E4	−0.38E4
SOCIA2	−0.55E3	0.0	0.28E2	0.17E2	0.10E2
OR	−0.95E3	0.0	0.32E1	0.10E1	0.59E2
RESB2	3.4	0.0	92.0	6.7	−73.0
HLA	0.59E2	0.0	−0.23E1	0.76E2	0.38E2
SG	−0.42E3	0.0	0.14E1	0.44E2	0.26E2
TB	−0.18E2	0.0	0.62E1	0.20E1	0.12E1
ATM	−0.58E2	0.0	0.19	0.62E1	0.36E1
R	0.66E1	0.0	−2.2	−0.70	−0.42
RLA	0.16E1	0.0	−0.53	−0.17	−0.98E1
R2	0.67	0.0	−6.4	3.5	1.6
USIS	0.17E1	0.0	−0.59	−0.19	−0.11
USIL	1.8	0.0	−59.0	−19.0	−11.0
PTA	−0.43	0.0	−10.0	4.7	2.3
PGMUS	0.15	0.0	−1.4	0.88	−870.0
PGMO	0.65E1	0.0	−0.57	0.37	−370.0
PGMCB	26.0	0.0	700.0	−430.0	−210.0
PMND	−32.0	0.0	110.0	−38.0	−19.0
PMD	4.8	0.0	−13.0	4.4	2.2
PGMIB	−29.0	0.0	−400.0	290.0	130.0
PGMIMB	0.0	0.0	0.0	0.0	0.0
PGMFLC	0.28	0.0	−150.0	−3.4	140.0
PMUSP1	−0.19E1	0.0	0.17	−410.0	410.0
CADULTM	−6.4	0.0	23.0	9.2	6.5
USIP	31.0	0.0	850.0	−640.0	33.0
BIP2	10.0	0.0	270.0	20.0	−220.0
WEJIP2	6.4	0.0	170.0	13.0	−140.0
OIP2	3.1	0.0	83.0	6.0	−66.0
CMARIN	0.12E3	0.0	−0.11E2	0.69E3	0.34E3
FA	0.37	0.0	−12.0	−3.9	−2.3
ACT	4.7	0.0	−45.0	24.0	11.0
W	1.2	0.0	−39.0	−12.0	−7.3

[a] The table employs a version of exponential format. Thus 0.xx*En* implies *n* decimal places to the right of the decimal. For example, 0.35E2 would be read as 0.0035.

	36 BS	37 FRSN	38 OTHERN	39 YDMC	40 YWC
GG	1.00E1	0.23E2	−0.73E10	0.48	0.39
GWASR	−0.83E1	0.15E2	−0.73E10	0.35	0.27
YMILIT	−0.11	0.30E2	0.0	1.1	0.89E1
XNATO	0.30E1	−0.33E1	0.0	0.12E1	0.61E2
TW	0.11	−0.30E2	0.0	−1.1	−0.89E1
TNW	0.57E1	−0.21E2	0.0	−0.91	0.51E1
SIFUD	61.0	0.92E1	0.38E7	99.0	52.0
OCO	−0.65	−0.25E2	0.0	−2.1	−1.4
OCBE	−0.66	−0.17E2	0.0	−2.2	−1.5
DLGC	−0.72	−0.20E2	0.0	−1.1	−0.60
SDINP	−26.0	−0.31E1	20.0	−17.0	−11.0
SOFIC2	−0.34E2	−0.27E5	0.0	−0.40E2	−0.30E2
SOCIA2	0.95E1	0.76E4	0.0	0.11	0.83E1
OR	0.29	0.44E3	0.22E9	0.47	0.25
RESB2	61.0	−2.3	0.0	140.0	87.0
HLA	−0.16E1	0.31E3	0.0	0.70E1	0.56E1
SG	0.13	0.19E3	0.0	0.21	0.11
TB	0.57	0.85E3	0.38E9	0.92	0.48
ATM	1.8	0.27E2	0.13E8	2.9	1.5
R	−20.0	−0.31E1	−0.14E7	−33.0	−17.0
RLA	−4.8	−0.73E2	−0.33E8	−7.8	−4.1
R2	−4.1	0.14	0.36	3.0	3.5
USIS	−5.4	−0.81E2	−0.40E8	−8.7	−4.6
USIL	−540.0	−0.82	−0.39E6	−880.0	−470.0
PTA	230.0	0.19	−0.15E5	96.0	57.0
PGMUS	26.0	−29.0	0.0	10.0	5.3
PGMO	11.0	−12.0	0.0	4.3	2.3
PGMCB	450.0	−17.0	0.25E6	−3700.0	1000.0
PMND	46.0	−1.5	0.21E6	−360.0	−290.0
PMD	−8.5	0.18	−0.72E8	51.0	41.0
PGMIB	−260.0	11.0	−0.13E6	−350.0	−150.0
PGMIMB	0.0	0.0	0.0	0.0	0.0
PGMFLC	−98.0	4.4	0.0	−150.0	−81.0
PMUSP1	−3.3	3.6	0.0	−1.3	−0.67
CADULTM	−6.9	0.44	0.17E6	1000.0	920.0
USIP	550.0	−14.0	0.0	1300.0	790.0
BIP2	180.0	−6.7	0.0	430.0	260.0
WEJIP2	110.0	−4.3	0.0	270.0	160.0
OIP2	55.0	−2.0	0.0	130.0	78.0
CMARIN	0.20E1	−0.23E1	0.0	0.80E2	0.41E2
FA	−110.0	−0.17	−0.85E7	−180.0	−98.0
ACT	−29.0	0.97	2.0	20.0	24.0
W	−360.0	−0.54	0.17E9	−580.0	−310.0

(continued on next page)

TABLE 7. Impact multipliers[a] (continued)

	41 YDWND	42 YDWD	43 YDWS	44 YNW	45 YDNWND
GG	0.43	0.39	0.48	0.14	0.15
GWASR	0.37	0.32	0.55	0.13	0.17
YMILIT	1.1	1.1	1.0	0.48E1	0.38E1
XNATO	0.79E2	0.75E2	0.10E1	0.34E2	0.40E2
TW	−1.1	−1.1	−1.0	−0.48E1	−0.38E1
TNW	0.54E1	0.45E1	0.34E1	0.11E1	−0.99
SIFUD	43.0	44.0	11.0	12.0	9.0
OCO	−1.1	−1.1	−0.26	−0.31	−0.20
OCBE	−1.1	−1.2	−0.28	−0.32	−0.21
DLGC	−0.50	−0.50	−0.12	−0.13	−0.10
SDINP	−9.9	−10.0	−7.4	−3.6	−3.4
SOFIC2	−0.22E2	−0.23E2	−0.55E3	−0.66E3	−0.41E3
SOCIA2	0.60E1	0.65E1	0.15E1	0.18E1	0.11E1
OR	0.21	0.21	0.54E1	0.56E1	0.43E1
RESB2	80.0	78.0	50.0	24.0	22.0
HLA	0.54E1	0.11	0.44E1	0.22E1	0.21E1
SG	0.91E1	0.92E1	0.24E1	0.25E1	0.19E1
TB	0.40	0.41	0.10	0.11	0.83E1
ATM	1.3	1.3	0.33	0.34	0.26
R	−15.0	−15.0	−3.8	−3.9	−3.0
RLA	−3.4	−3.5	−0.90	−0.93	−0.71
R2	4.3	3.7	6.3	1.5	1.8
USIS	−3.8	−3.9	−0.99	−1.0	−0.79
USIL	−390.0	−390.0	−100.0	−100.0	−80.0
PTA	71.0	41.0	−62.0	22.0	26.0
PGMUS	6.9	6.5	8.8	3.0	3.5
PGMO	2.9	2.8	3.7	1.3	1.5
PGMCB	770.0	820.0	420.0	260.0	190.0
PMND	−1100.0	−600.0	−290.0	−110.0	−360.0
PMD	46.0	−58.0	50.0	15.0	16.0
PGMIB	−320.0	−230.0	−330.0	−69.0	−120.0
PGMIMB	0.0	0.0	0.0	0.0	0.0
PGMFLC	−68.0	−68.0	−19.0	−18.0	−14.0
PMUSP1	−0.86	−0.82	−1.1	−0.37	−0.43
CADULTM	650.0	700.0	160.0	87.0	3.1
USIP	730.0	710.0	460.0	220.0	200.0
BIP2	240.0	230.0	150.0	70.0	64.0
WEJIP2	150.0	150.0	94.0	45.0	41.0
OIP2	73.0	70.0	45.0	21.0	20.0
CMARIN	0.54E2	0.51E2	0.69E2	0.23E2	0.27E2
FA	−81.0	−82.0	−21.0	−22.0	−17.0
ACT	30.0	26.0	44.0	11.0	13.0
W	−260.0	−260.0	−67.0	−69.0	−53.0

[a] The table employs a version of exponential format. Thus 0.xx*En* implies *n* decimal places to the right of the decimal. For examples, 0.35E2 would be read as 0.0035.

	46 YDNWD	47 YDNWS	48 SIF	49 DIVP	50 DIVR
GG	0.14	0.17	0.10E4	−0.44E2	−0.11
GWASR	0.15	0.22	0.92E5	−0.39E2	−0.95E1
YMILIT	0.44E1	0.23E1	0.10E4	−0.44E2	−0.11
XNATO	0.38E2	0.47E2	−0.40E6	0.17E3	0.42E2
TW	−0.44E1	−0.23E1	−0.10E4	0.44E2	0.11
TNW	−0.99	−1.0	−0.57E5	0.24E2	0.59E1
SIFUD	9.1	−1.1	1.0	2.7	66.0
OCO	−0.22	0.50E1	0.70E4	−0.30E1	−0.72
OCBE	−0.23	0.46E1	0.72E4	−0.31E1	−0.74
DLGC	−0.10	0.18E1	0.76E4	−0.32E1	−0.79
SDINP	−3.4	−2.6	0.39E3	−0.17	−4.0
SOFIC2	−0.46E3	0.11E3	0.63E7	0.29E2	−0.65E3
SOCIA2	0.13E1	−0.29E2	−0.17E5	0.74E3	0.98E1
OR	0.43E1	−0.54E2	−0.30E4	0.13E1	0.31
RESB2	21.0	12.0	−0.62E2	2.6	64.0
HLA	0.37E1	0.18E1	0.15E5	−0.65E3	−0.16E1
SG	0.19E1	−0.24E2	−0.13E4	0.57E2	0.14
TB	0.84E1	−0.10E1	−0.59E4	0.25E1	0.61
ATM	0.27	−0.33E1	−0.19E3	0.79E1	1.9
R	−3.0	0.38	0.21E2	−0.91	−22.0
RLA	−0.72	0.90E1	0.51E3	−0.21	−5.2
R2	1.6	2.4	0.37E3	−0.16	−3.9
USIS	−0.80	1.00E1	0.56E3	−0.24	−5.8
USIL	−81.0	10.0	0.57E1	−24.0	−590.0
PTA	16.0	−15.0	−0.32E2	1.4	33.0
PGMUS	3.4	4.1	−0.35E3	0.15	3.6
PGMO	1.4	1.7	−0.15E3	0.63E1	1.5
PGMCB	200.0	76.0	−0.47E1	20.0	480.0
PMND	−210.0	−110.0	−0.69E2	2.9	72.0
PMD	−16.0	18.0	0.89E3	−0.38	−9.2
PGMIB	−95.0	−120.0	0.25E1	−11.0	−260.0
PGMIMB	0.0	0.0	0.0	0.0	0.0
PGMFLC	−15.0	1.1	0.99E2	−4.2	−100.0
PMUSP1	−0.42	−0.51	0.43E4	−0.19E1	−0.45
CADULTM	22.0	−150.0	−0.15E2	0.65	16.0
USIP	190.0	110.0	−0.56E1	24.0	580.0
BIP2	62.0	36.0	−0.18E1	7.7	190.0
WEJIP2	39.0	23.0	−0.12E1	4.9	120.0
OIP2	19.0	11.0	−0.56E2	2.4	57.0
CMARIN	0.26E2	0.32E2	−0.27E6	0.12E3	0.28E2
FA	−17.0	2.1	0.12E1	−5.1	−120.0
ACT	11.0	17.0	0.27E2	−1.2	−28.0
W	−54.0	6.7	0.38E1	−16.0	−390.0

(continued on next page)

TABLE 7. Impact multipliers[a] (continued)

	51 CINTN	52 OCDPXB	53 BLK	54 PNIIC	55 DIC
GG	0.55E3	0.58E3	0.20E1	0.19E1	0.98E3
GWASR	0.49E3	0.73E3	0.16E1	0.17E1	−0.61E3
YMILIT	0.55E3	0.31E3	0.19E1	0.19E1	0.39E3
XNATO	−0.21E4	0.58E5	−0.82E3	0.73E3	−0.84E4
TW	−0.55E3	−0.31E3	−0.19E1	−0.19E1	−0.39E3
TNW	−0.30E3	−0.19E4	−0.11E1	−0.10E1	−0.28E3
SIFUD	−0.34	−0.17E1	70.0	−12.0	82.0
OCO	0.37E2	1.0	0.13	0.13	−0.14E2
OCBE	0.38E2	0.55E3	0.13	0.13	−0.13E2
DLGC	0.40E2	1.0	−0.86	0.14	0.43E2
SDINP	0.21E1	−0.80E3	0.74	0.71	0.24E1
SOFIC2	0.34E5	0.12E5	0.10E3	0.11E3	−0.12E4
SOCIA2	−0.93E4	−0.33E4	−0.28E2	−0.32E2	0.33E3
OR	−0.16E2	−0.82E4	−0.57E1	−0.55E1	−0.17E2
RESB2	−0.33	−0.19	−12.0	−11.0	−0.32
HLA	0.82E4	0.97E4	0.29E2	0.28E2	0.87E4
SG	−0.71E3	−0.36E4	0.15	0.15	−0.75E3
TB	−0.31E2	−0.16E3	0.67	0.68	−0.33E2
ATM	−0.99E2	−0.50E3	2.0	2.1	−0.10E1
R	0.11	0.58E2	−24.0	−24.0	0.12
RLA	0.27E1	0.14E2	−5.8	−5.8	0.28E1
R2	0.20E1	0.88E2	1.6	0.68	0.90
USIS	0.30E1	0.15E2	1.2	1.1	0.32E1
USIL	3.0	0.15	−630.0	−630.0	3.2
PTA	−0.17	0.74E1	−6.3	−5.9	−0.37
PGMUS	−0.19E1	0.51E2	−0.72	−0.64	−0.74E1
PGMO	−0.79E2	0.22E2	−0.30	−0.27	−0.31E1
PGMCB	−2.5	−0.46E1	−83.0	−85.0	1.9
PMND	−0.37	−0.46	−13.0	−13.0	−0.55
PMD	0.47E1	0.58E1	1.7	1.6	0.92E1
PGMIB	1.3	−0.55	72.0	45.0	26.0
PGMIMB	0.0	0.0	0.0	0.0	0.0
PGMFLC	0.53	0.26E1	19.0	18.0	0.56
PMUSP1	0.23E2	−0.64E3	0.89E1	0.80E1	0.92E2
CADULTM	−0.81E1	−0.38	2.7	−2.8	5.5
USIP	−3.0	−1.7	−110.0	−100.0	−2.9
BIP2	−0.97	−0.56	−34.0	−33.0	−0.95
WEJIP2	−0.62	−0.36	−22.0	−21.0	−0.61
OIP2	−0.30	−0.17	−10.0	−10.0	−0.29
CMARIN	−0.15E4	0.40E5	−0.56E3	−0.50E3	−0.57E4
FA	0.64	0.32E1	25.0	24.0	0.67
ACT	0.14	0.62E1	10.0	4.9	5.1
W	2.0	0.10	−420.0	−400.0	−19.0

[a] The table employs a version of exponential format. Thus 0.xx*En* implies *n* decimal places to the right of the decimal. For example, 0.35E2 would be read as 0.0035.

	56 PNIR	57 PTOS	58 TBN	59 HLAND	60 HLAD
GG	0.60E3	0.18E1	0.82E2	0.79E1	−0.26E2
GWASR	0.53E3	0.16E1	0.72E2	0.22	0.11
YMILIT	0.60E3	0.18E1	0.82E2	−0.65E1	−0.25E1
XNATO	−0.23E4	−0.71E3	−0.32E3	0.37E2	0.29E2
TW	−0.60E3	−0.18E1	−0.82E2	0.65E1	0.25E1
TNW	−0.33E3	−0.10E1	−0.45E2	0.58E2	−0.12E1
SIFUD	−0.37	−11.0	−5.0	−18.0	−17.0
OCO	0.40E2	0.12	0.55E1	0.74	0.60
OCBE	0.42E2	0.13	0.57E1	0.74	0.61
DLGC	0.44E2	0.13	0.60E1	0.22	0.20
SDINP	0.23E1	0.69	0.31	1.7	1.4
SOFIC2	0.36E5	0.11E3	0.50E4	0.17E2	0.14E2
SOCIA2	−0.10E3	−0.31E2	−0.14E2	−0.48E1	−0.38E1
OR	−0.18E2	−0.54E1	−0.24E1	−0.88E1	−0.83E1
RESB2	−0.36	−11.0	−4.9	−14.0	−19.0
HLA	0.89E4	0.27E2	0.12E2	1.0	1.1
SG	0.16	−0.99E2	−0.11E1	−0.39E1	−0.36E1
TB	0.50	0.17	−0.48E1	−0.17	−0.16
ATM	1.5	0.51	−0.15	−0.54	−0.51
R	−18.0	−6.2	1.7	6.2	5.8
RLA	−4.3	−1.5	0.41	1.5	1.4
R2	0.22E1	0.66	0.30	1.8	0.57
USIS	0.11	1.0	−0.41E1	1.6	1.5
USIL	−480.0	−150.0	45.0	160.0	150.0
PTA	−0.19	−5.7	−2.6	28.0	−33.0
PGMUS	−0.20E1	−0.62	−0.28	3.2	2.6
PGMO	−0.86E2	−0.26	−0.12	1.4	1.1
PGMCB	−2.7	−82.0	−37.0	−490.0	−400.0
PMND	−0.40	−12.0	−5.5	−1700.0	−660.0
PMD	0.51E1	1.6	0.70	10.0	−210.0
PGMIB	1.4	44.0	20.0	−360.0	−180.0
PGMIMB	0.0	0.0	0.0	0.0	0.0
PGMFLC	0.57	17.0	7.8	28.0	26.0
PMUSP1	0.25E2	0.78E1	0.35E1	−0.41	−0.32
CADULTM	−0.88E2	−2.7	−1.2	−560.0	−440.0
USIP	−3.3	−99.0	−45.0	−130.0	−170.0
BIP2	−1.1	−32.0	−14.0	−41.0	−56.0
WEJIP2	−0.67	−20.0	−9.2	−26.0	−35.0
OIP2	−0.32	−9.8	−4.4	−12.0	−17.0
CMARIN	−0.16E4	−0.48E3	−0.22E3	0.25E2	0.20E2
FA	2.3	22.0	−0.88	35.0	32.0
ACT	0.16	4.8	2.1	13.0	4.3
W	−240.0	−160.0	30.0	110.0	100.0

(continued on next page)

TABLE 7. Impact multipliers[a] (continued)

	61 HLAS	62 S	63 SO	64 RS	65 RSI
GG	0.17	0.21E3	0.21E3	−0.11E4	−0.11E4
GWASR	0.57	0.18E3	0.18E3	−0.99E5	−0.95E5
YMILIT	−0.18	0.21E3	0.21E3	−0.11E4	−0.11E4
XNATO	0.80E2	−0.80E5	−0.80E5	0.43E6	0.41E6
TW	0.18	−0.21E3	−0.21E3	0.11E4	0.11E4
TNW	−0.38E1	−0.11E3	−0.11E3	0.61E5	0.58E5
SIFUD	−89.0	−0.13	−0.13	0.69E2	0.66E2
OCO	2.5	0.14E2	0.14E2	−0.75E4	−0.72E4
OCBE	2.5	0.14E2	0.14E2	−0.78E4	−0.74E4
DLGC	1.1	0.15E2	0.15E2	−0.81E4	−0.78E4
SDINP	7.4	0.78E2	0.78E2	−0.42E3	−0.40E3
SOFIC2	0.53E2	0.13E5	0.13E5	−0.68E7	−0.65E7
SOCIA2	−0.15	−0.35E4	−0.35E4	0.19E5	0.18E5
OR	−0.42	−0.61E3	−0.61E3	0.33E4	0.31E4
RESB2	−82.0	−0.12	−0.12	0.66E2	0.64E2
HLA	1.0	0.31E4	0.31E4	−0.16E5	−0.16E5
SG	−0.19	0.66	−0.34	0.14E4	0.14E4
TB	−0.82	−0.69E1	−0.69E1	0.64E4	0.61E4
ATM	−2.6	−0.21	−0.21	0.20E3	0.19E3
R	30.0	2.5	2.5	−0.23E2	−0.22E2
RLA	7.0	0.59	0.59	−0.54E3	−0.52E3
R2	5.6	0.74E2	0.74E2	−0.40E3	−0.39E3
USIS	7.8	0.10E2	0.10E2	−0.60E3	−0.58E3
USIL	790.0	−0.99E1	−0.99E1	−0.61E1	−0.59E1
PTA	−250.0	−0.64E1	−0.64E1	0.35E2	0.33E2
PGMUS	7.0	−0.70E2	−0.70E2	0.38E3	0.36E3
PGMO	2.9	−0.30E2	−0.30E2	0.16E3	0.15E3
PGMCB	−1300.0	−0.93	−0.93	0.50E1	0.48E1
PMND	14.0	−0.14	−0.14	0.75E2	0.72E2
PMD	17.0	0.18E1	0.18E1	−0.96E3	−0.92E3
PGMIB	−360.0	0.49	0.49	−0.27E1	−0.26E1
PGMIMB	0.0	0.0	0.0	0.0	0.0
PGMFLC	140.0	0.20	0.20	−0.11E1	−0.10E1
PMUSP1	−0.87	0.88E3	0.88E3	−0.46E4	−0.43E4
CADULTM	−1600.0	−0.30E1	−0.30E1	0.16E2	0.16E2
USIP	−760.0	−1.1	−1.1	0.61E1	0.58E1
BIP2	−240.0	−0.36	−0.36	0.20E1	0.19E1
WEJIP2	−160.0	−0.23	−0.23	0.13E1	0.12E1
OIP2	−74.0	−0.11	−0.11	0.60E2	0.57E2
CMARIN	0.54E2	−0.55E5	−0.55E5	0.30E6	0.28E6
FA	170.0	0.22E1	0.22E1	−0.13E1	−0.12E1
ACT	41.0	0.54E1	0.54E1	−0.29E2	−0.28E2
W	520.0	−0.31E1	−0.31E1	−0.41E1	−0.39E1

[a] The table employs a version of exponential format. Thus 0.xx*En* implies *n* decimal places to the right of the decimal. For examples, 0.35E2 would be read as 0.0035.

	66 RSA	67 CRS	68 WCRS	69 RF	70 RFD
GG	−0.11E4	−0.11E4	−0.12E5	−0.11E4	0.21E6
GWASR	−0.10E4	−0.99E5	−0.11E5	−0.99E5	0.18E6
YMILIT	−0.11E4	−0.11E4	−0.12E5	−0.11E4	0.19E6
XNATO	0.44E6	0.43E6	0.45E7	0.43E6	−0.70E8
TW	0.11E4	0.11E4	0.12E5	0.11E4	−0.19E6
TNW	0.62E5	0.61E5	0.67E6	0.61E5	−0.96E7
SIFUD	0.70E2	0.69E2	0.76E3	0.69E2	−0.13E3
OCO	−0.76E4	−0.75E4	−0.83E5	−0.75E4	0.14E5
OCBE	−0.79E4	−0.78E4	−0.86E5	−0.78E4	0.14E5
DLGC	−0.83E4	−0.81E4	−0.90E5	−0.81E4	0.15E5
SDINP	−0.43E3	−0.42E3	−0.47E4	−0.42E3	0.77E5
SOFIC2	−0.69E7	−0.68E7	−0.75E8	−0.68E7	0.12E8
SOCIA2	0.19E5	0.19E5	0.21E6	0.19E5	−0.35E7
OR	0.33E4	0.33E4	0.36E5	0.33E4	−0.61E6
RESB2	0.68E2	0.66E2	0.74E3	0.66E2	−0.12E3
HLA	−0.17E5	−0.16E5	−0.17E6	−0.16E5	0.22E7
SG	0.15E4	0.14E4	0.16E5	0.14E4	−0.27E6
TB	0.98E4	0.64E4	0.71E5	0.96E4	−0.18E5
ATM	0.20E3	0.20E3	0.22E4	0.20E3	−0.37E5
R	−0.35E2	−0.23E2	−0.26E3	−0.35E2	0.64E4
RLA	−0.84E3	−0.54E3	−0.60E4	−0.82E3	0.15E4
R2	−0.41E3	−0.40E3	−0.45E4	−0.40E3	0.73E5
USIS	0.96E2	−0.60E3	−0.67E4	0.94E2	−0.17E3
USIL	−0.62E1	−0.61E1	−0.68E2	−0.61E1	0.11E2
PTA	0.36E2	0.35E2	0.39E3	0.35E2	−0.65E4
PGMUS	0.38E3	0.38E3	0.39E4	0.38E3	−0.61E5
PGMO	0.16E3	0.16E3	0.17E4	0.16E3	−0.26E5
PGMCB	0.51E1	0.50E1	0.56E2	0.50E1	−0.90E3
PMND	0.76E2	0.75E2	0.83E3	0.75E2	−0.14E3
PMD	−0.97E3	−0.96E3	−0.11E3	−0.96E3	0.18E4
PGMIB	−0.27E1	−0.27E1	−0.30E2	−0.27E1	0.50E3
PGMIMB	0.0	0.0	0.0	0.0	0.0
PGMFLC	−0.11E1	−0.11E1	−0.12E2	−0.11E1	0.20E3
PMUSP1	−0.46E4	−0.46E4	−0.29E5	−0.46E4	0.0
CADULTM	0.17E2	0.16E2	0.18E3	0.16E2	−0.30E4
USIP	0.62E1	0.61E1	0.67E2	0.61E1	−0.11E2
BIP2	0.20E1	0.20E1	0.22E2	0.20E1	−0.36E3
WEJIP2	0.13E1	0.13E1	0.14E2	0.13E1	−0.23E3
OIP2	0.61E2	0.60E2	0.67E3	0.60E2	−0.11E3
CMARIN	0.30E6	0.30E6	0.33E7	0.30E6	−0.54E8
FA	−0.13E1	−0.13E1	−0.14E2	−0.17E1	−0.37E2
ACT	−0.30E2	−0.29E2	−0.32E3	−0.29E2	0.53E4
W	−0.41E1	−0.41E1	−0.45E2	−0.41E1	0.75E3

(continued on next page)

TABLE 7. Impact multipliers[a] (continued)

	71 CRFD	72 CIS	73 CIL	74 DIL	75 PFS
GG	0.21E6	−0.82E5	−0.32E5	−0.32E5	0.81E5
GWASR	0.18E6	−0.72E5	−0.29E5	−0.29E5	−0.23E4
YMILIT	0.19E6	−0.81E5	−0.32E5	−0.32E5	−0.10E4
XNATO	−0.70E8	0.31E6	0.13E6	0.13E6	−0.89E6
TW	−0.19E6	0.81E5	0.32E5	0.32E5	0.10E4
TNW	−0.96E7	0.45E5	0.18E5	0.18E5	0.64E5
SIFUD	−0.13E3	0.50E2	0.20E2	0.20E2	0.62E2
OCO	0.14E5	−0.55E4	−0.22E4	−0.22E4	−0.18E3
OCBE	0.14E5	−0.57E4	−0.23E4	−0.23E4	−0.19E3
DLGC	0.15E5	−0.60E4	−0.24E4	−0.24E4	−0.72E4
SDINP	0.77E5	−0.31E3	−0.12E3	−0.12E3	−0.36E3
SOFIC2	0.12E8	−0.50E7	−0.20E7	−0.20E7	−0.39E6
SOCIA2	−0.35E7	0.14E5	0.55E6	0.55E6	0.11E4
OR	−0.61E6	0.24E4	0.96E5	0.96E5	0.29E4
RESB2	−0.12E3	0.49E2	0.19E2	0.19E2	0.72E2
HLA	0.22E7	−0.12E5	−0.47E6	−0.47E6	0.11E7
SG	−0.27E6	0.11E4	0.57E4	0.57E4	0.13E4
TB	−0.18E5	0.33E2	0.11E2	0.11E2	0.57E4
ATM	−0.37E3	0.15E3	0.33E2	0.33E2	0.18E3
R	0.64E4	−0.12	−0.39E1	−0.39E1	−0.21E2
RLA	0.15E4	−0.28E1	−0.93E2	−0.93E2	−0.49E3
R2	0.73E5	−0.29E3	−0.12E3	−0.12E3	−0.10E3
USIS	−0.17E3	0.41E4	−0.16E4	−0.16E4	−0.54E3
USIL	0.11E2	−0.45E1	0.16E2	−1.0	−0.55E1
PTA	−0.65E4	0.26E2	0.10E2	0.10E2	0.75E4
PGMUS	−0.61E5	0.27E3	0.11E3	0.11E3	−0.78E3
PGMO	−0.26E5	0.12E3	0.47E4	0.47E4	−0.33E3
PGMCB	−0.90E3	0.37E1	0.15E1	0.15E1	0.15
PMND	−0.14E3	0.55E2	0.22E2	0.22E2	−0.39E2
PMD	0.18E4	−0.70E3	−0.28E3	−0.28E3	0.10E2
PGMIB	0.50E3	−0.20E1	−0.78E2	−0.78E2	0.64E1
PGMIMB	0.0	0.0	0.0	0.0	0.0
PGMFLC	0.20E3	−0.78E2	−0.31E2	−0.31E2	−0.94E2
PMUSP1	0.0	−0.34E4	−0.12E4	−0.12E4	0.96E4
CADULTM	−0.30E4	0.12E2	0.48E3	0.48E3	0.12
USIP	−0.11E2	0.45E1	0.18E1	0.18E1	0.67E1
BIP2	−0.36E3	0.14E1	0.57E2	0.57E2	0.21E1
WEJIP2	−0.23E3	0.92E2	0.37E2	0.37E2	0.14E1
OIP2	−0.11E3	0.44E2	0.18E2	0.18E2	0.65E2
CMARIN	−0.54E8	0.22E6	0.86E7	0.86E7	−0.61E6
FA	−0.37E2	0.88E3	−0.35E3	−0.35E3	−0.12E1
ACT	0.53E4	−0.21E2	−0.85E3	−0.85E3	−0.79E3
W	0.75E3	−0.30E1	0.48E3	0.48E3	−0.37E1

[a] The table employs a version of exponential format. Thus 0.xx*En* implies *n* decimal places to the right of the decimal. For example, 0.35E2 would be read as 0.0035.

	76 PNDB	77 PDB	78 PSB	79 PNDPO	80 PDPO
GG	−0.98E5	0.33E6	−0.20E4	0.52E5	0.13E4
GWASR	−0.28E4	−0.13E4	−0.67E4	0.26E4	0.26E4
YMILIT	0.80E5	0.31E5	0.21E4	−0.82E5	−0.87E5
XNATO	−0.45E6	−0.36E6	−0.92E6	0.33E6	0.23E6
TW	−0.80E5	−0.31E5	−0.21E4	0.82E5	0.87E5
TNW	−0.72E6	0.14E5	0.45E5	−0.45E5	0.68E6
SIFUD	0.23E2	0.21E2	0.10E1	−0.61E2	−0.25E2
OCO	−0.91E4	−0.75E4	−0.29E3	0.15E3	0.76E4
OCBE	−0.92E4	−0.76E4	−0.30E3	0.15E3	0.76E4
DLGC	−0.27E4	−0.25E4	−0.12E3	0.72E4	0.30E4
SDINP	−0.21E3	−0.17E3	−0.87E3	0.48E3	0.24E3
SOFIC2	−0.21E6	−0.17E6	−0.62E6	0.30E6	0.16E6
SOCIA2	0.59E5	0.47E5	0.17E4	−0.82E5	−0.45E5
OR	0.11E4	0.10E4	0.49E4	−0.29E4	−0.12E4
RESB2	0.17E2	0.23E2	0.96E2	−0.62E2	−0.16E2
HLA	0.61E6	−0.13E4	0.34E5	0.18E5	−0.14E4
SG	0.48E5	0.45E5	0.22E4	−0.13E4	−0.52E5
TB	0.21E4	0.20E4	0.96E4	−0.56E4	−0.23E4
ATM	0.66E4	0.63E4	0.30E3	−0.18E3	−0.72E4
R	−0.76E3	−0.72E3	−0.35E2	0.20E2	0.83E3
RLA	−0.18E3	−0.17E3	−0.82E3	0.48E3	0.20E3
R2	−0.22E3	−0.71E4	−0.66E3	0.29E3	0.28E3
USIS	−0.20E3	−0.19E3	−0.91E3	0.53E3	0.22E3
USIL	−0.20E1	−0.19E1	−0.92E1	0.54E1	0.22E1
PTA	−0.35E2	0.41E2	0.29E1	−0.27E1	−0.17E2
PGMUS	−0.40E3	−0.31E3	−0.81E3	0.29E3	0.20E3
PGMO	−0.17E3	−0.13E3	−0.34E3	0.12E3	0.85E4
PGMCB	0.60E1	0.49E1	0.15	−0.65E1	−0.38E1
PMND	0.21	0.82E1	−0.16E2	0.19	−0.69E1
PMD	−0.12E2	0.26E1	−0.20E2	−0.71E2	0.27E1
PGMIB	0.45E1	0.22E1	0.42E1	0.77E2	−0.23E1
PGMIMB	0.0	0.0	0.0	0.0	0.0
PGMFLC	−0.34E2	−0.33E2	−0.16E1	0.93E2	0.38E2
PMUSP1	0.49E4	0.37E4	0.99E4	−0.34E4	−0.25E4
CADULTM	0.69E1	0.54E1	0.19	−0.87E1	−0.51E1
USIP	0.16E1	0.21E1	0.88E1	−0.56E1	−0.15E1
BIP2	0.50E2	0.69E2	0.28E1	−0.18E1	−0.49E2
WEJIP2	0.32E2	0.44E2	0.18E1	−0.12E1	−0.31E2
OIP2	0.15E2	0.21E2	0.87E2	−0.56E2	−0.15E2
CMARIN	−0.31E6	−0.25E6	−0.63E6	0.23E6	0.16E6
FA	−0.43E2	−0.40E2	−0.19E1	0.11E1	0.46E2
ACT	−0.16E2	−0.53E3	−0.47E2	0.21E2	0.20E2
W	−0.13E1	−0.13E1	−0.61E1	0.36E1	0.15E1

(continued on next page)

TABLE 7. Impact multipliers[a] (continued)

	81 PSPO	82 PNDS	83 PMCRPD	84 PDPCG	85 PTR
GG	−0.12E4	−0.14E4	0.20E4	−0.96E5	0.25E4
GWASR	−0.42E4	−0.43E4	0.38E4	−0.29E4	0.51E4
YMILIT	0.14E4	0.13E4	0.53E5	0.56E5	−0.98E6
XNATO	−0.49E6	−0.64E6	0.0	−0.43E6	0.16E6
TW	−0.14E4	−0.13E4	−0.53E5	−0.56E5	0.98E6
TNW	0.49E5	0.14E5	−0.70E5	0.11E5	−0.75E5
SIFUD	0.81E2	0.55E2	−0.11E1	0.38E2	−0.12E1
OCO	−0.21E3	−0.17E3	0.19E3	−0.11E3	0.24E3
OCBE	−0.21E3	−0.17E3	0.19E3	−0.12E3	0.24E3
DLGC	−0.96E4	−0.65E4	0.12E3	−0.46E4	0.14E3
SDINP	−0.66E3	−0.47E3	0.72E3	−0.31E3	0.88E3
SOFIC2	−0.42E6	−0.38E6	0.31E6	−0.25E6	0.42E6
SOCIA2	0.12E4	0.10E4	−0.86E5	0.68E5	−0.12E4
OR	0.39E4	0.26E4	−0.50E4	0.18E4	−0.58E4
RESB2	0.79E2	0.49E2	−0.99E2	0.34E2	−0.11E1
HLA	0.45E5	0.17E5	0.64E5	−0.48E5	0.63E7
SG	0.17E4	0.12E4	−0.22E4	0.81E5	−0.26E4
TB	0.75E4	0.51E4	−0.98E4	0.36E4	−0.11E3
ATM	0.24E3	0.16E3	−0.31E3	0.11E3	−0.36E3
R	−0.27E2	−0.18E2	0.35E2	−0.13E2	0.41E2
RLA	−0.65E3	−0.44E3	0.84E3	−0.30E3	0.97E3
R2	−0.46E3	−0.39E3	0.66E3	−0.27E3	0.78E3
USIS	−0.72E3	−0.48E3	0.93E3	−0.34E3	0.11E2
USIL	−0.73E1	−0.49E1	0.94E1	−0.34E1	0.11
PTA	0.32E1	0.96E2	−0.29E2	−0.55E3	1.0
PGMUS	−0.43E3	−0.56E3	0.0	−0.37E3	0.14E3
PGMO	−0.18E3	−0.24E3	0.0	−0.16E3	0.61E4
PGMCB	0.92E1	0.96E1	0.90	0.76E1	−0.14
PMND	−0.19	0.12	−0.37E1	0.30E1	−0.12
PMD	−0.42E2	−0.16E2	0.96E2	−0.87E2	0.24E2
PGMIB	0.14E2	0.44E1	−0.13E1	0.39E1	−0.14E1
PGMIMB	0.0	0.0	0.0	0.0	0.0
PGMFLC	−0.12E1	−0.84E2	0.16E1	−0.59E2	0.19E1
PMUSP1	0.53E4	0.68E4	0.0	0.46E4	−0.15E4
CADULTM	0.12	0.12	−0.77E1	0.76E1	−0.11
USIP	0.72E1	0.45E1	−0.90E1	0.31E1	−0.10
BIP2	0.23E1	0.14E1	−0.29E1	0.10E1	−0.34E1
WEJIP2	0.15E1	0.92E2	−0.19E1	0.64E2	−0.21E1
OIP2	0.71E2	0.44E2	−0.89E2	0.31E2	−0.10E1
CMARIN	−0.34E6	−0.44E6	−0.10E8	−0.29E6	0.11E6
FA	−0.15E1	−0.10E1	0.20E1	−0.72E2	0.23E1
ACT	−0.34E2	−0.28E2	0.48E2	−0.20E2	0.57E2
W	−0.48E1	−0.33E1	0.62E1	−0.23E1	0.72E1

[a] The table employs a version of exponential format. Thus 0.xx*En* implies *n* decimal places to the right of the decimal. For example, 0.35E2 would be read as 0.0035.

	86 PTC	87 PFC	88 PMNRC	89 PMIRPD	90 PDPIG
GG	−0.12E4	0.28E5	0.28E5	0.13E4	−0.16E5
GWASR	−0.38E4	−0.24E4	−0.24E4	0.55E4	−0.43E4
YMILIT	0.12E4	−0.79E5	−0.79E5	0.31E4	−0.18E4
XNATO	−0.57E6	−0.92E6	−0.92E6	0.85E6	−0.12E5
TW	−0.12E4	0.79E5	0.79E5	−0.31E4	0.18E4
TNW	0.12E5	0.31E5	0.31E5	−0.15E4	0.82E5
SIFUD	0.49E2	0.27E2	0.27E2	−0.15E1	0.79E2
OCO	−0.15E3	−0.12E3	−0.12E3	0.32E3	−0.23E3
OCBE	−0.15E3	−0.13E3	−0.13E3	0.33E3	−0.24E3
DLGC	−0.58E4	−0.32E4	−0.32E4	0.18E3	−0.93E4
SDINP	−0.42E3	−0.13E3	−0.13E3	0.88E3	−0.43E3
SOFIC2	−0.33E6	−0.30E6	−0.30E6	0.60E6	−0.51E6
SOCIA2	0.92E5	0.83E5	0.83E5	−0.17E4	0.14E4
OR	0.23E4	0.13E4	0.13E4	−0.73E4	0.38E4
RESB2	0.43E2	0.31E2	0.31E2	−0.15E1	0.84E2
HLA	0.15E5	−0.65E6	−0.65E6	0.36E5	−0.19E5
SG	0.10E4	0.57E5	0.57E5	−0.32E4	0.17E4
TB	0.45E4	0.25E4	0.25E4	−0.14E3	0.73E4
ATM	0.14E3	0.79E4	0.79E4	−0.45E3	0.23E3
R	−0.16E2	−0.90E3	−0.90E3	0.51E2	−0.26E2
RLA	−0.39E3	−0.21E3	−0.21E3	0.12E2	−0.63E3
R2	−0.35E3	0.46E3	0.46E3	−0.13E3	0.50E3
USIS	−0.43E3	−0.24E3	−0.24E3	0.13E2	−0.70E3
USIL	−0.44E1	−0.24E1	−0.24E1	0.14	−0.71E1
PTA	0.86E2	−0.21E2	−0.21E2	−0.20E2	−0.14E2
PGMUS	−0.50E3	−0.81E3	−0.81E3	0.74E3	−0.11E2
PGMO	−0.21E3	−0.34E3	−0.34E3	0.31E3	−0.45E3
PGMCB	0.85E1	0.10	0.10	−0.25	0.19
PMND	0.11	0.16E3	0.15E3	−0.12E1	0.43E2
PMD	−0.14E2	0.38E3	0.38E3	0.86E3	0.86E4
PGMIB	0.39E1	0.44	0.43	1.0	0.89E1
PGMIMB	0.0	0.0	0.0	0.0	0.0
PGMFLC	−0.75E2	−0.40E2	−0.40E2	0.23E1	−0.12E1
PMUSP1	0.62E4	0.99E4	0.99E4	−0.93E4	0.13E3
CADULTM	0.10	0.10	0.10	−0.17	0.16
USIP	0.40E1	0.28E1	0.28E1	−0.14	0.77E1
BIP2	0.13E1	0.91E2	0.91E2	−0.46E1	0.25E1
WEJIP2	0.81E2	0.58E2	0.58E2	−0.29E1	0.16E1
OIP2	0.39E2	0.28E2	0.28E2	−0.14E1	0.76E2
CMARIN	−0.39E6	−0.63E6	−0.63E6	0.58E6	−0.83E6
FA	−0.91E2	−0.51E2	−0.51E2	0.28E1	−0.15E1
ACT	−0.25E2	0.32E2	0.32E2	−0.68E3	0.34E2
W	−0.29E1	−0.16E1	−0.16E1	0.90E1	−0.47E1

(continued on next page)

TABLE 7. Impact multipliers[a] (continued)

	91 PWIM	92 PDPIM	93 PXB	94 PXC	95 PMGSR
GG	0.52E5	0.26E5	−0.62E4	−0.49E4	0.66E5
GWASR	−0.21E5	−0.75E5	−0.77E4	−0.60E4	0.59E5
YMILIT	0.12E5	−0.32E5	−0.32E4	−0.25E4	0.66E5
XNATO	−0.33E6	−0.28E6	−0.61E6	−0.48E6	−0.25E6
TW	−0.12E5	0.32E5	0.32E4	0.25E4	−0.66E5
TNW	−0.47E6	0.20E5	0.20E5	0.15E5	−0.36E5
SIFUD	−0.75E3	0.20E2	0.18E2	0.14E2	−0.41E2
OCO	−0.17E4	−0.59E4	−0.51E4	−0.40E4	0.45E4
OCBE	−0.17E4	−0.59E4	−0.58E4	−0.46E4	0.46E4
DLGC	0.90E5	−0.23E4	−0.15E4	−0.12E4	0.49E4
SDINP	0.50E4	−0.12E3	0.84E4	0.66E4	0.25E3
SOFIC2	−0.66E7	−0.13E6	−0.13E6	−0.99E7	0.40E7
SOCIA2	0.18E5	0.35E5	0.35E5	0.28E5	−0.11E5
OR	−0.36E5	0.94E5	0.87E5	0.68E5	−0.20E4
RESB2	−0.44E3	0.23E2	0.20E1	0.16E1	−0.40E2
HLA	0.51E6	0.46E8	−0.10E4	−0.81E5	0.98E6
SG	−0.16E5	0.42E5	0.38E5	0.30E5	−0.86E5
TB	−0.70E5	0.18E4	0.17E4	0.13E4	−0.38E4
ATM	−0.22E4	0.58E4	0.53E4	0.42E4	−0.12E3
R	0.25E3	−0.66E3	−0.61E3	−0.48E3	0.14E2
RLA	0.60E4	−0.16E3	−0.14E3	−0.11E3	0.33E3
R2	0.10E3	−0.32E4	−0.93E3	−0.73E3	0.24E3
USIS	0.66E4	−0.17E3	−0.16E3	−0.13E3	0.36E3
USIL	0.67E2	−0.18E1	−0.16E1	−0.13E1	0.37E1
PTA	−0.11E2	0.24E4	−0.78E2	−0.61E2	−0.21E2
PGMUS	−0.29E3	−0.25E3	−0.53E3	−0.42E3	−0.22E3
PGMO	−0.12E3	−0.10E3	−0.23E3	−0.18E3	−0.94E4
PGMCB	0.18E1	0.48E1	0.49E2	0.38E2	0.28
PMND	−0.32E2	−0.13E2	0.48E1	0.38E1	−0.45E2
PMD	0.52E3	0.32E3	−0.62E2	−0.48E2	0.57E3
PGMIB	0.22E1	0.21E1	0.58E1	0.46E1	0.34
PGMIMB	0.32	0.0	0.0	0.0	0.0
PGMFLC	0.12E2	−0.30E2	−0.27E2	−0.21E2	0.64E2
PMUSP1	0.34E4	0.31E4	0.65E4	0.53E4	0.28E4
CADULTM	0.27E1	0.39E1	0.40E1	0.31E1	−0.98E3
USIP	−0.40E2	0.21E1	0.18	0.14	−0.36E1
BIP2	−0.13E2	0.69E2	0.59E1	0.46E1	−0.12E1
WEJIP2	−0.84E3	0.44E2	0.38E1	0.30E1	−0.75E2
OIP2	−0.40E3	0.21E2	0.18E1	0.14E1	−0.36E2
CMARIN	−0.23E6	−0.20E6	−0.42E6	−0.33E6	−0.18E6
FA	0.14E2	−0.37E2	−0.34E2	−0.27E2	0.77E2
ACT	0.73E3	−0.25E3	−0.66E2	−0.52E2	0.17E2
W	0.45E2	−0.12E1	−0.11E1	−0.85E2	0.24E1

[a] The table employs a version of exponential format. Thus 0.xx*En* implies *n* decimal places to the right of the decimal. For example, 0.35E2 would be read as 0.0035.

	96 PMNDR	97 PMDR	98 PMKR	99 PMIMR	100 FORCEM
GG	0.11E4	0.11E4	0.11E4	0.11E4	0.28E4
GWASR	0.97E5	0.97E5	0.95E5	0.98E5	0.38E4
YMILIT	0.11E4	0.11E4	0.11E4	0.11E4	0.15E4
XNATO	−0.43E6	0.42E6	−0.41E6	−0.43E6	0.11E5
TW	−0.11E4	−0.11E4	−0.11E4	−0.11E4	−0.15E4
TNW	−0.60E5	−0.60E5	−0.59E5	−0.61E5	−0.25E6
SIFUD	−0.67E2	−0.67E2	−0.66E2	−0.68E2	−0.64E4
OCO	0.74E4	0.73E4	0.72E4	0.75E4	0.43E5
OCBE	0.76E4	0.76E4	0.75E4	0.77E4	0.34E5
DLGC	0.80E4	0.79E4	0.78E4	0.81E4	0.16E5
SDINP	0.41E3	0.41E3	0.41E3	0.42E3	−0.64E3
SOFIC2	0.66E7	0.66E7	0.65E7	0.67E7	0.85E8
SOCIA2	−0.18E5	−0.18E5	−0.18E5	−0.19E5	−0.23E6
OR	−0.32E4	−0.32E4	−0.31E4	−0.33E4	−0.30E6
RESB2	−0.65E2	−0.65E2	−0.64E2	−0.66E2	0.22E2
HLA	0.16E5	0.16E5	0.16E5	0.16E5	0.48E5
SG	−0.14E4	−0.14E4	−0.14E4	−0.14E4	−0.13E6
TB	−0.62E4	−0.62E4	−0.61E4	−0.63E4	−0.59E6
ATM	−0.20E3	−0.20E3	−0.19E3	−0.20E3	−0.19E5
R	0.23E2	0.22E2	0.22E2	0.23E2	0.21E4
RLA	0.53E3	0.53E3	0.52E3	0.54E3	0.51E5
R2	0.39E3	0.39E3	0.39E3	0.40E3	0.39E3
USIS	0.59E3	0.59E3	0.58E3	0.60E3	0.56E5
USIL	0.60E1	0.60E1	0.59E1	0.61E1	0.57E3
PTA	−0.34E2	−0.34E2	−0.34E2	−0.35E2	0.46E2
PGMUS	−0.37E3	−0.36E3	−0.36E3	−0.37E3	0.94E3
PGMO	−0.16E3	−0.15E3	−0.15E3	−0.16E3	0.40E3
PGMCB	−0.49E1	−0.49E1	−0.48E1	−0.50E1	0.16E1
PMND	1.0	−0.73E2	−0.72E2	−0.74E2	−0.23E1
PMD	0.94E3	1.0	0.92E3	0.95E3	0.29E2
PGMIB	0.26E1	0.26E1	1.1	0.27E1	−0.19E1
PGMIMB	0.0	0.0	0.0	1.0	0.0
PGMFLC	0.10E1	0.10E1	0.10E1	0.11E1	−0.50E4
PMUSP1	0.46E4	0.46E4	0.43E4	0.46E4	−0.12E3
CADULTM	−0.16E2	−0.16E2	−0.16E2	−0.16E2	0.55
USIP	−0.60E1	−0.59E1	−0.58E1	−0.60E1	0.20E1
BIP2	−0.19E1	−0.19E1	−0.19E1	−0.20E1	0.65E2
WEJIP2	−0.12E1	−0.12E1	−0.12E1	−0.12E1	0.41E2
OIP2	−0.59E2	−0.59E2	−0.58E2	−0.59E2	0.20E2
CMARIN	−0.29E6	−0.29E6	−0.28E6	−0.29E6	0.74E6
FA	0.13E1	0.13E1	0.12E1	0.13E1	0.12E3
ACT	0.29E2	0.29E2	0.28E2	0.29E2	0.28E2
W	0.40E1	0.40E1	0.39E1	0.40E1	0.38E3

(continued on next page)

TABLE 7. Impact multipliers[a] (continued)

	101 EMPM	102 EMPNM	103 PEREMP	104 UNEMPM	105 AHP
GG	0.21	0.12E3	0.54E4	−0.31E3	0.69E2
GWASR	0.29	0.16E3	0.73E4	−0.42E3	0.93E2
YMILIT	0.11	0.61E4	0.28E4	−0.16E3	0.36E2
XNATO	0.80E2	0.44E5	0.20E5	−0.12E4	0.26E3
TW	−0.11	−0.61E4	−0.28E4	0.16E3	−0.36E2
TNW	−0.19E2	−0.11E5	−0.48E6	0.29E5	−0.63E4
SIFUD	−0.47	−0.26E3	−0.12E3	0.70E3	−0.16E1
OCO	0.32E1	0.17E4	0.81E5	−0.47E4	0.10E2
OCBE	0.26E1	0.14E4	0.65E5	−0.38E4	0.84E3
DLGC	0.12E1	0.66E5	0.30E5	−0.18E4	0.39E3
SDINP	−4.8	−0.26E2	−0.12E2	0.71E2	−0.16
SOFIC2	0.63E4	0.35E7	0.16E7	−0.94E7	0.21E5
SOCIA2	−0.17E2	−0.96E6	−0.44E6	0.26E5	−0.57E4
OR	−0.23E2	−0.13E5	−0.58E6	0.34E5	−0.74E4
RESB2	16.0	0.89E2	0.41E2	−0.24E1	0.53
HLA	0.36E1	0.20E4	0.92E5	−0.53E4	0.12E2
SG	−1.00E3	−0.55E6	−0.25E6	0.15E5	−0.33E4
TB	−0.44E2	−0.24E5	−0.11E5	0.65E5	−0.14E3
ATM	−0.14E1	−0.77E5	−0.35E5	0.21E4	−0.45E3
R	0.16	0.88E4	0.41E4	−0.24E3	0.52E2
RLA	0.38E1	0.21E4	0.96E5	−0.56E4	0.12E2
R2	2.9	0.16E2	0.74E3	−0.43E2	0.94E1
USIS	0.42E1	0.23E4	0.11E4	−0.62E4	0.14E2
USIL	4.2	0.23E2	0.11E2	−0.63E2	0.14
PTA	34.0	0.19E1	0.87E2	−0.50E1	1.1
PGMUS	7.0	0.39E2	0.18E2	−0.10E1	0.23
PGMO	3.0	0.16E2	0.76E3	−0.44E2	0.97E1
PGMCB	120.0	0.67E1	0.31E1	−0.18	4.0
PMND	−170.0	−0.93E1	−0.43E1	0.25	−5.5
PMD	21.0	0.12E1	0.54E2	−0.31E1	0.69
PGMIB	−140.0	−0.76E1	−0.35E1	0.20	−4.5
PGMIMB	0.0	0.0	0.0	0.0	0.0
PGMFLC	−3.7	−0.20E3	−0.94E4	0.55E3	−0.12E1
PMUSP1	−0.88	−0.48E3	−0.22E3	0.13E2	−0.29E1
CADULTM	−21.0	−94.0	−0.12	0.74	−0.70
USIP	150.0	0.81E1	0.37E1	−0.22	4.8
BIP2	48.0	0.26E1	0.12E1	−0.71E1	1.6
WEJIP2	31.0	0.17E1	0.78E2	−0.45E1	1.0
OIP2	15.0	0.81E2	0.37E2	−0.22E1	0.48
CMARIN	0.55E2	0.30E5	0.14E5	−0.81E5	0.18E3
FA	0.89	0.49E3	0.23E3	−0.13E2	0.29E1
ACT	20.0	0.11E1	0.52E2	−0.30E1	0.67
W	2.8	0.15E2	0.72E3	−0.42E2	0.92E1

[a] The table employs a version of exponential format. Thus 0.xx*En* implies *n* decimal places to the right of the decimal. For example, 0.35E2 would be read as 0.0035.

	106 AHN	107 WR	108 WRS
GG	0.46E2	0.15E4	−0.50E4
GWASR	0.62E2	−0.51E4	−0.14E3
YMILIT	0.24E2	−0.23E4	0.52E4
XNATO	0.17E3	−0.18E5	−0.16E5
TW	−0.24E2	0.23E4	−0.52E4
TNW	−0.42E4	0.15E4	0.66E5
SIFUD	−0.10E1	0.14E1	0.20E1
OCO	0.69E3	−0.40E3	−0.56E3
OCBE	0.56E3	−0.40E3	−0.56E3
DLGC	0.26E3	−0.17E3	−0.24E3
SDINP	−0.10	−0.84E3	−0.17E2
SOFIC2	0.14E5	−0.84E6	−0.12E5
SOCIA2	−0.38E4	0.23E4	0.33E4
OR	−0.49E4	0.68E4	0.95E4
RESB2	0.35	0.16E1	0.18E1
HLA	0.78E3	−0.30E6	0.77E5
SG	−0.22E4	0.30E4	0.42E4
TB	−0.95E4	0.13E3	0.18E3
ATM	−0.30E3	0.42E3	0.58E3
R	0.34E2	−0.48E2	−0.66E2
RLA	0.82E3	−0.11E2	−0.16E2
R2	0.63E1	−0.29E3	−0.14E2
USIS	0.91E3	−0.13E2	−0.17E2
USIL	0.92E1	−0.13	−0.18
PTA	0.74	0.87E3	0.66E1
PGMUS	0.15	−0.16E2	−0.14E2
PGMO	0.64E1	−0.66E3	−0.59E3
PGMCB	2.6	0.22	0.25
PMND	−3.7	−0.66E2	−0.15E2
PMD	0.46	0.19E2	−0.51E2
PGMIB	−3.0	0.19E1	0.59E1
PGMIMB	0.0	0.0	0.0
PGMFLC	−0.80E2	−0.22E1	−0.30E1
PMUSP1	−0.19E1	0.19E3	0.17E3
CADULTM	−0.47	0.26	0.36
USIP	3.2	0.15	0.16
BIP2	1.0	0.49E1	0.52E1
WEJIP2	0.66	0.31E1	0.33E1
OIP2	0.32	0.15E1	0.16E1
CMARIN	0.12E3	−0.12E5	−0.11E5
FA	0.19E1	−0.27E1	−0.37E1
ACT	0.44	−0.23E2	−0.10E1
W	0.61E1	−0.85E1	−0.12

Strictly speaking, one cannot interpret this result as the increase in R required to offset the increase in CIL induced by a one percent rise in USIL, because impact multipliers are interpreted as *partial* derivatives. The notation $\partial E_i/\partial P_j$ is used to remind one that all P_k, $k \neq j$, are constant (at $\overline{P}_k$). However, the above interpretation may be made if (1) it is assumed that interactions are small and (2) it is accepted that the result is only an approximation. Then the change in R, measured in percentage points of the ratio of excess banking cash to actual liabilities, must be 0.041 times as great as the change in USIL, measured in percent per quarter.

4. *Debt management cum monetary policy*

Assume that for some autonomous reason (the Conversion Loan situation?) the government decides to increase the average term to maturity of its long-term debt (ATM). This has an effect—even if undesired—upon the interest rate (CIL). $\partial\text{CIL}/\partial\text{ATM}$ is positive. What increase in R is required per unit change (that is, a one month change) in ATM in order to offset the rise in CIL?

$$\frac{\partial\text{CIL}/\partial\text{ATM}}{-\partial\text{CIL}/\partial\text{R}} = \frac{0.0033}{0.039} = 0.085$$

This answer is subject to the qualifications noted with respect to example 3.

Apart from their use in the determination of relative efficiencies of policy tools, other aspects of the impact multipliers are of interest, namely, (1) the light they shed on the model from which they are derived, (2) their individual values as indicating absolute efficiencies of policy instruments or impacts of foreign and autonomous variables, and (3) relationships among large *sets* of impact multipliers, these relationships interpreted analogously to the relative efficiency conclusion pertaining to a set of two multipliers. It is from these standpoints that the tabulated impact multiplier matrix is considered in the remainder of this chapter. The examination is systematically arranged according to columns of the matrix, that is, by determined variables in order. However, it is often necessary to escape these confines within the analysis itself.

1. YR

$\partial YR/\partial GWASR > \partial YR/\partial GG$. An important reason for this divergence is the differential effects on BI (a component of YR). GG—but not GWASR—is a component of YG, and the direct effect of YG on BI is negative. The two multipliers are analogous to Keynes' investment multiplier. Their small sizes (1.4 and 1.1, respectively) are due to the fact they are initial impact multipliers. These multipliers portray the differential effect on determined variables *in the current quarter only*. Goldberger obtains 1.4 as the impact of government expenditure on goods and services on gross national expenditure,[6] and his structural model is annual rather than quarterly.

$\partial YR/\partial YMILIT$ and $\partial YR/\partial XNATO$ are expected to be of positive sign but less than the first two multipliers, which is so. YMILIT is in current—not constant—dollars. This might have accounted for the fact it is less than one, were military pay and allowances included in YR.

The XNATO multiplier is 0.04—much less than one. Again, XNATO is not included in YR. It is expected that its multiplier is less than that even of YMILIT. After all, YMILIT involves spending on the part of the government, and hence respending, while XNATO is a mere transfer of goods.

$\partial YR/\partial TW$ and $\partial YR/\partial TNW$ have proper sign. $\partial YR/\partial TW$ is larger in absolute value, reflecting the fact that the marginal propensity to spend out of wage exceeds that out of non-wage personal income.

$\partial YR/\partial OCO > \partial YR/\partial OCBE$. The reason is that OCO is stimulatory in two respects. (1) OCO is a subtraction from BM. Thus it lowers demand for Canadian dollars, hence depresses RS, therefore increases the effective price of Canadian imports, and finally decreases GM, a negative component of YR. (Although GMI is stimulated, it is outweighed by the decrease in GMC. GMIM is affected only to a lower order of magnitude because its price effect is lagged.) (2) OCO stimulates XO through OCDPXB. OCBE has only effect (1) associated with it.

6. *Ibid.*, p. 31.

OCO and OCBE are *subtractions* from YM (equation 72). This explains their relatively low multipliers for that variable. They are, however, not subtractions from YR, nor from YG.

∂YR/∂OR < 0 is explained by an effect similar to (1) above. A decline in reserves (increase in OR) implies a higher RS and therefore increased GM.

∂YR/∂SG, ∂YR/∂TB, ∂YR/∂ATM < 0; corresponding multipliers for YM are >0. ∂YR/∂R, ∂YR/∂RLA, ∂YR/∂R2 are all >0. Because R2 (and not R) appears in the CNR and EM equations, ∂YR/∂R2 is much greater than ∂YR/∂R. In fact the changeover in signs of corresponding multipliers of YR and YM does not extend to R2, which indeed retains its very value.

Multipliers with respect to USIS and USIL reverse signs when acting on YR and YM.

Considering price indexes of imports, those corresponding to a country breakdown (PGMUS and PGMO) yield positive multipliers; those corresponding to a commodity breakdown give multipliers of mixed sign. The signs correspond to the *direct* effects of these price changes on imports. Thus ∂YR/∂PGMCB > 0 and PMCRPD has a negative coefficient in equation 8 (substitution price effect between imports and domestic production); ∂YR/∂PGMIB < 0 and PMIRPD has a positive coefficient in equation 9 (complementary effect).

Similarly the sign of ∂YR/∂PGMFLC is consistent with that of the coefficient of PFLPD1 in equation 11, this in spite of the fact PGMFLC differs from its analogy which appears in PFLPD1 in both weighting schema (current- rather than base-weighted) and lag (nil as against one period).

∂YR/∂PMUSP1 > 0, indicating that on balance Canadian output responds positively to a switch of imports from U.S. to non-U.S. sources via a change in PMUSP1, and negatively to the reverse switching.

The sign of ∂YR/∂CADULTM appears unusual, until it is realized that in the model under consideration the only *direct* effect of CADULTM is on FORCEM, thus increasing unemployment.

The interesting feature of the foreign output multipliers is the close correspondence between direct effects and ultimate multipliers and the similarity of these relationships. This is shown in Table 8.

TABLE 8. Foreign output multipliers of YR.

Direct effect	Impact effect	Ratio
dXUS/dUSIP = 700	∂YR/∂USIP = 730	1.04
dXB/dBIP2 = 230	∂YR/∂BIP2 = 240	1.04
dXWEJ/dWEJIP2 = 140	∂YR/∂WEJIP2 = 150	1.07
dXO/dOIP2 = 69	∂YR/∂OIP2 = 73	1.06

∂YR/∂ACT > 0 is expected from the direct effects of ACT on construction, residential (RC) and non-residential (CNR).

W is basically favorable to YR, as shown by ∂YR/∂W > 0. But the net effect is a conglomeration of several effects—some favorable, some unfavorable, as is indicated by the varying signs of multipliers of components of YR.

2. PROD

Signs of corresponding multipliers are the same as those of YR. It is not surprising that division of YR by EMPM (yielding PROD) has this property even though EMPM is current endogenous, because EMPM is directly dependent on YR with a positive coefficient (equation 36).

3. YG

∂YG/∂GWASR < ∂YG/∂GG, in contradiction to corresponding multipliers of YR. In fact ∂YG/∂GWASR is even <1. The explanation: YR is inclusive of GWASR while YG is not; both include GG.

∂YG/∂TNW > 0. This is surprising. Note, however, that ∂YR/∂TNW is (in absolute value) small compared to ∂YR/∂TW. YG by definition is a sum of terms all of which are included in YR. The effect of TNW on that part of YR not included in YG must therefore be negative, and sufficiently negative to outweigh ∂YG/∂TNW.

The foreign output multipliers are uniformly greater for YG than for YR.

4. YM

∂YM/∂TNW > 0, as is ∂YG/∂TNW. In fact the former is rather larger, indicating that price effects—as well as differences in (real) components—account for the sign.

∂YM/∂OCO, ∂YM/∂OCBE < 0. This is partly explained by the fact OCO and OCBE enter negatively in the definition of YM. DLGC does not enter YM; yet ∂YM/∂DLGC < 0. However, it is smaller (in absolute value) than the former two multipliers.

∂YM/∂OR > 0, the opposite sign from the multipliers on real income. In this case, as in some others, real income and monetary income move in opposite directions, albeit components are not quite identical.

Again, multipliers of SG, TB, ATM differ in sign between YM and YR, YG. All three variables tend to tighten security markets (raise interest rates) as a direct effect (SG working through S). A priori signs for multipliers on income variables are not obvious. Real investment is a function of R2, not CIS, CIL. Otherwise this factor would make for a priori negativity of real income multipliers (which indeed occurs).

Again, the R, RLA, USIS, and USIL multipliers of YM differ in sign from those of YR and YG.

∂YM/∂CADULTM > 0 (and relatively large) while ∂YR/∂CADULTM, ∂YG/∂CADULTM < 0. With respect to foreign output multipliers, for each exogenous variable P, $\partial YM/\partial P > \partial YG/\partial P > \partial YR/\partial P$.

Changeovers in sign again occur for the multipliers with respect to FA and W.

What can account for so many changeovers in sign as between real and monetary income multipliers? It has been remarked that YG is a subset of YR in terms of components. Therefore let us compare YM and YR. Looking at equations 72 and 74, the differences are: (1) YM is a current-dollar while YR is a constant-dollar aggregate. (2) The final six terms of YM represent flows which do not appear in YR—even in their constant-dollar equivalents.

(1) allows price effects to influence the multipliers differently; (2) permits the six extra flows to act in a similar fashion.

5. CND; 6. CD; 7. CS

All consumption multipliers with respect to personal taxes are negative, the expected result. Furthermore, the TW multipliers are uniformly larger (in absolute value) than the TNW multipliers, again an expected relationship. The interesting feature here is the small size of the CD multiplier relative to the corresponding CND and CS multipliers. This is especially so for the TW multipliers: $\partial CD/\partial TW$ is only one tenth the size of $\partial CS/\partial TW$ and even a smaller fraction of $\partial CND/\partial TW$. TW and TNW are subtractions from disposable wage and non-wage incomes, respectively. Therefore it is possible to compare the direct effects of disposable income on consumer expenditures with its full impact effects via net personal taxes (Table 9).

TABLE 9. Income effects on consumer expenditures.

Expenditure	Wage income		Non-wage income	
	Direct effect	Impact effect	Direct effect	Impact effect
CND	0.37	0.39	0.062	0.045
CD	0.077	0.032	0.015	0.0087
CS	0.31	0.32	0.038	0.027

$\partial CND/\partial HLA$, $\partial CD/\partial HLA$, $\partial CS/\partial HLA$ all reflect a positive liquid assets effect on consumption, with $\partial CD/\partial HLA > \partial CND/\partial HLA > \partial CS/\partial HLA$, which corresponds to the relationship of the direct effect coefficients.

Viewing the CND, CD, and CS multipliers from an overall scope, two interesting results are apparent:

(1) Corresponding multipliers of CND and CS have the same sign. The only exception is the PTA multipliers.

(2) No such tendency to correspond exists for the multipliers of CD. In fact, if we exclude the PTA and PGMIMB multipliers from consideration (the former because of the mixed signs of the CND and CS multipliers, the latter because of its null effects), twenty-five of the CD multipliers differ in sign from the corresponding CND and CS multipliers, sixteen have the same sign.

8. TRN

It cannot be said that on the basis of a direct income effect ∂TRN/∂GG, ∂TRN/∂GWASR, and ∂TRN/∂TNW have unexpected signs, while ∂TRN/∂TW has the expected sign. This is because Canadian disposable income enters equation 12 only as part of a predetermined (lagged) variable (RYD1); thus there is no direct income effect.

However, the full impact effect of the foreign price variable PTA has not only the same sign but a slightly larger magnitude than its direct price effect (via PTR).

9. CNDFS; 10. CDFS; 11. SFS

The CNDFS, CDFS, and SFS multipliers have relationships similar to those among the CND, CD, and CS multipliers. Thus corresponding multipliers of CNDFS and SFS are of the same sign, excepting the PTA and PMND multipliers. Hence a second exception is added to PTA (the sole exception in the CND-CS relationship). However, in twelve cases there is a changeover in the common CNDFS-SFS sign with respect to the common CND-CS sign. The behavior of the CDFS multipliers in relation to CNDFS-SFS is similar to that of the CD multipliers in relation to CND-CS. CDFS multipliers differ in sign from the corresponding CNDFS-SFS multipliers in twenty-seven cases and have the same sign in thirteen instances.

12. GDI; 13. CME; 15. RC; 16. CNR; 17. EM; 20. FI; 21. XUS; 22. XB; 23. XWEJ; 32. GMFL

In the case of equations all of whose explanatory variables are predetermined, initial impact multipliers are identical to corresponding direct coefficients. There are eight current endogenous variables explained by such equations: RC, CNR, EM, FI, XUS, XB, XWEJ, GMFL. The current endogenous variable CME is defined as the sum of CNR and EM (equation 77). Its impact multipliers are the sums of corresponding multipliers of its component variables. Similarly, GDI is the sum of RC, CNR, EM and AGDI, where AGDI is predetermined. Hence, again, its impact multipliers are the sums of corresponding multipliers of RC, CNR, and EM.

14. MNRCC

∂MNRCC/∂TW, ∂MNRCC/∂TNW > 0. The corresponding CND, CD, and CS multipliers are <0. Thus increased personal direct taxes tend to increase current-dollar business investment (machinery, equipment, and non-residential construction) while decreasing constant-dollar consumption expenditure. A statement in terms of comparable units (deflated or non-deflated dollars) for consumption and investment cannot be made. *Constant-dollar* investment is independent of TW and TNW, depending, as it does, solely on *other* predetermined variables. *Current-dollar* consumption as a set of variables does not enter the model.

∂MNRCC/∂SIFUD > 0. This is a fact tending to make for a large ∂DIC/∂SIFUD, since SIF and MNRCC both stimulate DIC directly (equation 18).

∂MNRCC/∂R2 = ∂CME/∂R2. The multipliers, however, are not identically the same. A similar remark applies to ∂MNRCC/∂ACT and ∂CME/∂ACT.

∂MNRCC/∂PGMIB is positive and substantial. This is a logical result. Real (that is, constant-dollar) investment cannot be affected by PGMIB, depending as it does solely on a set of predetermined variables (exclusive of PGMIB). Because of the positive effect of PGMIB on PMNRC, the current-dollar cost of a determined constant-dollar investment expenditure must increase upon an increase in PGMIB.

18. FKFS

Its multipliers are interesting not for their own sake but rather for analyzing those of PFC in relation to PWIM.

19. BI

$\partial BI/\partial GG = -0.31$. This may be compared with the direct effect of YG on BI—a coefficient of -0.26. GG, of course, is an additive component of YG (equation 75).

All foreign activity multipliers are <0. This is logical because these variables stimulate merchandise exports, which are components of YG.

24. XO

Notice that $\partial XO/\partial OCO = \partial XO/\partial DLGC$. This is not obvious, since although the variables appear in OCDPXB in the same way, they enter other variables differently. Because PXB, the current endogenous component of OCDPXB, itself depends on two current endogenous variables, the way may be open for divergent multipliers. However, the direct effect of OCDPXB on XO is equal to the full impact effect of OCO or DLGC.

Again, the direct effect of OIP2 is equal to its full impact effect.

25. XFS

Note that $\partial XFS/\partial OCO \neq \partial XFS/\partial DLGC$. In fact the one is negative, the other positive. This is interesting in the light of the comments in the above paragraph.

The relationship of signs of corresponding multipliers of XO and XFS is interesting, especially when compared to analogous relationships. Excluding PGMIMB (which yields null effects), XO and XFS multipliers have the same sign in only three out of forty-two cases, two of which are DLGC and OIP2. In contrast to this, twenty-nine of corresponding CND-CNDFS multipliers are of the same sign, twenty-eight in the CS-SFS set, and forty in the CD-CDFS set. The CS-SFS pair of variables is not strictly analogous to the others because the numerator of SFS is not CS alone, but CS − TRN (equation 82). TRN is quantitatively small compared to CS. However, it is current endogenous and depends directly on a current endogenous variable, namely, PTR.

Consider, now, the relationship between XO and XFS. The numerator of XFS is not XO, but the sum of XO and four other variables. These variables are either predetermined (as is XC) or directly dependent on predetermined variables only (as are XUS, XB, and XWEJ). It has been remarked that variables which enter the model in the latter fashion have impact multipliers which are identical to corresponding direct coefficients. This implies an overwhelming proportion of the multipliers are identically zero. Therefore it is not enlightening (although it is legitimate) to consider the impact multipliers on the joint variable (XO + XUS + XB + XWEJ + XC). However, if desired, such joint multipliers could be obtained simply by summing the corresponding individual multipliers. In fact this procedure is valid even if more than one component variable of the sum is a function of a current endogenous variable. This follows from the fact that differentiation—even if partial—is a linear operator; thus $\partial \sum_i E_i/\partial P_j = \sum_i \partial E_i/\partial P_j$, where the E_i are current endogenous variables and P_j is a predetermined variable. (In particular, the CS and TRN multipliers may be subtracted to obtain the multipliers on (CS − TRN).) However, it is not true that the joint effect of a *set* of predetermined variables on a given current endogenous variable can be obtained as the sum of the impact multipliers of each variable in the set. An arbitrary impact multiplier, say, $\partial E_i/\partial P_j$, is valid only on the assumption that all predetermined variables other than P_j are unchanging. In the special case of a completely linear model the above reservation does not apply, because partial derivatives reduce to ordinary derivatives; and the joint effect of a number of predetermined variables is indeed the sum of their individual impact multipliers.

Returning to the fact that the set of (CS — TRN) multipliers may be derived by simply subtracting corresponding multipliers of CS and TRN, it is apparent from the tabulation that this involves only a unit change in the above count of twenty-eight cases of the same sign of the CS and SFS multipliers when the extension is made from CS to (CS — TRN). With only one exception, the absolute value of an arbitrary TRN multiplier is less than that of the corresponding CS multiplier. The exception is PTA, and because, further, $\partial CS/\partial PTA$ and $\partial TRN/\partial PTA$ are both negative, there is a changeover of sign in the transformation from CS to (CS — TRN). It is natural that $|\partial TRN/\partial PTA| > |\partial CS/\partial PTA|$, because of the large direct effect of PTA on TRN. The outcome is that the twenty-eight cases reduce to twenty-seven under the transformation.

26. GMUS; 27. GMO

GG and GWASR, expenditure policy variables, are stimulatory to both GMUS and GMO—a natural consequence of the dependence of imports on real income. Impact multipliers with respect to personal direct taxes are depressing—again the expected result.

R2, the direct effects of which are on real (constant-dollar) investment, stimulates GMUS and GMO, while R, the direct effect of which is on the short-term interest rate, is depressing.

USIS and USIL depress GMUS and GMO. This might ostensibly be explained by the fact increased USIL and USIS implies decreased DIL and RFD, respectively (via equations 66, 54, and 55), hence decreased autonomous capital inflows (equations 19, 20, and 21), therefore a depreciation of the Canadian dollar (via equation 1). However, a fall in the value of the dollar does not affect all imports negatively. The price effect is negative for GMC (equation 8) and GMIM (equation 10), positive for GMI (equation 9) and GMFL (equation 11).

Moreover, in equations 10 and 11 the price variable is lagged. Thus the explanation reduces to a comparison of the impact multipliers on GMC and GMI. The GMC impact multipliers are negative, the GMI positive—correct signs according to the above analysis—and the size (absolute value) of each of the GMC multipliers exceeds that of the corresponding GMI multiplier. The USIS and USIL multipliers of GMIM are positive (not a contradiction of the above argument since PIMPD1 is a lagged variable) but relatively small. The multipliers of GMFL are, as indicated above, zero. Now

$$\text{GM} = \text{GMC} + \text{GMI} + \text{GMIM} + \text{GMFL} + \text{GMR} + \text{CGRK} \quad \text{(equation 61)}$$

For any predetermined variable the impact on GM is the sum of the impact multipliers of the components of GM. Because GMR and CGRK are predetermined and $\partial\text{GMFL}/\partial\text{USIS}$, $\partial\text{GMFL}/\partial\text{USIL} = 0$, $\partial\text{GM}/\partial\text{USIL} = \partial\text{GMC}/\partial\text{USIL} + \partial\text{GMI}/\partial\text{USIL} + \partial\text{GMIM}/\partial\text{USIL}$, and similarly for USIS. Thus $\partial\text{GM}/\partial\text{USIL}$, $\partial\text{GM}/\partial\text{USIS} < 0$. However, it is not legitimate to pass from this to the *strong presumption* that $\partial\text{GMUS}/\partial\text{USIL}$, $\partial\text{GMO}/\partial\text{USIL}$ and $\partial\text{GMUS}/\partial\text{USIS}$, $\partial\text{GMO}/\partial\text{USIS}$ are negative, and to the *certainty* that their respective sums are of this sign because the relationship

$$\text{GMO} + \text{GMUS} = \text{GMC} + \text{GMI} + \text{GMIM} + \text{GMFL} + \text{GMR} + \text{CGRK}$$

is *not* a valid identity. Rather, a complicated identity in current dollars is valid (equation 62). This true relationship includes several current endogenous variables other than those in the spurious identity. However, a presumption may be put forward in favor of a tendency for sums of corresponding multipliers of GMO and GMUS to have values not widely divergent from corresponding multipliers of GM. ("Corresponding" multipliers means multipliers with respect to the same predetermined variable.) Let P be an arbitrary predetermined variable in our set of forty-three. Define the divergence between (∂GMUS/∂P + ∂GMO/∂P) and ∂GM/∂P to be

$$\begin{matrix}\text{small}\\ \text{large}\end{matrix}\ \text{according as}\ \frac{\partial \mathrm{GM}/\partial P - (\partial \mathrm{GMUS}/\partial P + \partial \mathrm{GMO}/\partial P)}{\partial \mathrm{GM}/\partial P}\ \begin{matrix}\leqq 1\\ \geqq 25\end{matrix}$$

According to this criterion the difference is small (and in many cases even very small) for all but three predetermined variables. These are PGMUS, PGMO, and PGMFLC. Now compare the signs of ∂GMUS/∂P and ∂GMO/∂P for all P. These signs are the same for all variables except four, namely, PGMUS, PGMO, PGMFLC (the three stated above) and PMUSP1. It is further interesting that sign (∂GMUS/∂P) = sign (∂GMO/∂P) $\Rightarrow$ sign (∂GM/∂P) = sign (∂GMUS/∂P) = sign (∂GMO/∂P).

Consider the GMUS and GMO impact multipliers with respect to PGMUS and PGMO. The fact that ∂GMUS/∂PGMUS > 0 and ∂GMO/∂PGMUS < 0 must not be taken as a contradiction of a negative price effect. In equation 7 the price ratio (PMUSP1) is a *lagged* variable. The fact that the size of ∂GMO/∂PGMUS is extremely large relative to that of ∂GMUS/∂PGMUS may be partially explained by the predetermined nature of PMUSP1 *and* the fact that PGMUS enters equation 62 (which defines GMO) as part of a negative term. A similar explanation pertains to the relationship of ∂GMUS/∂PGMO and ∂GMO/∂PGMO, for equation 62 may be rewritten:

$$\begin{aligned}\mathrm{GMO} = {} & (\mathrm{GMC} * \mathrm{PGMCC} + \mathrm{GMI} * \mathrm{PGMIC}\\ & + \mathrm{GMIM} * \mathrm{PGMIMC} + \mathrm{GMFL} * \mathrm{PGMFLC}\\ & + \mathrm{CGRK} * \mathrm{PXCL} * \mathrm{RSI} + \mathrm{GMR} * \mathrm{PGMR}\\ & - \mathrm{GMUS} * \mathrm{PGMUS})/\mathrm{PGMO} \quad \text{(equation 62')}\end{aligned}$$

PGMO enters positively but as a *denominator* to each term in the parentheses, and six of the seven terms are themselves positive.

A feature—in addition to the lagged nature of PMUSP1—which explains the relatively small size of the multipliers of

GMUS with respect to PGMUS and PGMO is the fact that the PGMUS and PGMO impact multipliers of GM, the only current endogenous variable upon which GMUS directly depends (equation 7), are themselves small compared to such multipliers of GMO.

∂GMUS/∂PMUSP1 and ∂GMO/∂PMUSP1 are equal in size, but opposite in sign. ∂GMUS/∂PMUSP1 has a value indistinguishable from that of the direct coefficient of PMUSP1 on GMUS. The intriguing result, however, is rather the equivalence of ∂GMO/∂PMUSP1 to ∂GMUS/∂PMUSP1 in size. That the sign of ∂GMO/∂PMUSP1 should be negative is quite consistent with equation 62 (or 62′, as it is written above). That the magnitude of ∂GMO/∂PMUSP1 should be equal to the magnitude of ∂GMUS/∂PMUSP1 is obvious only from a consideration of the effect of GMUS (itself decreased by PMUSP1) upon GMO, coupled with an average value of PGMO in the order of unity. In fact the mean of PGMO over the relevant time period is 0.98. Thus, other things being equal, the rise in GMO should be slightly greater than the fall in GMUS consequent upon an increase in PMUSP1. However, this assessment ignores many other indirect effects. These effects may be roughly (but only roughly) summarized by the multiplier ∂GM/∂PMUSP1. (This is an incomplete summarizer because it ignores the price variables in equation 62.) This approximation is equivalent to the false identity GMO = GM − GMUS. However, accepting this approximation momentarily, we notice that ∂GM/∂PMUSP1 is relatively small, but *negative*. The fall in GM (which variable we take as representing the six positive terms in equation 62′) compensates for the excess rise in GMO beyond that of GMUS due to the deviation of the mean value of PGMO from unity.

GM has a direct and "true" effect on GMUS. However, the small size of ∂GM/∂PMUSP1 implies an imperceptible effect of PMUSP1 upon GMUS via GM and/or that its effect is cancelled by a "gross" effect of PMUSP1 (exclusive of its operation via GM) in excess of the impact multiplier ∂GMUS/∂PMUSP1.

GMUS and GMO multipliers with respect to the foreign activity variables (USIP, BIP2, WEJIP2, and OIP2) are positive, presumably in part a reflection of the foreign trade multiplier. Increased foreign output increases Canadian exports, which add to Canadian output, hence increase Canadian imports. However, this hypothesis is better tested in the light of the multipliers of GM and its component variables (because of the direct role of Canadian activity variables in their explanation).

28. GM; 29. GMC; 30. GMI; 31. GMIM

As mentioned above, for any predetermined variable P

$$\partial \text{GM}/\partial P = \partial \text{GMC}/\partial P + \partial \text{GMI}/\partial P + \partial \text{GMIM}/\partial P$$

Multipliers of GMC, GMI, and GMIM (and hence GM) with respect to GG and GWASR are all positive, again (as in the case of the corresponding GMUS and GMO multipliers) reflecting a positive real income effect on imports.

TW and TNW multipliers are negative in all cases except GMIM (for which variable the TNW multiplier is positive but very small). However, the GMC multipliers are the largest—a reflection of the role of TW and TNW in the definition of YDMC, which directly enters equation 8 (explaining GMC). Furthermore, for each of the four import variables under consideration the size of the TW multiplier exceeds that of the TNW multiplier—presumably a consequence of the higher marginal propensity to spend out of wage than out of non-wage personal income. In addition, only the TNW—and not the TW—multiplier of GMIM is of positive sign.

It is interesting to consider the various import multipliers of SDINP. This autonomous variable, which reflects the growth of the stock of foreign direct investment in Canada, has a *positive* impact multiplier only for GMI—imports of investment goods—a relationship between foreign direct investment (the cause) and Canadian imports of goods for *real* investment (the effect). This relationship is apparently inexorable. It occurs in the face of negative signs for all other import multipliers with respect to SDINP, including those of GMUS and GMO. It occurs even though the model does not include direct investment as a cause of real investment. Indeed the model reverses the direction of causation: direct investment is a function of (current-dollar) real investment (equation 18). It is true that GMI is directly dependent on GDI (equation 9). However, the impact multiplier of GDI with respect to SDINP is zero, since GDI, though current endogenous, is a sum of predetermined variables and variables which themselves depend only on predetermined variables. The inexorability of the phenomenon is further demonstrated by the various impact multipliers with respect to SOFIC2: the GMI multiplier is again positive (and it is joined in its sign only by that of GMIM). It is true that neither SDINP nor SOFIC2 is purely the stock of foreign direct investment. The former variable is the *ratio* of this stock to that of Canadian direct investment abroad; the latter is the *sum* of this stock and part of foreign portfolio investment in Canada. However, it is noticed that the sign of the GMI multiplier is preserved even though the *lags* of SDINP and SOFIC2 differ.

The final manifestation of the inexorability occurs in the impact multipliers of SOCIA2. Among the import variables ∂GMI/∂SOCIA2 and ∂GMIM/∂SOCIA2 are the only multipliers with *negative* sign. SOCIA2 is the *Canadian investment abroad* analogue of SOFIC2. Hence there is a presumption that the "Canadian investment abroad" components of SDINP and SOFIC2 tend to give their GMI impact multipliers a *negative* sign. Because their signs are in fact *positive*, the influence of *foreign direct investment in Canada* upon GMI must be of sufficient strength to overcompensate the "Canadian investment abroad" effect. Furthermore, foreign investment in Canada—both direct and portfolio upon which dividends are received—are larger and grow faster than the Canadian equivalent abroad.

An increase in OR appreciates RS. The price effect on GMC is positive, on GMI negative. The GMC and GMI multipliers have the same sign as these respective direct effects of RS. GMIM's price effect is negative; however, $\partial\text{GMIM}/\partial\text{OR} < 0$ is not an anomaly since PIMPD1 is a *lagged* variable.

There is a positive impact effect of HLA on all merchandise import variables—from GMUS to GMIM. HLA has no direct effect on any import variable. Presumably this uniform impact results from the beneficial effect of HLA directly on CND, CD, CS and thence on other activity variables. The equations explaining GMC, GMI, and GMIM each contain an activity variable which is *unlagged*, thus giving scope to the effect.

R2 stimulates all import variables. As in the case of HLA, the explanation is again activity effects; however, the initial stimulus to activity takes the form of investment as distinct from consumption expenditure.

The GMC, GMI, GMIM, and (hence) GM impact multipliers with respect to PGMUS and PGMO are positive. They take the sign of the corresponding GMUS—rather than GMO—multiplier. However, their sizes, like those of the GMUS multipliers, are small relative to the GMO multipliers.

∂GMC/∂PGMCB = -550 as compared with a -280 direct effect of PMCRPD on GMC.

∂GMI/∂PGMIB = 490 as compared with a 480 direct effect of PMIRPD on GMI.

PMUSP1 has a negative impact effect on GMC, GMI, GMIM, and (hence) GM. Thus the commodity import variables follow the sign of ∂GMUS/∂PMUSP1 rather than ∂GMO/∂PMUSP1; however, the *size* of ∂GM/∂PMUSP1 (and hence of its components) is small relative to ∂GMUS/∂PMUSP1. Consequences of these features are outlined above.

Impact multipliers of import variables (excepting, of course, GMFL) with respect to foreign activity variables are positive except for the GMI multipliers, which are uniformly negative. How can this divergence be explained? A foreign activity variable has a stimulatory effect (through a direct effect on exports) on YDMC and YG—domestic activity variables respectively entering the equations explaining GMC and GMIM. However, its effect on GDI, the activity variable in the equation explaining GMI, is nil. Thus GMC and GMIM—but not GMI—tend to be positively affected by this route. Consider, now, price effects. PIMPD1, the price variable in the GMIM equation, is predetermined. PMCRPD and PMIRPD, price variables for GMC and GMI, respectively, have a direct effect that is positive and negative, respectively. Increase in exports raises RS, a price effect in addition to income effects. Increased RS implies increased RSI, which itself implies *decreased* PMCRPD and PMIRPD. Because of the varying signs of the direct effects of the latter two variables, GMC is increased through this effect and GMI decreased. Variables entering the direct explanation of GMC, GMI, and GMIM and unmentioned here are predetermined. Thus, in summary, *two* forces (both an income and price effect) increase GMC, *one* force (an activity effect) increases GMIM, and one force (price effect) *decreases* GMI. This analysis is reflected not only in the signs of the multipliers but also in their relative sizes. Thus for each of the foreign activity variables the GMC multiplier exceeds the GMIM multiplier.

Impact multipliers of import variables with respect to ACT are uniformly positive, due to the stimulatory direct effect of ACT on GDI (via RC and CNR) and subsequent multiplier effects on activity variables, thus inducing imports.

33. BM

Impact multipliers with respect to GG, GWASR, YMILIT and XNATO are negative, reflecting the negative effect of income growth on the balance of trade. $\partial BM/\partial GWASR > \partial GM/\partial GG$, which is commensurate with the relationship of $\partial YR/\partial GWASR$ to $\partial YR/\partial GG$. The tax multipliers are positive, again the expected effect, and $\partial BM/\partial TW > \partial BM/\partial TNW$.

$\partial BM/\partial R2 < 0$, again through the positive effect of R2 on investment and hence on income. However, the foreign output variables yield positive multipliers, because their direct favorable effect on exports outweighs the indirect income effects.

34. BMTUS; 35. BMTO

BMTUS and BMTO differ from BM in several respects. (1) They are defined in constant dollars while BM is a current-dollar flow. (2) Their sign is negative upon a favorable balance whereas that of BM is positive. (3) Each of BMTUS and BMTO has a component variable not present in BM, and vice-versa. (4) The import variables entering BMTUS or BMTO represent an "area" breakdown while those entering BM refer to a "commodity" breakdown. (1), (3), and (4) imply the invalidity of the relationship.

$$\text{BM} = -(\text{BMTUS} + \text{BMTO})$$

These facts, together with the definitions of BMTUS and BMTO (equations 63 and 64, respectively) suffice to explain the impact multipliers of BMTUS and BMTO in relation to those of BM. Thus, for example, the signs of the BMTUS and BMTO multipliers of GG, GWASR, YMILIT, XNATO, TW, and TNW are the opposite of the signs of the corresponding BM multipliers, with the exception of ∂BMTO/∂XNATO, which itself is explained by the fact XNATO is a (negative) component of BMTO and not of the other variables.

36. BS

BS is composed of such a motley group of flows that it is difficult to discuss its multipliers intelligently without reference to its component variables. Although BS is defined by means of a non-linear identity, it is a summation of terms each of which involves no more than one current endogenous variable. Thus the impact multiplier of BS with respect to an arbitrary predetermined variable is a *linear combination* of the multipliers of its current endogenous components: $\partial(\sum_i c_i E_i)/\partial P_j = \sum_i (\partial c_i E_i/\partial P_j)$. Because of the fact the (current endogenous) service flows (TRN, FRSN, OTHERN, DIVP and DIVR) are subject to such different determinants, the way to understand the impact multipliers of BS is to understand those of its component flows, and look upon the latter as linear combinations of the former.

∂BS/∂GG > ∂BS/∂GWASR, contrary to the relationship of the corresponding BM multipliers. But the relationships of the TW and TNW multipliers are the same.

Both the USIS and USIL multiplier are negative, but the latter is greater in size by a multiple of a hundred, principally due to the large size of ∂DIVR/∂USIL (itself discussed below).

37. FRSN

Because of the direct dependence of FRSN on BMTUS and BMTO, it occurs that for a given predetermined variable P sign (∂BMTUS/∂P) = sign (∂BMTO/∂P) ⇒ each = sign (∂FRSN/∂P). The sole exception concerns CMARIN, whose direct depressing effect swamps the stimulating effect via BMTUS and BMTO.

38. OTHERN

The only current endogenous variable upon which OTHERN depends is CME. CME itself has non-zero impact multipliers (among our forty-three variables) only with respect to RS and ACT. SDINP directly affects OTHERN. Computed impact multipliers with respect to predetermined variables other than these three are very small, and, in fact, should be zero. Naturally the R2 and ACT multipliers have sign commensurate with their direct effect on CME; and the impact effect of SDINP is identical to its direct effect.

39. YDMC

YWC is the predominant variable in the definition of YDMC (equation 89). With respect to any predetermined variable P, sign (∂YDMC/∂P) = sign (∂YWC/∂P), with the exception of TNW and PGMCB. These latter variables, although stimulatory to YWC, have depressing *direct* effects on YDMC. Similarly the signs of the YMILIT and TW multipliers are commensurate with those of their direct effects. A further interesting comparison of corresponding YDMC and YWC multipliers: |∂YDMC/∂P| > |∂YWC/∂P|, again with two exceptions: R2 and ACT, the only predetermined variables (among those listed) which affect

GDI. But the influence of this fact (if indeed it is relevant) is apparently not easy to trace.

40. YWC

Because of the direct dependence of YWC on YM and PEREMP, it is expected that predetermined variables which stimulate (depress) activity (as measured by YM and PEREMP) should have positive (negative) impact multipliers. Then how is the sign of $\partial \text{YWC}/\partial \text{TNW}$ to be explained? Simply by recalling that TNW has a positive effect on YM.

44. YNW

YNW depends only on YM and predetermined variables (equation 26). Thus for every predetermined variable P, $\partial \text{YNW}/\partial P = C1 + C2 * \partial \text{YM}/\partial P$, where $C1$ and $C2$ are constants. Hence the observed facts that (1) sign $(\partial \text{YNW}/\partial P)$ = sign $(\partial \text{YM}/\partial P)$ and (2) $\dfrac{\partial \text{YM}/\partial P}{\partial \text{YNW}/\partial P}$ = approximately a constant (in the order of 9) are not unreasonable (though not necessary).

41. YDWND; 42. YDWD; 43. YDWS; 45. YDNWND; 46. YDNWD; 47. YDNWS

Each of these variables is defined by a relationship involving only two current endogenous variables: one of YWC or YNW in the numerator, and one of PNDB, PDB, or PSB in the denominator.

Relationships among the impact multipliers of these variables are apparently anomalous, because

$$\text{sign}\ (\partial \text{YDWND}/\partial P) = \text{sign}\ (\partial \text{YDNWND}/\partial P)$$

and

$$\text{sign}\ (\partial \text{YDWD}/\partial P) = \text{sign}\ (\partial \text{YDNWD}/\partial P)$$

for all predetermined variables except TNW. Yet

$$\text{sign}\ (\partial \text{YDWS}/\partial P) \neq \text{sign}\ (\partial \text{YDNWS}/\partial P)$$

in not only one (as in the above relationships) but in nineteen cases. How is this phenomenon to be explained? The above relationships are grouped by common price variable. Consider, now, groupings by income variable. Sign (∂YDWND/∂P) = sign (∂YDWD/∂P) = sign (∂YDWS/∂P) for all P except PTA and PMD. But the relationship sign (∂YDNWND/∂P) = sign (∂YDNWD/∂P) = sign (∂YDNWS/∂P) fails to be fulfilled in twenty—as distinct from two—cases. The income groupings indicate that the core of the anomaly is the set of impact multipliers of YDNWS rather than YDWS. This may be manifested again as follows. The relationship sign (∂YDWND/∂P) = sign (∂YDWD/∂P) = sign (∂YDNWND/∂P) = sign (∂YDNWD/∂P) is false in two cases (TNW and PMD). Adding a fourth equality, sign (∂YDWS/∂P), makes the extended relationship invalid in only one additional case (PTA). But the addition of a fifth equality, sign (∂YDNWS/∂P), invalidates the relationship in a total of twenty-one cases—an increase of eighteen. The fact that sign changeovers are associated with YDNWS rather than both YDWS and YDNWS indicates that the anomaly is not caused by differential behavior of the PSB multipliers relative to the PNDB and PDB multipliers. In fact the relationship sign (∂PNDB/∂P) = sign (∂PDB/∂P) ≠ sign (∂PSB/∂P) holds in only one case (PMND).

To discover the basis of the anomaly, one must transcend relationships of sign and investigate those of *size*. The three relations |∂YDWND/∂P| > |∂YDNWND/∂P|, |∂YDWD/∂P| > |∂YDNWD/∂P|, |∂YDWS/∂P| > |∂YDNWS/∂P| hold for all P except TNW. Consider, now, the relative sizes of

$$|\partial \text{YDWND}/\partial P|,\ |\partial \text{YDWD}/\partial P|, \text{ and } |\partial \text{YDWS}/\partial P|.$$

|∂YDWND/∂P|, |∂YDWD/∂P| > |∂YDWS/∂P| is true for thirty predetermined variables and false for twelve (excluding PGMIMB). *For the twelve predetermined variables with respect to which*

the relations do not hold, sign $(\partial\text{YDWS}/\partial P)$ = *sign* $(\partial\text{YDNWS}/\partial P)$. Thus the nineteen differences in sign of corresponding YDWS and YDNWS multipliers are associated with predetermined variables which satisfy $|\partial\text{YDWND}/\partial P| > |\partial\text{YDWS}/\partial P|$ and $|\partial\text{YDWD}/\partial P| > |\partial\text{YDWS}/\partial P|$. Therefore a small $|\partial\text{YDWS}/\partial P|$ (relative to $|\partial\text{YDWND}/\partial P|$, $|\partial\text{YDWD}/\partial P|$) may imply (and in nineteen of thirty cases does so) a $|\partial\text{YDNWS}/\partial P|$ so small that removal of the absolute value reveals a sign changeover.

48. SIF

SIF = SIFUD/RSI. Therefore $\partial\text{SIF}/\partial P = -\text{C} * \partial\text{RSI}/\partial P$, where C is a positive constant, except for P = SIFUD. Hence sign $(\partial\text{SIF}/\partial P) = -$sign $(\partial\text{RSI}/\partial P)$, again with that exception.

49. DIVP; 50. DIVR; 51. CINTN

It is truly an amazing result that sign $(\partial\text{DIVP}/\partial P)$ = sign $(\partial\text{DIVR}/\partial P) = -$sign $(\partial\text{CINTN}/\partial P)$ for all P with but one exception: SOFIC2, a predetermined variable that directly enters the explanation of DIVP. However, the explanation is simple. CRS and WCRS are the only current endogenous variables directly explaining these variables. Both enter the equations which determine DIVP and DIVR; CRS alone enters the equation explaining CINTN. The sign of the coefficient of CRS is positive for both DIVP and DIVR, negative for CINTN. The sign of the coefficient of WCRS is negative for both DIVP and DIVR.

Another intriguing result: $|\partial\text{DIVR}/\partial P| > |\partial\text{DIVP}/\partial P|$, again with the exception of SOFIC2. The relative *sizes* of the corresponding CRS and WCRS coefficients provide the explanation of this phenomenon. The coefficient for DIVR is greater than that for DIVP for each variable; but the one of CRS (the positive coefficient) is larger by a factor of nearly twenty, while that of WCRS (the negative coefficient) is larger by a factor of less than two.

52. OCDPXB

OCDPXB is the ratio of the sum of two predetermined variables to a determined variable (PXB). Hence there exists a relationship between ∂OCDPXB/∂*P* and ∂PXB/∂*P* analogous to that discussed above between ∂SIF/∂*P* and ∂RSI/∂*P*.

55. DIC

The impact of GG on DIC is positive, that of GWASR negative. This changeover in sign does not occur in the case of the other capital inflows (PNIR, PTOS, TBN). However, for each flow the GWASR multiplier is less than the GG multiplier.

Increased personal direct taxes are depressing to all capital inflows. SIFUD has a positive impact on DIC slightly greater than the direct effect of SIF. It adversely affects other capital flows.

Investment flow multipliers with respect to investment stock variables are of interest. SDINP, the ratio of foreign to Canadian direct investments, is stimulatory to all capital flows. SOFIC2, a stock of foreign direct plus some portfolio investment in Canada, has a *negative* impact on DIC, a positive one on all other capital flows; SOCIA2, the analogous stock of Canadian investment abroad, has precisely opposite effects with respect to sign. The fact that SOFIC2 is not stimulating to DIC while SDINP is, involves no contradiction, even though SOFIC2 and SDINP both increase, *ceteris paribus*, with increased (past) foreign investment in Canada. It must be recalled that DIC is not explained by an autoregressive structure. The *direct* effects of SDINP, SOFIC2, and SOCIA2 pertain to OTHERN, DIVP, and DIVR, respectively. From these variables their impacts on DIC, PNIR, and PTOS may be traced.

OR, the direct effect of which is appreciation of the dollar, has a negative effect on all investment flows. Hence *increasing* official reserves, that is, decreasing OR, which *depreciates* the dollar, results—after all interactions—in an *increase* in all capital inflows.

This is clearly of relevance to an understanding of the effects of the government's exchange fund policy. Similarly, other variables which appreciate the dollar, even though indirectly, adversely affect all capital inflows. These variables and their *modi operandi* are tabulated in Table 10.

TABLE 10. Impacts on the exchange rate.

Variable	Direct effect is on	Impact on RS is via
RESB2	XB	BM
USIP	XUS	BM
BIP2	XB	BM
WEJIP2	XWEJ	BM
OIP2	XO	BM
CMARIN	FRSN	BS

56. PNIR; 57. PTOS; 58. TBN

Sign $(\partial \text{PNIR}/\partial P)$ = sign $(\partial \text{PTOS}/\partial P)$, with one exception: SG. Both the uniformity and the exception are expected; for of the eight (direct) determinants of PNIR and the eight of PTOS, seven are identical. Consider the remaining two: FIA, explaining PTOS (but not PNIR), is a predetermined variable but not one of the forty-three. S, explaining PNIR (but not PTOS), is the sum of SO and SG. It has a positive coefficient. SG, though depressing SO, has a net positive effect on S. Hence the explanation of $\partial \text{PNIR}/\partial \text{SG} > 0$.

The influence of monetary policy on capital flows should be examined. Effects of SG have been noted. TB, the analogous instrument in the (short-term) money market, directly raises CIS and hence CIL (via the latter's dependence on CIS). Therefore DIL is increased, and hence PNIR and PTOS are stimulated. But TBN, the short-term capital flow, is depressed. The crucial variable in explaining TBN is not a short-term interest differential (analogous to DIL in the explanation of PNIR and PTOS), but rather RFD, the forward exchange differential. Even though the rise in CIS *by itself* tends to lower RSA and hence increase RFD (equation 55), the impact of TB on RS involves a *rise* in RSA. Though RF, too, rises, the net effect on RFD is depressing (though very small). The *direct* effects of CRS and WCRS on TBN are negative and positive, respectively, and the size of the WCRS coefficient is nearly *three* times that of the CRS coefficient. TB has positive impact on both CRS and WCRS, but the size of the CRS impact is *nine* times that of the WCRS one, which more than compensates for the relative direct effects. Hence one has a second factor explaining the sign of ∂TBN/∂TB.

The direct effect of ATM is to increase CIL. Hence DIL is increased, and PNIR and PTOS stimulated.

R and RLA lower CIS, hence CIL, and therefore DIL. Therefore their impact on PNIR and PTOS is depressing. Yet they stimulate TBN, hence remarks analogous to the ones made above in connection with the impact of TB are in order.

The influence of foreign monetary variables is of interest. USIS has a direct stimulating influence on RSA; its impact on RFD is negative, as expected. ∂TBN/∂USIS < 0. But USIS has positive impact on PNIR and PTOS.

USIL has opposite effects. PNIR and PTOS are depressed (via a fall in DIL), and TBN is stimulated.

54. PNIIC

From equation 60, $\partial\text{PNIIC}/\partial P = \partial\text{PNIR}/\partial P + \partial\text{PTOS}/\partial P$, for all P.

53. BLK

From equation 59, $\partial\text{BLK}/\partial P = \partial\text{DIC}/\partial P + \partial\text{PNIR}/\partial P + \partial\text{PTOS}/\partial P$, for all P (of our forty-three) except DLGC. Though DLGC has positive impact on all three endogenous components of BLK, its negative direct effect on BLK dominates the impact effect.

59. HLAND; 60. HLAD; 61. HLAS

HLAND, HLAD, and HLAS are each defined (equations 69, 70, and 71, respectively) as the ratio of a predetermined to a current endogenous variable. Hence an assessment of their impact multipliers similar to that concerning the variable SIF is applicable.

62. S; 63. SO

S = SO + SG, where SO is current endogenous and SG predetermined. Hence $\partial \text{S}/\partial P = \partial \text{SO}/\partial P$ except for $P = \text{SG}$, in which case $\partial \text{S}/\partial \text{SG} = 1 + \partial \text{SO}/\partial \text{SG}$.

CIL, the direct effect of which is negative, is the only current endogenous variable upon which SO depends, and SG is the only predetermined variable of our set of forty-three which directly affects CIL. Hence, again excepting only SG, sign $(\partial \text{SO}/\partial P) = -\text{sign}\ (\partial \text{CIL}/\partial P)$.

There is an interesting feature regarding the relationship between general economic activity (measured, say, by YR) and net new security issues. Variables that *stimulate* (depress) activity by directly (to at most one degree removed) affecting domestic demand have a *positive* (negative) effect on SO. These variables are GG, GWASR, YMILIT, TW, TNW, HLA, R2, and ACT. By "directly (to at most one degree removed) affecting domestic demand" is meant that one of three events is true: (1) The variable is a component of YR but not an item in the balance of payments. (2) The variable directly enters the explanation of a category (1) variable. (3) The variable directly enters the explanation of a variable in category (2). Variables that stimulate activity by directly (to at most one degree removed) affecting balance of payments variables have a *negative* effect on SO. These variables are RESB2, PGMCB, PGMIB, USIP, BIP2, WEJIP2, OIP2, and CMARIN.

64. RS

At last the set of impact effects on RS is reached. A priori it can be said that a variable which has a *positive* (negative) direct (to at most one degree removed) effect on one of BM, BS, BLK, or TBN is likely to *appreciate* (depreciate) RS. Thus RESB2 and the foreign activity variables (via merchandise exports and BM) have positive impact multipliers. PGMCB and PGMIB give positive and negative multipliers, respectively. The one variable increases BM (via decreasing GMC); the other decreases BM (via increasing GMI). The opposite signs of their direct effects should be recalled. CMARIN (via FRSN and BS) has a positive effect. USIL (via PNIR, PTOS, and BLK) depreciates RS. Included here is the second subset of variables used to delineate multipliers of SO.

Variables that directly (to at most one degree removed) *stimulate* (depress) domestic activity are expected to *depreciate* (appreciate) RS, via income-import effects. Is this expectation fulfilled? Yes, for GG, GWASR, YMILIT, TW, TNW, HLA, R2, and ACT—the first subset mentioned above in connection with the SO multipliers.

The *impact* effect of OR on RS is less than its *direct* effect. The explanation is to be found in the impact of OR on the current endogenous determinants of RS. Its positive effect on BM and BS is outweighed by its negative impact on BLK and TBN.

65. RSI

$\partial \mathrm{RSI}/\partial P = \text{constant} * \partial \mathrm{RS}/\partial P$, upon differentiating equation 51.

66. RSA; 69. RF

With but five exceptions, the values of corresponding impact multipliers of RSA and RF are indistinguishable or almost indistinguishable from that of RS. Both the uniformity and the particular exceptions are easily explained. RS, RSA, and RF are "similar" variables in two senses. *First*, RS, RSA, and RF are comparable in units and have significantly similar observations (size). Thus the respective means are 1.0151, 1.0146, and 1.0135. This similarity is only logical. RS and RF are measurements of the same phenomenon, the actual exchange rate—only the one is the spot, the other the forward rate. RSA is defined (equation 54) as RS adjusted essentially by the ratio of the United States to the Canadian treasury bill rate. Again, USIS and CIS have similar means—0.558 and 0.605, respectively. *Second*, the three variables are closely related in terms of causation. RSA is by definition RS adjusted multiplicatively by an interest rate ratio. RSA is the only current endogenous variable determining RF, and its coefficient is close to unity.

Now the exceptions to the uniformity may be discussed. Four predetermined variables—TB, R, RLA, and USIS—disturb the similarity between multipliers of RS and RF cum RSA, but *not* between those of RF and RSA. The reason is clear. USIS directly enters the definition of RSA; the other three predetermined variables directly enter the determination of CIS, which itself is a term in the definition of RSA. (And they are the only predetermined variables of our forty-three to do so.) Furthermore, RF is directly dependent upon RSA; not so is RS: in fact the direction of causation is reversed in this case.

The fifth exception concerns FA, which is the only predetermined variable (of our set) to enter the explanation of RF. It does not enter that of RS and RSA. Hence $\partial RF/\partial FA$ is dissimilar from $\partial RS/\partial FA$ and $\partial RSA/\partial FA$, but the latter two retain their indistinguishability.

OR is a predetermined variable which directly enters the explanation of RS but not of RSA or RF. Yet the three impact multipliers are indistinguishable because RS is causally linked to both RSA and RF. The *direction* of causation is RS $\rightarrow$ RSA $\rightarrow$ RF.

67. CRS

CRS = RS − RS1 (equation 52), where RS1 is predetermined but not one of the forty-three. Hence $\partial CRS/\partial P = \partial RS/\partial P$, all P.

68. WCRS

For $P \neq W$,

$$\partial WCRS/\partial P = \text{constant} * \partial CRS/\partial P$$

For P = W,

$$\partial \text{WCRS}/\partial P = \overline{\text{W}} * \partial \text{CRS}/\partial \text{W} + \overline{\text{CRS}}$$

where $\overline{\text{W}}$ is the above constant. These relationships are based on equation 53.

70. RFD

Differentiating equation 55,

$$\partial \text{RFD}/\partial P = \partial \text{RF}/\partial P - \partial \text{RSA}/\partial P$$

Because corresponding RF and RSA multipliers are generally close to equality, the RFD multipliers are small.

71. CRFD

Differentiating equation 56, ∂CRFD/∂P = ∂RFD/∂P, all P. (RFD1, though predetermined, is not one of the forty-three.)

72. CIS; 73. CIL

CIS and CIL are positively correlated (via impact multipliers) with USIS and USIL, respectively. This causal relation between Canadian and American interest rates is not direct; increased USIS or USIL causes decreased capital inflow (TBN or PNIIC, respectively) and thus increased CIS or CIL. Although ∂CIL/∂USIL, ∂CIS/∂USIS > 0, ∂CIS/∂USIL, ∂CIL/∂USIS < 0. As noted in the discussion of multipliers of PNIR, PTOS, and TBN, ∂TBN/∂USIL, ∂PNIR/∂USIS, ∂PTOS/∂USIS are all >0. Because of the direct positive dependence of CIL on CIS, cases of sign (∂CIL/∂P) $\neq$ sign (∂CIS/∂P) are expected to be rare events. Yet this occurs not only for USIS and USIL but also for FA and W, since these variables also affect TBN and PNIIC in opposite directions. The impact on PNIIC is of sufficient strength in these two cases (FA and W) to offset the impact via not only CIS but also S (the third current endogenous variable, after CIS and PNIIC, entering the explanation of CIL), both of which operate in the direction of moving CIL in the same direction as CIS.

$|\partial \text{CIS}/\partial P| > |\partial \text{CIL}/\partial P|$, with but two exceptions: SG and ATM. The latter is the only predetermined variable (apart from the seasonals) which enters the equation explaining CIL, and it does so with a positive coefficient. Though the former variable does not enter the equation itself, it is a component of S, which does so, and again with a positive coefficient. Apart from these two exceptions, which are due to direct effects working for CIL but not CIS, the result of greater responsiveness of short-term relative to long-term rate is obtained (upon a disturbance in the system), which is the normal expectation.

74. DIL

DIL = CIL − USIL (equation 66), where USIL is predetermined. Hence $\partial \text{DIL}/\partial P = \partial \text{CIL}/\partial P$, except for P = USIL, in which case $\partial \text{DIL}/\partial \text{USIL} = \partial \text{CIL}/\partial \text{USIL} - 1$.

75. PFS

In general, it is expected that forces generating expansion in the economy would involve a rise in the general price level (demand-pull inflation). This is true in the case of PFS with, however, several exceptions: the predetermined variables directly explaining the components of GDI (R2 and ACT), the personal tax variables (TW and TNW), and government wage expenditure (GWASR). In the model current endogenous variables which directly explain PFS are WR and PMGSR. Economic activity enters via WR, which is defined as the ratio of YWC to EMPM, adjusted by a multiplicative constant. Thus the direct effect of activity on PFS is not a simple one: WR is a ratio of two different measures of activity.

In commensurate with their direct effects explicit in the definition of PMGSR (equation 99), PGMIB and PGMCB have positive multipliers. Although they enter the definition of PMGSR symmetrically except for constant term (and in fact

PGMIB is multiplied by the larger constant), ∂PFS/∂PGMCB is more than twice the size of ∂PFS/∂PGMIB. ∂PMGSR/∂PGMIB > ∂PMGSR/∂PGMCB, as expected. But ∂WRS/∂PGMCB is eleven times the size of ∂WRS/∂PGMIB (both being positive). This can be traced to a much stronger effect of PGMCB on YWC. (In fact ∂YWC/∂PGMIB, ∂EMPM/∂PGMIB < 0, though ∂YWC/∂PGMCB, ∂EMPM/∂PGMCB > 0.) And this differential effect can be traced to |∂YM/∂PGMCB| being nearly four times the size of |∂YM/∂PGMIB|, where YM is a direct determinant of YWC. Thus ultimately one reaches the fact that PGMIB decreases YM while PGMCB increases it, both via GM in equation 72. Here the opposite behavior of GMC and GMI in response to their price variables is the explanation, the one decreasing, the other increasing.

Because of the presence of RSI in the definition of PMGSR (equation 99), the impact of OR is of interest. OR increases RS (hence RSI); by equation 99 this decreases PMGSR, and therefore, by equation 40, should decrease PFS. However, ∂PFS/∂OR > 0. ∂WR/∂OR is positive and outweighs ∂PMGSR/∂OR in affecting PFS. Why is ∂WR/∂OR positive? One follows the same line of causation as discussing the PGMCB and PGMIB multipliers above. Looking at the components of WR, ∂YWC/∂OR > 0 but ∂EMPM/∂OR < 0. Hence one must investigate the former variable, because it outweighs EMPM's deliterious effect. Considering the determinants of YWC, ∂PEREMP/∂OR < 0 (as might be expected from the sign of ∂EMPM/∂OR), so there is only hindrance here, but ∂YM/∂OR > 0, as is noted in the discussion of the YM multipliers.

76. PNDB; 77. PDB

Despite the widely differing coefficients of corresponding explanatory variables of PNDB and PDB (albeit their equations have the same basic structure), in only five cases does sign (∂PNDB/∂P) ≠ sign (∂PDB/∂P). Considering the positive direct effect of PFS on both PNDB and PDB, it is of interest to note the three exceptions to the relationship sign (∂PNDB/∂P) = sign (∂PDB/∂P) $\Rightarrow$ each = sign (∂PFS/∂P). These are YMILIT, TW, and PMND; there does not appear to be a pattern in these exceptions.

78. PSB

In view of the direct dependence of PSB on PFS (equation 46), the cases in which sign (∂PSB/∂P) $\neq$ sign (∂PFS/∂P) are worthy of investigation. There are four such events. The amazing thing is that these involve variables that entail either opposite-signed PNDB and PDB multipliers (GG and PMD) or exceptions to the rule sign (∂PNDB/∂P) = sign (∂PDB/∂P) $\Rightarrow$ each = sign (∂PFS/∂P) (YMILIT and TW). The fact is amazing because there is no uniformity in the WRS and PNDB cum PDB equations, apart from dependence on PFS and seasonal variables.

79. PNDPO; 80. PDPO; 81. PSPO

Impact multipliers of PNDPO, PDPO, and PSPO are related to corresponding ones of PNDB, PDB, and PSB by means of equations 90, 91, and 92, appropriately differentiated. Some interesting sign relationships: sign (∂PNDPO/∂P) $\neq$ sign (∂PDPO/∂P) for five variables, three of which are among the five for which sign (∂PNDB/∂P) $\neq$ sign (∂PDB/∂P). However, sign (∂PNDPO/∂P) = sign (∂PDPO/∂P) $\Rightarrow$ each $\neq$ sign (∂PSPO/∂P) *always* holds. This may be compared with the fact that sign (∂PNDB/∂P) = sign (∂PDB/∂P) $\Rightarrow$ each $\neq$ sign (∂PSB/∂P) holds in but one case (PMND).

82. PNDS

$\partial\text{PNDS}/\partial P = 0.6 * \partial\text{PNDB}/\partial P + 0.4 * \partial\text{PSB}/\partial P$, by equation 100.

84. PDPCG; 90. PDPIG; 92. PDPIM

These three variables are explained by the semi-identities, which are similarly structured. Of interest here is the effect of import prices. Looking at the equations, it is observed that the direct effect of foreign import prices (albeit adjusted by the exchange rate) is *negative*. However, the theory underlying these relationships is that foreign import prices (again so adjusted) have a *positive* effect on the corresponding *overall* price indexes (PNDB, PDB, PFC, and PWIM) via equations 41, 42, 43, and 45, respectively. In fact, by the construction of the semi-identities, the *direct* effects of the import price on the overall price and on the "domestically produced" price are equal in size but opposite in sign, providing one neglects the constant multiple on the right-hand side of each semi-identity. Now, because the appropriate *overall* price index *enters* each semi-identity, the combined *direct* effect of the foreign price is zero. However, it is the full *impact* effect which is at issue. Only in a special case does the combined direct effect equal the impact. That case is PDPIM. Differentiating equation 108 with respect to PGMIMB,

$$\begin{aligned} \partial \text{PDPIM}/\partial \text{PGMIMB} &= (\partial \text{PWIM}/\partial \text{PGMIMB} \\ &\qquad - 0.31 * \partial \text{PMIMR}/\partial \text{PGMIMB})/0.69 \\ &= (0.32 - 0.31 * 1.0)/0.69 = 0 \end{aligned}$$

(The roundedness of the impact multipliers and coefficients obscures the fact that the bracketed expression is zero.)

This phenomenon is due to the fact that PDPIM, PWIM, and PMIMR are "extraneous determined variables," linked to the rest of the system by a predetermined—and not a current endogenous—variable. (See Diagrams I and II and the accompanying text in chapter III.)

∂PDPIG/∂PGMIB is positive; this is due to the fact ∂PFC/∂PGMIB exceeds the mere direct effect of PGMIB on PFC (this effect being 0.36 * ∂PMKR/∂PDPIG). Scope is given to indirect effects because PFC is neither extraneously determined nor a function of only predetermined variables, and the indirect effects are stimulatory to PFC.

Concerning ∂PDPCG/∂PMND and ∂PDPCG/∂PMD there is a second reason (that is, in addition to the non-identically zero indirect effects on PNDB and PDB, respectively) why they are not zero. Equation 106 is an average of two expressions each of which is analogous to the right-hand side of equation 107 or 108. Hence ∂PDPCG/∂PMND and ∂PDPCG/∂PMD are linear functions of not two but four impact multipliers. It then occurs that ∂PDPCG/∂PMND is positive and ∂PDPCG/∂PMD negative.

83. PMCRPD; 89. PMIRPD

Equations 93 and 94 show that PMCRPD and PMIRPD have mutually analogous definitions. Hence it is not surprising that sign (∂PMCRPD/∂P) ≠ sign (∂PMIRPD/∂P) in but five cases. (However, there are four variables—in addition to PGMIMB—which have zero impact on PMCRPD but not on PMIRPD.) Comparing signs of ∂PDPCG/∂P and ∂PDPIG/∂P, one finds they are unequal in five cases, but the overlap with the above group consists of two variables only: R2 and ACT.

86. PTC

PNDS is the only variable (other than seasonals) upon which PTC depends. Therefore ∂PTC/∂P = constant * ∂PNDS/∂P, where the constant is the direct effect of PNDS upon PTC, namely, 0.89.

85. PTR

Sign (∂PTR/∂P) = −sign (∂PTC/∂P), with but two exceptions (one of which is PTA). The tendency is not surprising in view of equation 101, which, upon differentiation by P ≠ PTA, becomes

$$\partial \mathrm{PTR}/\partial P = -C1 * \partial \mathrm{PTC}/\partial P - C2 * \partial \mathrm{RSI}/\partial P$$

where $C1$ and $C2$ are positive constants.

Since RSI and PTC enter the equation symmetrically, again there is the rule sign (∂PTR/∂P) = −sign (∂RSI/∂P), with, however, eight exceptions. There are, in fact, only nine instances in which sign (∂PTC/∂P) ≠ sign (∂RSI/∂P).

87. PFC

PFC is similarly structured to PNDB and PDB. Like them, its positive direct dependence on PFS is largely retained in terms of impact effects. Thus sign $(\partial \mathrm{PFC}/\partial P)$ = sign $(\partial \mathrm{PFS}/\partial P)$ is false in only five cases.

It is reasonable to expect prices of capital goods to be more similar in behavior to prices of durable consumer goods than those of non-durables. This expectation is fulfilled in the following simple test: sign $(\partial \mathrm{PFC}/\partial P) \neq$ sign $(\partial \mathrm{PDB}/\partial P)$ in five cases, although sign $(\partial \mathrm{PFC}/\partial P) \neq$ sign $(\partial \mathrm{PNDB}/\partial P)$ in eight cases.

88. PMNRC

The relationship between the impact multipliers of PMNRC and those of PFC is identical to that between those of PTC and PNDS (discussed above), except that the direct effect is 1.0 (equation 50), which implies $\partial \mathrm{PMNRC}/\partial P = \partial \mathrm{PFC}/\partial P$, all P.

91. PWIM

PWIM is directly dependent upon PFS, as are PNDB, PDB, and PFC. However, there are twenty-five cases in which sign $(\partial \mathrm{PWIM}/\partial P) \neq$ sign $(\partial \mathrm{PFS}/\partial P)$. What accounts for the lack of sign uniformity here, when compared with the behavior of, say, $\partial \mathrm{PFC}/\partial P$, which has one fifth such cases? Viewing the equations which explain PFC and PWIM (43 and 45, respectively), it is clear that the answer does not lie in the mutually exclusive predetermined variables—SIK and SIX—neither of which are in the set—nor in the seasonals. Consider the corresponding variables PMKR and PMIMR. They are not a cause of the varying behavior because their corresponding impact multipliers are always of the same sign and close to equality in size, except for those of PGMIB and PGMIMB. Furthermore, their direct effects are not significantly different—0.36 and 0.31, respectively.

Then the reason in question is probably a twofold one. (1) The direct effect of PFS is much greater on PFC than on PWIM—

0.82 versus 0.22. (2) PWIM lacks a sectoral demand variable such as FKFS, which may play a role in the relationship. There are twice as many cases (28) in which sign (∂FKFS/∂P) = sign (∂PFS/∂P) holds as in which it doesn't (14). The direct effect of FKFS on PFC is positive, and there are nine variables for which sign (∂PFC/∂P) $\neq$ sign (∂FKFS/∂P). In any event these variables satisfy sign (∂PFS/∂P) = sign (∂PFC/∂P). Thus where FKFS is a hindrance rather than a help, it does not destroy the sign uniformity.

93. PXB

The equations explaining PXB (44) and PWIM (45) each differ from the structure of those explaining PNDB, PDB, and PFC in a mutually exclusive respect. Equation 44 lacks a *current endogenous* variable comparable to the adjusted import price (say, PMKR in equation 43); instead it has the *predetermined* variable PXO1. However, it retains a sectoral demand variable, namely, XFS. Comparing corresponding impact multipliers of PXB and PFS, it is seen that signs are unequal in six cases, compared to the twenty-five cases of PWIM. Equation 45, explaining PWIM, lacks the sectoral demand variable, though it possesses a current endogenous adjusted import price index. In the PXB multipliers there is a further illustration of the workings of the sectoral demand variable in equating signs of corresponding multipliers of the overall price index (PFS) and particular price index (in this case, PXB): sign (∂XFS/∂P) $\neq$ sign (∂PFS/∂P) in only eight cases.

94. PXC

The relationship between ∂PXC/∂P and ∂PXB/∂P is analogous to that between ∂PTC/∂P and ∂PNDS/∂P.

95. PMGSR

Differentiating equation 99 for $P \neq$ PGMIB or PGMCB,

$$\partial \text{PMGSR}/\partial P = -\text{constant} * \partial \text{RSI}/\partial P$$

where the constant involves only the coefficients 0.313 and 0.303 and the means of PGMIB, PGMCB, and RSI, and is a positive quantity. Hence, in particular, sign (∂PMGSR/∂P) = −sign (∂RSI/∂P).

When P = PGMCB or PGMIB, ∂PMGSR/∂P is no longer proportional to ∂RSI/∂P but is related to it as follows:

$$\partial \text{PMGSR}/\partial P = C1 - C2 * \partial \text{RSI}/\partial P$$

where $C1$, $C2$ are positive constants and $C2$ has different values for P = PGMCB and P = PGMIB. It is noticed that PGMCB and PGMIB yield by far the largest multipliers of PMGSR, the largest not only in algebraic but also in absolute value.

96. PMNDR; 97. PMDR; 98. PMKR; 99. PMIMR

These variables are defined by equations of the form

$$E = F/\text{RSI}$$

where E = the explained variable

F = the corresponding foreign import price

For $P \neq F$ the impact multipliers are

$$\partial E/\partial P = -\text{constant} * \partial \text{RSI}/\partial P$$

where the constant = $\overline{F}/(\overline{\text{RSI}} * \overline{\text{RSI}}) > 0$

For $P = F$ the multiplier becomes

$$\partial E/\partial F = C1 - C2 * \partial \text{RSI}/\partial P$$

where $C1 = 1/\overline{\text{RSI}}$

$C2 = \overline{F}/(\overline{\text{RSI}} * \overline{\text{RSI}})$

are positive constants.

In particular, for E = PMIMR, F = PGMIMB

$$\partial \text{PMIMR}/\partial \text{PGMIMB} = 1/\overline{\text{RSI}}$$

because ∂RSI/∂PGMIMB = 0

At this point it is opportune to indicate why impact multipliers with respect to PGMIMB are identically zero for all variables except PWIM and PMIMR. PGMIMB enters the model only in the definition of PMIMR (equation 98). PMIMR, in turn, is an explanatory variable only in equations 45 (which determines PWIM) and 108 (determining PDPIM). Now, PMIMR, PWIM, and PDPIM form a set of extraneous determined variables; no current endogenous variable connects this set to the rest of the system. (See Diagrams I and II and the accompanying text in chapter III.) Hence the only possible non-zero multipliers of PGMIMB are those of PMIMR, PWIM, and PDPIM. It is explained above why the PDPIM multiplier is zero; thus only ∂PMIMR/∂PGMIMB and ∂PWIM/∂PGMIMB have non-zero magnitude.

100. FORCEM; 104. UNEMPM

UNEMPM is the only current endogenous variable determining FORCEM and the explanatory predetermined variables are not in the set. Hence, differentiating equation 35,

$$\partial \text{FORCEM}/\partial P = -0.091 * \partial \text{UNEMPM}/\partial P$$

However, UNEMPM itself is explained by an identity involving FORCEM (equation 104). Because FORCEM enters equation 104 in its pure form, differentiating this equation and substituting for ∂FORCEM/∂P yields:

$$\partial \text{UNEMPM}/\partial P = (-1.0/1.091) * \partial(\text{EMPM}/\text{AHP} + \text{EMPNM}/\text{AHN})/\partial P \qquad \text{(i)}$$

An interesting question is: Do forces which stimulate (depress) activity cause an expansion (contraction) in the labor force? In view of the proportionality between ∂FORCEM/∂P and ∂UNEMPM/∂P the question may be rephrased: do forces which stimulate (depress) activity cause a decrease (increase) in unemployment? Let YR be the measure of activity and define stimulation to be a positive effect on a component of YR, the effect direct to at most one degree removed. A glance at the

FORCEM or UNEMPM impact multipliers with respect to the relevant variables (namely, GG, GWASR, TW, TNW, RESB2, HLA, R2, USIP, BIP2, WEJIP2, OIP2, CMARIN, ACT, PGMCB, and PGMIB) reveals an affirmative answer to the question. Incidentally, again viewing the YR multipliers with respect to the above bracketed variables, it is seen that their impact effects are of the same sign as their corresponding direct effects. Therefore there is no contradiction in assessing the effect of YR on the right-hand side of (i). In terms of direct effects, $\partial\text{EMPM}/\partial\text{YR} > 0$ (equation 36), $\partial\text{EMPNM}/\partial\text{YR} < 0$ (equation 37), $\partial\text{AHP}/\partial\text{YR} > 0$ (equation 38), and $\partial\text{AHN}/\partial\text{AHP} > 0$ (equation 39) $\Rightarrow \partial\text{AHN}/\partial\text{YR} > 0$. Without differentiating the important term (EMPM/AHP + EMPNM/AHN), it is noticed that YR directly increases three of the four component variables. And it also increases the exception (EMPNM) by the strength of an indirect effect: EMPNM is a function of not only YR but also UNEMPM, the coefficient of UNEMPM is negative, and sign $(\partial\text{UNEMPM}/\partial P) = -\text{sign } (\partial\text{YR}/\partial P)$, where P is any of the "relevant variables" enumerated above.

Because AHP and AHN enter the expression only as reciprocals, their effect is a tendency to negate the relationship in question, but this is offset by the workings of EMPM and EMPNM, especially the former variable. In fact

$$\begin{aligned} &\partial(\text{EMPM}/\text{AHP} + \text{EMPNM}/\text{AHN})/\partial P \\ &= C1 * \partial\text{EMPM}/\partial P + C2 * \partial\text{EMPNM}/\partial P \\ &\quad - C3 * \partial\text{AHP}/\partial P - C4 * \partial\text{AHN}/\partial P \end{aligned}$$

where the Ci are positive constants (combinations of means of the variables). For each of the relevant variables, Table 7 shows $\partial\text{EMPM}/\partial P$ is of a far greater magnitude than $\partial\text{AHP}/\partial P$ or $\partial\text{AHN}/\partial P$ (or, for that matter, $\partial\text{EMPNM}/\partial P$).

101. EMPM

EMPM is determined only by YR and the seasonals. Hence, differentiating equation 36,

$$\partial\text{EMPM}/\partial P = 0.20 * \partial\text{YR}/\partial P$$

In particular, sign (∂EMPM/∂P) = sign (∂YR/∂P), confirming the fact that the impact of the relevant variables on EMPM is favorable for the negativity of ∂UNEMPM/∂P not only in terms of magnitude (discussed above) but also in terms of sign.

102. EMPNM

It is remarked above that YR has divergent influences on EMPNM: a direct negative effect and an indirect positive effect (via UNEMPM). It happens that for every P, sign (∂EMPNM/∂P) = sign (∂YR/∂P). The preponderance of the indirect effect should have been guessed by the fact that the size of the coefficient of UNEMPM in equation 37 is greater than that of YR by a factor of over 3000.

103. PEREMP

In view of the fact the right-hand sides of equations 103 and 104 are rearrangements of the same variables, the one yielding the proportion of the labor force employed, the other unemployment, it is reasonable to expect sign (∂PEREMP/∂P) = −sign (∂UNEMPM/∂P), for all P, which in fact occurs.

105. AHP

The current endogenous variables which determine AHP are YR and PROD (equation 38). The coefficient of YR is positive and that of PROD negative; but the size of the latter is about 2000 times greater than that of the former. It is known that sign (∂PROD/∂P) = sign (∂YR/∂P), all P. Furthermore, no predetermined variable in the set enters the equation. On the basis of these observations it would be expected that ∂AHP/∂P and ∂YR/∂P are of opposite sign, but in fact they are of the same sign for all P. The explanation can only lie in the relative *sizes* of ∂YR/∂P and ∂PROD/∂P. For every P (excluding, of course, PGMIMB) the former multiplier is sufficiently greater than the latter to more than compensate for the discrepancy in the values of the direct coefficients.

106. AHN

AHP is the only variable (other than the seasonals) upon which AHN depends. Hence differentiation of equation 39 yields

$$\partial \mathrm{AHN}/\partial P = 0.66 * \partial \mathrm{AHP}/\partial P$$

107. WR

WR is defined (equation 102) as the ratio of two current endogenous variables adjusted by a constant factor. Its impact multipliers are linear functions of those of its components; thus:

$$\partial \mathrm{WR}/\partial P = C1 * \partial \mathrm{YWC}/\partial P - C2 * \partial \mathrm{EMPM}/\partial P$$

where *C1* and *C2* are positive constants.

It is interesting that the wage rate impact of government expenditure on goods exceeds that of government wage payments. This is a consequence of both that

$$\partial \mathrm{YWC}/\partial \mathrm{GG} > \partial \mathrm{YWC}/\partial \mathrm{GWASR}$$

and that

$$\partial \mathrm{EMPM}/\partial \mathrm{GWASR} > \partial \mathrm{EMPM}/\partial \mathrm{GG}$$

In fact ∂WR/∂GG is positive though ∂WR/∂GWASR is negative. Before one is disposed to dismiss the value of ∂WR/∂GWASR as nonsense—both with respect to sign and in relation to the value of ∂WR/∂GG—it must be remembered that GG and GWASR are real and not monetary expenditures. They are defined in units of constant—rather than current—dollars. It is the *current-dollar* equivalent of GWASR that is of necessity part of YWC. In common sense terms there is no reason why ∂WR/∂GG cannot exceed ∂WR/∂GWASR or why the latter cannot be negative.

CHAPTER IV

108. WRS

In conformity with the relationship of the corresponding WR multipliers, $\partial WRS/\partial GWASR < \partial WRS/\partial GG$, although both multipliers are negative. It may be remarked that service industries do not incorporate government; hence the current-dollar equivalent of GWASR is not incorporated in the wage bill from which the variable WRS is constructed.

Appendix A / Construction of Variables

A complete outline of sources of data and methods of construction of variables is presented in the dissertation.[1] Furthermore, the matrix of observations is tabulated therein.[2] What follows here is a summary of the main features of the sources and methods.

With respect to Canadian data, the principal sources are the Dominion Bureau of Statistics (D.B.S.) and the Bank of Canada. Quarterly national accounts are in the D.B.S. publications: *National Accounts, Income and Expenditure by Quarters, 1947–61* and *National Accounts, Income and Expenditure*. Corresponding tabulations of the balance of payments are in a second group of D.B.S. periodicals: *The Canadian Balance of International Payments in the Post-War Years, 1946–1952; The Canadian Balance of International Payments and International Investment Position;* and *Quarterly Estimates of the Canadian Balance of International Payments*. Detailed information on certain categories of the capital account are in *Sales and Purchases of Securities Between Canada and Other Countries* (D.B.S.). For the commodity classification of imports the Bank of Canada and its *Statistical Summary* publications are the principal sources, although basic data are in the D.B.S. monthly periodical *Imports by Commodities*.

1. Lawrence H. Officer, "An Econometric Model of the Canadian Economy under the Fluctuating Exchange Rate," unpub. diss. Harvard University, 1964, ch. IV.
2. *Ibid.*, chs. IV and V (appendix).

Financial data are obtained principally from the Bank of Canada and its *Statistical Summary Supplement*. Price series are provided by D.B.S. and found in several publications: *Prices & Price Indexes; Industry Selling Price Indexes, 1956–59;* and *Review of Foreign Trade*. Labor information is in *The Labour Force*, *Man-Hours and Hourly Earnings*, and *Employment and Payrolls*, publications of D.B.S.

Concerning non-Canadian data, there are three groups: United States, Britain, and other countries (or international).

United States national accounts data are obtained from the Department of Commerce publications: *U.S. Income and Output* and *Survey of Current Business*, and from the Office of Business Economics. An index of unit value of exports is provided by the Bureau of International Commerce of the United States Department of Commerce. Wage rate information is found in *Survey of Current Business*, the related *Business Statistics*, and the Department of Labor periodical *Employment and Wages*. Industrial production series are in *Industrial Production—1957–59 Base* and *Federal Reserve Bulletin*, publications of the Board of Governors. The *Treasury Bulletin* contains series useful for developing the variable TBN; *Survey of Current Business* and the Bureau of Labor Statistics' *Wholesale Prices and Price Indexes* and *Consumer Price Index* provide data employed in the construction of Canadian import price indexes.

The chief sources of British data are three publications of the Central Statistical Office: *National Income and Expenditure*, *Monthly Digest of Statistics*, and *Economic Trends*. Industrial production series are in *The Index of Industrial Production, Method of Compilation*, published by the same office, and the *Monthly Digest of Statistics*.

There are five sources for the series used to construct the foreign output variables WEJIP2 and OIP2. These are two organizations: Australia and New Zealand Bank Limited and the Statistical Office of the United Nations; and three publications: the United Nations' *Monthly Bulletin of Statistics*, the International Monetary Fund's *International Financial Statistics*, and the International Labour Office's *Yearbook of Labour Statistics*. Price series of international exports or of exports from other countries are obtained from *International Financial Statistics*, *Monthly Bulletin of Statistics*, and the Statistical Office of the United Nations.

The actual process of variable construction involves varying degrees of artistry. The observations on some variables are identical to existing series, or are related to them in a trivial way by means of, say, an averaging of monthly into quarterly data. Development of other variables involves a careful selection and use of available information. The main contributions of the study in this area concern the variables FI, TBN, and the several indexes of prices of merchandise imports.

Construction of FI involves the removal of a spurious intensity in the seasonal pattern because the comparable national accounts' variable represents the totality of the addition to grain inventories in any year as occurring in the period in which the crop is harvested, that is, the third quarter.

Development of TBN requires a component series, the change in Canadian treasury bill holdings of foreigners, which is published only from the first quarter of 1959 onward. The strategy used to extend the series to the preceding period is to construct two flows. The first is the change in foreign holdings of government of Canada securities *inclusive* of treasury bills; the second is the change in foreign holdings of these securities *exclusive* of treasury bills. Subtraction of the second from the first movement yields the desired series.

The Bank of Canada's series of merchandise imports classified by end-use are in current-dollar form. The construction of current-weighted and base-weighted price indexes of these flows enables them not only to be expressed in constant dollars but also to be explained by testable hypotheses.

Appendix B / Estimators of Parameters

Associated with each parameter of the model is not a unique estimate but rather a set of estimates, the elements of which represent different methods of estimation each of which entails its own assumptions regarding error terms and criteria of good estimators. It is true that chapter II presents only one estimated form of each equation; bases for these selections are discussed in Appendix C. Because parameters of the semi-identities are functions of parameters that enter stochastic equations, it suffices to outline estimators of the latter relationships. The various methods of estimation are discussed in the order in which they were actually performed.

The first procedure is ordinary least squares (LS). One interpretation of this method is that it produces a line according to a well-established criterion of goodness of fit. A refined justification is given by the statement that its parameter estimates are best linear unbiased. However, this requires that the assumptions of the Markov theorem hold. In some equations explanatory variables are endogenous but enter in lagged form. No distinction is made between such variables and those that are exogenous, although the Markov theorem requires the exogeneity of all explanatory variables. Attention is focused rather on the fact that equations include more than one *current* endogenous variable. This is the simultaneous equation problem. It occurs in 42 of the 50 stochastic equations. According to the order condition, all these relationships are greatly overidentified. There are a total of 109 predetermined variables in the system, but no equation has even a tenth that number of explanatory variables. Furthermore, there are only 45 observations—less than half the number of predetermined variables. Even given that it has been decided to adopt the two-stage least squares method of estimating overidentified equations, this procedure cannot be applied in its pristine form because degrees of freedom in reduced form estimation are negative!

The solution to this problem is based on suggestions put forward by Kloek and Mennes.[1] The explanatory variables of the first stage (reduced form) regressions associated with a given structural equation are (1) the predetermined variables included in that equation and (2) a number of principal components of a subset of *all* the predetermined variables. For precision, this subset should include only those predetermined variables that do not enter the structural equation. However, because of the large number of variables involved, extraction of components to serve all structural equations is performed from a unique subset of predetermined variables. It is desired to maximize the number of variables included in this subset, subject to computational limitations. The latter considerations limit the number to 99, given that there are 45 observations. The ten predetermined variables omitted are:

Q1	SMANI	PIMPD1	FIA
Q2	T		HLARC2
Q3	W		PXRPO1

The seasonal dummy variables are excluded because they enter every stochastic equation; they are always part of group (1) above. SMANI, W, and T are omitted on analogous grounds: they represent the only predetermined variables (exclusive of the seasonals) that are included in more than one stochastic equation.

1. T. Kloek and L. B. M. Mennes, "Simultaneous Equations Estimation Based on Principal Components of Predetermined Variables," *Econometrica*, 28: 45–61 (January 1960).

PIMPD1 cannot be computed until the parameter d_{45} is estimated; the remaining exclusions are arbitrary.

The principal components of a set of variables are a new set of variables constructed as linear combinations of elements of the original set such that the first component extracted has maximum variance, the second has maximum variance subject to the constraint that it be uncorrelated with the first, and in general the nth component has maximum variance subject to uncorrelatedness with the $(n - 1)$ components the variances of which exceed that of the nth. There are several works which rigorously outline the construction of principal components.[2] In general, principal components are void of economic (or other substantial) interpretation.[3] Their function is to reproduce a given proportion of the total variation of the original set of variables by means of a small number of new variables. For purposes of reduced form estimation, in the case at hand this means a large increase in degrees of freedom. However, principal components possess one undesirable feature: they are not invariant under changes in the units in which the original variables are measured. If all original variables were measured in a unique unit, say, in millions of current dollars, there would be no problem. However, the predetermined variables under consideration are expressed in a variety of non-comparable measures. Therefore they are reduced to standardized form (zero mean and unit variance) before the components are extracted. The sum of the variances of the principal components equals the sum of the variances of the original (standardized) variables; but the economy in the presentation of a given proportion of the total variation is evident from Table 11.

2. Examples are: T. W. Anderson, *Introduction to Multivariate Statistical Analysis* (New York, 1962), pp. 272–286; M. G. Kendall, *A Course in Multivariate Analysis* (New York, 1961), pp. 10–36; Gerhard Tintner, *Econometrics* (New York, 1952), pp. 102–114, and Lester D. Taylor, "A Note on the Mathematical Derivation of Principal Components," unpub. ms., Cambridge, Mass., December 1962. Discussion in the text assumes absence of degeneracy (equal variances of components).

3. A famous exception is Richard Stone's study "On the Interdependence of Blocks of Transactions," *Journal of the Royal Statistical Society, Supplement*, 9: 1–32 (1947).

TABLE 11. Principal components.

Number of component	Proportion of total variation	Number of component	Proportion of total variation
1	0.421	6	0.042
2	0.095	7	0.036
3	0.084	8	0.027
4	0.056	9	0.022
5	0.049	10	0.021

The first ten principal components represent over 85 percent of the total variation. Because the first component alone accounts for nearly half that amount, it is interesting that it can be given an interpretation, which is evident from Table 12.

TABLE 12. First principal component.

Year/Quarter	1	2	3	4
1951	—9.52	—9.37	—9.81	—9.15
1952	—9.00	—8.56	—7.61	—6.18
1953	—6.92	—6.54	—5.93	—5.14
1954	—5.67	—5.38	—4.61	—4.26
1955	—4.02	—4.10	—2.69	—1.44
1956	—0.95	—0.64	—0.31	0.98
1957	1.87	1.79	2.64	3.68
1958	3.62	2.93	3.26	4.28
1959	4.86	5.59	6.21	7.57
1960	7.79	7.30	7.06	7.79
1961	9.27	9.18	9.58	10.32
1962	10.22			

The first principal component is essentially a time trend. This factor is inherent in many economic time series. Further analysis might identify other components as representatives of cyclical and seasonal patterns as well as interactions among these and a trend; but this hypothesis is not tested in the present study.

There remains one degree of arbitrariness in estimation, namely, the selection of principal components included as independent variables in the first stage of two-stage least squares. It is clear that given a decision to use *n* components, the first *n* of the components ranked in order of variance would be selected.[4] The problem is the value of *n*. To avoid underidentification, *n* cannot be less than the number of current endogenous explanatory variables. An obvious solution is to create a just identified situation, that is, to let *n* equal the number of current endogenous explanatory variables. The resulting method of estimation of the structural equation is called just-identified two-stage least squares and denoted as JT. Under this procedure the value of *n* is not a given constant for all stochastic equations. A third method of estimation involves this invariance, and results from a criterion based upon the very function of principal components. The procedure is as follows: given a certain proportion of the total variation represented by the set of principal components, select *n* equal to the minimum number of components necessary to attain this proportion. The proportion chosen is 85 percent and the corresponding *n* is ten. This procedure is known as overidentified two-stage least squares (OT), since in practice *n* of this magnitude implies universal overidentification in the model.

Thus far the Markov assumption of independence of the error terms of an equation is maintained. However, examination of the calculated Durbin-Watson coefficients as well as perusal of the estimated residuals themselves suggested that in many equations strong serial correlation exists.[5] This suggests adoption of a class of estimation methods corresponding to LS, JT, and OT, but

4. Kloek and Mennes suggest a refined procedure involving a reranking of the principal components for each structural equation on the basis of regressions of the components on the predetermined variables included in the equation. See pages 52–53 of their study. The method is at least as good as the invariant ranking approach, but is rejected because of the large number of computations involved with no guarantee of reranking.

5. The Durbin-Watson test assumes that all explanatory variables are nonstochastic. Therefore given such variables that are endogenous, it cannot be applied in a precise manner. However, the fact that the two-stage least squares procedure involves the elimination of the (estimated) current endogenous "part" of explanatory variables implies that the Durbin-Watson statistic is more appropriate than under some other method of estimating overidentified equations.

involving the assumption that the error term follows the autoregressive law

$$E_t = \mathrm{P} * E_{t-1} + U_t$$

where the error terms U are uncorrelated with one another. The parameter P is estimated as

$$p = \frac{\sum_{t=2}^{45} (e_t * e_{t-1})}{\sum_{t=2}^{45} e_{t-1}^2}$$

where the e_t are calculated residuals of the structural equation estimated by LS, JT, or OT. Corresponding methods of estimation are the same as the three stated above except that all variables *in the structural equation* are transformed as follows. Let V_t be the tth observation on an arbitrary variable V. Then V_t is replaced by $(V_t - p * V_{t-1})$. The new estimation procedures are called autoregressive least squares (ALS), autoregressive just-identified two-stage least squares (AJT), and autoregressive overidentified two-stage least squares (AOT). ALS estimates are calculated only for the stochastic equations that do not involve the simultaneous equation problem. Autoregressive least squares is an established econometric technique. It usually takes the form of "estimating" P by assuming it to be unity, that is, first-differencing variables. However, the use of the autoregressive technique in connection with two-stage least squares is not conventional; it involves certain assumptions of integration of two divergences from the Markov assumptions, namely, (i) correlation between the error term and explanatory variables and (ii) autoregression of the error terms themselves. Using analysis of variance terminology, it can be said that the adopted methods of estimation under such circumstances assume no interaction between the two effects.[6]

6. It would be better to utilize methods of estimation which do not exclude these interactions. Such procedures are developed by J. D. Sargan in his article "The Maximum Likelihood Estimation of Economic Relationships with Autoregressive Residuals," *Econometrica*, 29: 414–426 (July 1961). However, his results depend on the assumption of normality of the residuals; they represent extensions of full and limited information rather than two-stage least squares.

Therefore equations that contain more than one current endogenous variable possess five sets of parameter estimates: LS, JT, OT, AJT, and AOT. Those which limit current endogeneity to the dependent variable involve only two such sets: LS and ALS. In the cases of ALS, AJT, and AOT the estimated intercept and its standard error are adjusted to apply to the equation involving non-transformed variables. Let C be the true constant term. Under autoregressive methods the computed intercept estimates not C but $(1 - p) * C$. Division of the estimate and its standard error by $(1 - p)$ produces the desired conversion. The Durbin-Watson statistic (DW) is presented as an indicator of the presence of autoregression in the error terms. It may be used as follows. A value less than 1.6 indicates the presence of positive autocorrelation $(P > 0)$, while one greater than 2.4 suggests negative autocorrelation $(P < 0)$. If DW is between 1.6 and 2.4, the hypothesis of absence of autoregression $(P = 0)$ may be accepted.[7]

The remaining statistics are various measures of squared correlation between actual and estimated values of the dependent variable. In one case the actual and predicted values are represented as they appear in the method of estimation under consideration. No account is taken of the transformed nature of the variables (under ALS, AJT, and AOT) or the replacement of current endogenous explanatory variables by their estimated predetermined parts (under JT, OT, AJT, and AOT). The resulting statistic is denoted as RSQ. A second measure of the coefficient of determination involves correction of these factors. Thus all variables—dependent and explanatory—are expressed in pristine form, and where appropriate the calculated intercept is divided by $(1 - p)$ in order to produce the estimate of the true constant term. This second measure of multiple correlation is called RSQC: it is applicable to all methods of estimation except

7. The critical points apply to a 1 percent significance level. Naturally they vary with the number of explanatory variables in the equations and with the number of observations (44 or 45). However, because assumptions of the Durbin-Watson test are not precisely fulfilled, the statistic itself should be used in only a rough manner, and the procedure indicated in the text suffices.

ordinary least squares. The statistics RSQ and RSQC apply only to structural equations. An analogous statistic is computed for the estimated first stage equations under JT, OT, AJT and AOT. Because transformation of variables does not take place until the second stage estimation, RSQ and RSQC are identical for the first stage, and the measure is denoted as RSQT. RSQ is a conventional indicator of goodness of fit; the significances of RSQC and RSQT are discussed in Appendix C.

Special techniques are used in the estimation of certain parameters; these are now discussed. Equation 2 is

$$\text{RF} = a_2 + b_2 * \text{RSA} + c_2 * \text{CRFD} + d_2 * \text{FA} + e_2 * \text{Q1} + f_2 * \text{Q2} + g_2 * \text{Q3} + E_2$$

Now by definition

$$\text{CRFD} = \text{RF} - \text{RSA} - \text{RFD1}$$

Hence not only does RSA enter two explanatory variables, but RF, the dependent variable, is included on both sides of the equation. These considerations suggest that direct estimation of parameters should apply to not equation 2 but rather equation 2′ which is

$$\text{RF} = a_2' + b_2' * \text{RSA} + c_2' * \text{RFD1} + d_2' * \text{FA} + e_2' * \text{Q1} + f_2' + \text{Q2} + g_2' * \text{Q3} + E_2'$$

and the estimates for equation 2 are obtained by means of the following relationships.

$$a_2 = a_2'/(1 - c_2')$$

$$b_2 = (b_2' - c_2')/(1 - c_2')$$

$$c_2 = -c_2'/(1 - c_2')$$

$$d_2 = d_2'/(1 - c_2')$$

$$e_2 = e_2'/(1 - c_2')$$

$$f_2 = f_2'/(1 - c_2')$$

$$g_2 = g_2'/(1 - c_2')$$

The estimated form of equation 2′ (insofar as it is not reflected in that of equation 2) is

$$\begin{aligned} RF = {} & \underset{(0.086)}{0.018} + \underset{(0.085)}{0.98} * RSA + \underset{(0.89)}{0.71} * RFD1 - \underset{(0.0081)}{0.0040} * FA \\ & - \underset{(0.0034)}{0.00062} * Q1 + \underset{(0.0036)}{0.0000060} * Q2 - \underset{(0.0033)}{0.00026} * Q3 \end{aligned}$$

$$RSQT(RSA) = 0.92$$

Both wage and non-wage income variables enter the consumer expenditure equations (27, 28, and 29). It is expected that this dual inclusion would involve serious multicollinearity and therefore imprecise estimates. Experimentation confirmed this assessment; the solution involves yet another use of principal components. Consider the sets of variables (i)YDWND, YDNWND: (ii) YDWD, YDNWD: (iii) YDWS, YDNWS. Extract the first principal component from each of these groups. The components are constructed as follows.

$$\left.\begin{aligned} PCND &= 0.986 * YDWND + 0.164 * YDNWND \\ PCD &= 0.983 * YDWD + 0.185 * YDNWD \\ PCS &= 0.993 * YDWS + 0.120 * YDNWS \end{aligned}\right\} \text{(iv)}$$

The *proportion* of the total variation of each set of variables *represented* by the corresponding first principal component is tabulated in Table 13.

TABLE 13. Principal components of income variables.

Principal component	Proportion of variation
PCND	0.880
PCD	0.903
PCS	0.710

Now in each equation replace the two income variables by the corresponding principal component. Thus not only is collinearity among the income measures avoided but one less explanatory variable enters the estimation process. The estimates of the parameters of PCND, PCD, and PCS combine with relationships (iv) to provide estimates of b_{27}, c_{27}, b_{28}, c_{28}, b_{29} and c_{29}. The former estimates are presented in Table 14.

TABLE 14. Coefficients of principal components of income variables.

Principal component	Coefficient		RSQT
	Estimate	Standard error	
PCND	0.38	0.074	0.99
PCD	0.078	0.12	0.99
PCS	0.31	0.11	0.99

This procedure is not substantively original; but the early suggestion advocated extraction of components from the set of *all* explanatory variables of the equation under consideration.[8] In cases in which the source of collinearity is limited to a subset of these variables, it is reasonable to construct the components accordingly. Furthermore, the original variables in the above instances are not standardized, because the elements of each set are measured in comparable units.

Similar treatment is applied to equation 42. General methods invariably yielded esimates of e_{42}, the signs of which were negative. This result is unacceptable because the presence of that parameter in equation 106 requires that its estimate possess the theoretically correct sign. It was suspected that peculiar relationships among explanatory variables were the cause of this phenomenon because it did not arise in other price equations of the same nature. The solution involves extraction of principal components from the four non-dummy explanatory variables, where the latter are expressed in standardized form (because the units of measurement are not comparable among all four

8. Kendall, *Multivariate Analysis*, pp. 70–74.

variables). The proportion of the total variation of the standardized variables accounted for by the various principal components is presented in Table 15.

TABLE 15. Principal components for equation 42.

Principal component	Proportion of total variation
PCC1	0.622
PCC2	0.271
PCC3	0.089
PCC4	0.018

The first two components account for over 89 percent of the total variation. They replace the four original variables in equation 42. Estimates of parameters of the latter variables are obtained using the relationships:

$$\begin{aligned} \text{PCC1} &= 0.505 * \text{SID}' - 0.546 * \text{PMDR}' - 0.573 * \text{PFS}' \\ &\quad - 0.344 * \text{CDFS}' \end{aligned}$$

$$\begin{aligned} \text{PCC2} &= 0.380 * \text{SID}' + 0.432 * \text{PMDR}' + 0.362 * \text{PFS}' \\ &\quad - 0.733 * \text{CDFS}' \end{aligned}$$

where a prime denotes standardization.[9] Thus for example,

$$\text{SID}' = (\text{SID} - \text{SIDM})/\text{SIDS}$$

where SIDM = mean of SID

SIDS = standard deviation of SID

9. For purposes of extraction of principal components from both the 99 predetermined variables and the four explanatory variables of equation 42, the definition of the standard deviation of a variable an observation on which is denoted by X is

$$\sqrt{\frac{\Sigma(X - \overline{X})^2}{N - 1}}$$

where N is the number of observations ($N = 45$). Division by some number (say, N) other than $(N - 1)$ would not affect estimates of parameters of the model because it would alter observations of principal components by only a multiplicative factor.

Estimates of the coefficients of the principal components together with associated statistics are outlined in Table 16.

TABLE 16. Statistics of principal components for equation 42.

Principal component	Coefficient		RSQT
	Estimate	Standard error	
PCC1	0.0061	0.0024	0.99
PCC2	0.015	0.0030	0.92

The final special procedure concerns parameters corresponding to WCRS. This current endogenous variable serves merely to alter the slope of CRS; hence presence of WCRS as an explanatory variable implies that of CRS. Accordingly, in the two-stage least squares methods, the estimated predetermined part of WCRS that replaces WCRS in the second stage is obtained not by the usual calculation but as identical to (i) the predetermined part of CRS for the last five observations, and (ii) zero in the earlier period.

Appendix C / Estimates of Parameters

For general commentary on the estimates it is useful to divide the stochastic equations into two groups:

(i) equations estimated by LS and ALS. These are equations 3, 4, 5, 11, 30, 31, 32, and 34;

(ii) equations estimated by LS, JT, OT, AJT, and AOT. The remaining relations are in this category.

For the presentation of the estimated form of a given equation in chapter II, a best method of estimation is chosen. A tabulation of the results of all methods is included in the dissertation.[1] In order to select the best estimate, obvious criteria based on the following statistics (and ranked in the usual order of importance) are adopted: (1) the Durbin-Watson statistic, (2) the ratio of each estimated coefficient to its standard error (given that the former possesses the theoretically correct sign), (3) the estimated (in relation to the a priori) sign of a coefficient, (4) the RSQ statistic, and (5) the RSQC measure. A summary of the selections is given in Table 17.

An important feature of the estimates is the prevalence of positive serial correlation under those methods that assume the error terms are mutually independent. Though the autoregressive techniques improve the situation substantially, even these procedures are not sufficiently powerful to destroy all autocorrelation in the residuals. The general picture is presented

1. Officer, *Econometric Model*, pp. 383–408.

TABLE 17. Best methods of estimation.

Method	Number of equations
Group (i)	
LS	2
ALS	6
Group (ii)	
JT	1
OT	9
AJT	7
AOT	25

in a tabulation of all the calculated Durbin-Watson statistics (Table 18).

TABLE 18. Durbin-Watson statistic: all estimates.

Method/DW	Number of equations		
	Less than 1.6	1.6 to 2.4	Greater than 2.4
Group (i)			
LS	6	2	0
ALS	2	6	0
Group (ii)			
LS	30	10	2
JT	32	8	2
OT	29	11	2
AJT	13	28	1
AOT	7	34	1

Considering only best estimates, the situation reduces to that portrayed in Table 19.

The third manifestation of the phenomenon is the fact that autoregressive methods constitute best estimates for 38 of the 50 equations.

The presence of autoregression has predominantly theoretical rather than statistical implications. Systematic movements in residuals suggest non-random omitted effects. However, a quarterly model is expected to be plagued with autocorrelated

TABLE 19. Durbin-Watson statistic: best estimates.

Method/DW	Number of equations		
	Less than 1.6	1.6 to 2.4	Greater than 2.4
LS	0	2	0
ALS	2	4	0
JT	0	1	0
OT	1	8	0
AJT	2	4	1
AOT	4	21	0

residuals to a far greater extent than a corresponding annual model. "If it is true in economic life that *natura non facit saltum*, then the shorter the time intervals at which economic variables are observed, the more highly correlated will each variable be with its own past values. Since the residuals in the stochastic equations represent the net effects of many small influences which have been omitted, these too will tend to be more highly serially correlated the shorter the interval of observation."[2] Now consider the following heuristic criterion of theoretical implications of non-random computed residuals. If autoregression is *persistent*, that is, if it cannot be removed by the "*p*th-differencing" of variables underlying ALS, AJT, and AOT, then systematic relationships in the residuals are due not to adoption of a short unit of observation but rather to omission of relevant variables from the relationship and/or inclusion of irrelevant variables. It is this criterion which implies that autoregression may be a phenomenon entailing theoretical rather than statistical deficiencies. To the extent that autocorrelated residuals are a function of the selected measure of time, the ALS, AJT, or AOT techniques are assumed to correct them. Suppose the criterion is used in the following manner. To the Durbin-Watson statistic of the best estimate of a given equation is associated that of its complement on autoregressive grounds; that is, the applicable one of the sets (LS, ALS), (JT, AJT), or (OT, AOT) is considered. Then it must be concluded that equations explaining the variables RS, CINTN, CIS, CIL, CD, RC, CNR, PNDB, PDB, and PXB are

2. *Nerlove*, "Quarterly Econometric Model," p. 166.

capable of theoretical improvement. It is interesting that apart from CD (whose Durbin-Watson is 1.54—the closest to 1.6), persistent positive autoregression is confined to equations explaining prices (of goods, securities, and currencies) and construction, both residential and non-residential. The only case of negatively autocorrelated residuals concerns CINTN.

Because (JT, AJT) and (OT, AOT) are sets of estimation methods that differ only in the number of principal components selected as independent variables in the first stage, it is interesting to compare their results. According to Table 17, overidentified methods give best estimates for 34 of the 42 relationships which involve a simultaneous equation problem. The obvious conclusion to be drawn from the superiority of (OT, AOT) over (JT, AJT) in the bulk of the equations is that methods involving overidentification are generally superior to those that imply strict identification. The results may be given another interpretation as follows. Concerning the simultaneous equation problem in itself, that is, assuming random error terms, the two-stage least squares procedure is usually a desirable method *only as it approaches ordinary least squares!* This is because the RSQT associated with every current endogenous explanatory variable must increase (or at the limit remain unchanged) as n (the number of principal components entering the first-stage regressions) increases. The argument assumes that ordering of components remains fixed, a practice that this study follows. (See Appendix B.) Now, RSQT is a measure of the divergence of the second-stage set of observations on the current endogenous explanatory variable under consideration from the corresponding set of pristine observations. An RSQT of unity for all current endogenous explanatory variables implies the identity of two-stage and ordinary least squares. As stated above, there are some equations for which the two-stage least squares procedures involving *smaller* values of RSQT are superior. It can be said that these relations involve a serious (as distinct from moderate) simultaneous equation problem.

RSQ is presented as a conventional measure of goodness of fit. Compared to the Durbin-Watson statistic, it is of little use in evaluation of theories because economic data are in general highly correlated due to pervasive trend-cycle-seasonal factors. Thus RSQ usually has an inflated value. In any event an RSQ greater than, say, 0.95 is devoid of meaning because the a priori assessment of the applicability of the theoretical equation to the actual economy can rarely exceed that number. However, the statistic has some interest for purposes of comparing different estimates of an equation. In this respect it may be used in conjunction with RSQC. Now the RSQ of ordinary least squares cannot be less than RSQC of any other method because the computation of LS estimates involves maximization of RSQ, where observations on all variables are in their natural form. It is possible for RSQ under some other method to exceed the RSQ of ordinary least squares, because the former procedure does not fulfill the condition of unchanged observations. However, the interesting comparison concerns RSQ of ordinary least squares and RSQC of another method. The closer RSQC of JT, OT, AJT, AOT, or ALS is to the RSQ of LS, the greater is the similarity between the former method and ordinary least squares. Thus this correspondence yields a second measure of the difference between least squares and other methods of estimating a given equation. It is superior to RSQT (the first measure) because of general applicability: the comparison is not restricted to two-stage least squares.

The remaining discussion concerns the economic rather than mere statistical interpretation of estimates. The interesting feature of equation 1 (RS) is the large size of the coefficient of TBN relative to those of other balance of payments flows. This does not mean that autonomous short-term capital is the predominant influence on the fluctuating exchange rate, because the *size* of TBN is in general smaller than that of BM, BS, or BLK. Beta coefficients could be computed to take account of size differences, but even these might be interpreted as overestimating the effect of TBN. Although BM, BS, BLK, TBN, and OR are constructed as net flows, the sum of the absolute values of gross (inward and outward) flows is perhaps a superior measure of size. Then the movement underlying the coefficient of TBN would be dwarfed by those relating to BM, BS, and BLK.

Most of the other comments concern unsatisfactory or unexpected results and attempt to explain their causes. Those estimates that conform to a priori designations do not require discussion.

In the merchandise export equations (3, 4, 5, and 6) the only theoretically incorrect sign of a price effect pertains to equation 3 (XUS). This phenomenon can be explained theoretically. It is a case of harmful collinearity. Assume that USIP rises. This increases the demand for Canadian exports, that is, XUS, hence induces a rise in the price of Canadian exports (PXB) through the variables SIX and XFS (equation 44). Therefore PXRPO1 increases in the next period. The fact that PXRPO1 is a lagged variable while XUS and USIP are current does not suffice to destroy the relationship, because USIP net of seasonality tends to be positively autocorrelated due to the presence of a trend. Dummy variables correct for the seasonality. The collinearity between price and income variables in the export equation is pronounced and harmful in this one case because exports to the United States are of predominant importance relative to exports to any other area.

In equation 6 the insignificance of the coefficient of OCDPXB is perhaps due to the small size of Canada's foreign aid—the ratio of OCDPXB to XO is less than 7 percent, taking total values over the years 1951 to 1961—but the concentration of this aid is also a factor. Asian Commonwealth countries are the principal recipients of the aid represented by OCDPXB, although exports to that area are only a part of XO.

The pattern followed by the coefficients of CRS and WCRS in the five equations in which the variables appear is worthy of note. Considering the estimates of equations 15 (DIVP), 16 (DIVR), 19 (PNIR), and 20 (PTOS), it is seen that the coefficient of CRS is uniformly positive while that of WCRS is uniformly negative. However, the signs are reversed in equation 21 (TBN). Furthermore, the size of the coefficient of WCRS is greater than that of CRS in every equation except 16 (DIVR).

These coefficients shed light on the extent to which expectations of exchange rate movements are elastic or inelastic. DIVR,

PNIR, PTOS, and TBN are transactions which involve demand for (purchase of) Canadian currency, whereas DIVP is a transaction which involves its supply (sale). If a rise in the exchange rate (CRS $>$ 0) induces the (elastic) expectation that the rate will increase even more, purchases will be expedited and sales postponed; if a rise induces the (inelastic) expectation that the rate will fall, purchases will be postponed and sales expedited. In view of the signs and sizes of the coefficients of CRS and WCRS in the equations under consideration, it is clear that *before the first quarter of 1961* expectations were inelastic for DIVP and TBN and elastic for DIVR, PNIR, and PTOS, while *from that quarter onward* expectations were inelastic for PNIR and PTOS and elastic for DIVR, DIVP, and TBN. Thus the withholding tax changes and the aggressive exchange fund policy reversed the type of expectations for all but one of the flows.

Inelastic expectations are associated with stabilizing speculation and elastic expectations with destabilizing speculation, where reference is to the *dynamic* stability of the foreign exchange market. On balance, then, is speculation stabilizing or destabilizing? One way to answer this question is via the autoregressive coefficient of RS1 on RS. If this coefficient is less (greater) than unity, movements in RS will be damped (explosive), and the foreign exchange market is stable (unstable). Such an autoregressive framework is not part of the structure of the model, but the impact multiplier of RS with respect to RS1 is an analogous concept. $\partial RS/\partial RS1 = 0.79$, indicating that the foreign exchange market is dynamically stable.

Estimation of equation 17 (CINTN) yields unsatisfactory results. The reason may lie in the construction of BNI2, BRTO1, and OINT1, which involves simplification of interest rate weighting schemes. In addition, the assumption of linearity may be incorrect. A principal reason is the fact that BNI2, BRTO1, and OINT1 refer to securities that give rise to only a minute part of gross payments and receipts of interest, while CRS refers to interest transfers from *all* securities denominated in foreign currency. Non-linearity would probably center on the variable CRS. This equation is the only one that involves persistent negative autoregression. A significant Durbin-Watson ratio may be interpreted as indicating a divergence from linearity rather than the omission of relevant variables. However, it is recalled that BNI2, BRTO1, and OINT1 are exclusive of influences on one type of official interest, namely, loans granted by the government of Canada.

Equation 23 involves an inconclusive sign of the estimated coefficient of PNIIC. Apart from the omitted effects implicit in persistent serial correlation, a reason is the fact that a rise in CIL induces an increase in PNIIC, even while the latter movement tends to depress the interest rate. A similar remark applies to the coefficient of TBN in equation 22 (CIS). It is the function of two-stage least squares to reduce the two-way relationship to a unidirectional causality running from the explanatory variable (PNIIC or TBN) to the dependent variable (CIL or CIS). The fact that this task is not successfully performed may be due to the interactions of autoregressive residuals with correlations between the residuals and current endogenous explanatory variables. It is recalled that the methods of estimation assume that no such interactions exist.

Another case of reciprocal causality opposite in sign of effect concerns the variables CIL and SO of equation 24. Because this relation is interpreted as a supply curve, it is expected that the coefficient of CIL is negative. But another factor tends to produce a positive coefficient: the necessity to lower security prices in order to successfully place new issues in the market. Again, this latter relationship represents the effect of the dependent variable (SO) on an explanatory variable (CIL) that is current endogenous; this causality should be suppressed by the adoption of two-stage least squares or some other simultaneous equation method.

With respect to the consumer expenditure equations (27, 28, and 29) the imposing result is the persistence of a positive price effect. The cause is not easy to determine. One argument is that the inclusion of a price influence in the two other principal explanatory variables of each relation suffices to represent the influence of prices; the addition of a third non-dummy variable, namely, a price ratio, is superfluous. But this explains *inconclusive* price effects; it is *significant* positive price effects that are at issue.

A second explanation, namely, the irrationality of consumer response to changes in relative prices, is absurd for the broad categories of purchases under consideration. The true answer may well be reflected in the particular methods of estimation. The three expenditure equations are estimated by single equation procedures. It may be that a method—say, a variant of three-stage least squares—which takes account of the fact that spending decisions on the three categories of consumer goods and services are interrelated (as reflected in correlated error terms of the equations) would produce proper signs for the price effects. In the same context, quasi-determination of personal saving as a residual may be inferior to an approach that first determines the spending-saving mix of disposable income and then explains the division of expenditure among the three classes.[3]

Concerning the fixed investment equations 31 (CNR) and 32 (EM), the insignificance of external sources of funds (represented by R2) relative to internal sources (the liquidity or net income variables) is apparent, although all coefficients have the theoretically correct sign.

With respect to relations explaining prices of goods and services, only equations 41 (PNDB) and 42 (PDB) yield unexpected results. In both cases the coefficient of the inventory-shipment ratio has the theoretically incorrect sign—a phenomenon which is prevalent under no other specification of such variables. Furthermore, the coefficient of CDFS in equation 42 is negative—an unreasonable estimate. It may be concluded that the theories underlying prices of consumer goods are deficient. In the case of PNDB this is indicated by autocorrelated residuals; in that of PDB it is reflected in both this and the fact that a special procedure had to be adopted merely to produce a positive coefficient of PMDR.

3. The model does not determine personal saving. This flow is defined as the difference between total disposable income and total personal expenditure on consumer goods and services, where both are measured in current dollars. Variables composing the latter flow enter the model only in constant-dollar form. Therefore personal saving could be explained only if current-weighted price indexes of consumer non-durable goods, durable goods, and services were included as variables in the model. This action is not taken because it is contrary to the methodological approach adopted.

Index of Variables

ACE adjustment for consumer expenditure, in millions of constant dollars: role in model, 177; in identities, 158–159, 161, 163, 164

ACT 1 if second quarter 1954 or beyond, 0 otherwise: role in model, 198, 208; in stochastic equations, 103, 104, 105, 108–109, 110; impact multipliers, 210–231, 235, 239, 249, 251–252, 258, 259, 262, 266, 271

AGDI adjustment for business gross fixed capital formation, in millions of constant dollars: role in model, 178; in identities, 162

AHN number of hours worked per unpaid worker: role in model, 195, 201; in stochastic equations, 123; in identities, 171; impact multipliers, 231, 271, 273

AHP number of hours worked per paid worker: role in model, 195, 201; in stochastic equations, 121–122, 123; in identities, 171; impact multipliers, 230, 271, 272–273

AINV adjustment for change in inventories, in millions of constant dollars: role in model, 178; in identities, 161

ATM average term to maturity of government of Canada long-term marketable securities at beginning of quarter, in months: role in model, 188, 207; in stochastic equations, 88–90; impact multipliers, 210–231, 232, 234, 236, 257, 262

BI change in non-farm business inventories, in millions of constant dollars: role in model, 178, 201, 202; in stochastic equations, 111–114; in identities, 161; impact multipliers, 213, 240

BIP2 index of industrial production of the United Kingdom, 1957 = 1, lagged two quarters: role in model, 196, 208; in stochastic equations, 27, 29; impact multipliers, 210–231, 235, 236, 240, 245–246, 248–249, 256, 258, 259, 271

PMIRPD ratio of base-weighted price index of imports of investment goods divided by index of spot exchange rate to price index of domestically produced investment goods: role in model, 191, 201, 203; in stochastic equations, 42, 43; in identities, 168; impact multipliers, 227, 266

PMKR base-weighted price index of imports of investment goods divided by index of spot exchange rate: role in model, 193, 201; in stochastic equations, 129, 130; in identities, 169, 173; impact multipliers, 229, 265, 267, 269–270

PMND base-weighted price index of imports of consumer non-durable goods, 1957 = 1: role in model, 194, 208; in identities, 168; impact multipliers, 210–231, 238, 253, 264, 265–266.

PMNDR base-weighted price index of imports of consumer non-durable goods divided by index of spot exchange rate: role in model, 193, 201; in stochastic equations, 127, 128; in identities, 168, 172, 173; impact multipliers, 229, 269–270

PMNRC current-weighted price index of new machinery, equipment, and non-residential construction, 1957 = 1: role in model, 191, 201; in stochastic equations, 137–139; in identities, 162; impact multipliers, 227, 267

PMUSP1 ratio of price index of United States exports to price index of exports of other countries exporting to Canada, lagged one quarter: role in model, 194, 208; in stochastic equations, 36, 37, 38; impact multipliers, 210–231, 234, 244, 245, 248

PNDB base-weighted price index of consumer non-durable goods, 1957 = 1: role in model, 190, 201; in stochastic equations, 126–128, 292–293, 298; in identities, 157, 166, 167, 168, 170, 172, 173; impact multipliers, 225, 253, 263–264, 267

PNDPO ratio of base-weighted price index of consumer non-durable goods to weighted average of base-weighted price indexes of consumer durable goods and services: role in model, 190, 201; in stochastic equations, 97–98, 99, 297–298; in identities, 167; impact multipliers, 225, 264

PNDS base-weighted price index of consumer services and non-durable goods, 1957 = 1: role in model, 190, 201; in stochastic equations, 136, 137; in identities, 170; impact multipliers, 226, 264, 266, 267

156, 158, 161, 162, 163, 164; impact multipliers, 214, 238–239, 241

YDMC disposable income divided by base-weighted price index of imports of consumer goods itself divided by the index of the spot exchange rate, in millions of deflated dollars: role in model, 181, 201; in stochastic equations, 38–39, 41, 42; in identities, 166–167; impact multipliers, 217, 251–252

YDNWD disposable non-wage income divided by base-weighted price index of consumer durable goods, in millions of deflated dollars: role in model, 182, 201; in stochastic equations, 99, 100, 286–287; in identities, 166; impact multipliers, 219, 252–254

YDNWND disposable non-wage income divided by base-weighted price index of consumer non-durable goods, in millions of deflated dollars: role in model, 182, 201; in stochastic equations, 97, 98, 99, 286–287; in identities, 166; impact multipliers, 218, 252–254

YDNWS disposable non-wage income divided by base-weighted price index of consumer services, in millions of deflated dollars: role in model, 182, 201; in stochastic equations, 100, 101, 286–287; in identities, 166; impact multipliers, 219, 252–254

YDRC2 disposable income divided by base-weighted price index of residential construction, in millions of deflated dollars, lagged two quarters: role in model, 181; in stochastic equations, 102, 104, 105

YDWD disposable wage income divided by base-weighted price index of consumer durable goods, in millions of deflated dollars: role in model, 182, 201; in stochastic equations, 99, 100, 286–287; in identities, 166; impact multipliers, 218, 252–254

YDWND disposable wage income divided by base-weighted price index of consumer non-durable goods, in millions of deflated dollars: role in model, 182, 201; in stochastic equations, 97, 98, 99, 286–287; in identities, 164–166; impact multipliers, 218, 252–254

YDWS disposable wage income divided by base-weighted price index of consumer services, in millions of deflated dollars: role in model, 182, 201; in stochastic equations, 100, 101, 286–287; in identities, 166; impact multipliers, 218, 252–254